CHICHESTER COLLEGE

STUDYING LITERATURE

STUDYING LITERATURE: A PRACTICAL INTRODUCTION

Edited by Graham Atkin, Chris Walsh and Susan Watkins

Chester College of Higher Education

HARVESTER
WHEATSHEAF

New York   London   Toronto   Sydney   Tokyo   Singapore

First published 1995 by
Harvester Wheatsheaf
Campus 400, Maylands Avenue
Hemel Hempstead
Hertfordshire HP2 7EZ
A division of
Simon & Schuster International Group

© Graham Atkin, Chris Walsh, Susan Watkins 1995

Typeset in 10/12pt Erhardt by Dorwyn Ltd, Rowlands Castle, Hants

Printed and bound in Great Britain by
Biddles Ltd, Guildford and King's Lynn

Library of Congress Cataloging in Publication Data

Studying literature: a practical introduction / edited by Graham
    Atkin, Chris Walsh, and Susan Watkins.
        p.   cm.
    Includes bibliographical references and index.
    ISBN 0-7450-1627-8
    1. Literature—Study and teaching. I Atkin, Graham. II. Walsh,
Chris. III. Watkins, Susan.
PN59.S89 1995
807—dc20   94-30015
                                                                       CIP

British Library Cataloguing in Publication Data

A catalogue record for this book is available from
the British Library
ISBN 0-7450-1627-8 (pbk)

---

1 2 3 4 5   99 98 97 96 95

What one knows is, in youth, of little moment; they know enough who know how to learn.

Henry Adams, *The Education of Henry Adams* (1907)

. . . literature is the human activity that takes the fullest and most precise account of variousness, possibility, complexity, and difficulty.

Lionel Trilling, *The Liberal Imagination* (1950)

Contents

List of contributors   xi
Preface   xiii
Acknowledgements   xvii

Introduction   1

Part I   Practical skills for studying literature

1   Studying literature   *Merritt Moseley*   9
      Attitudes   9
      Knowledge and skills   13
      Behaviour   18

2   Discussing literature   *Bill Hughes*   25
      Talking and listening   25
      The lecture   27
      The seminar   29
      The student presentation   34
      Small group work   39
      Conclusion: The active learner   44
      Appendix A: Student questionnaire   46
      Appendix B: Record of presentation meetings   46

3   Writing about literature   *Jo Pryke*   48
       Writing critical essays   48
       Preparatory work   50
       Reading, note-taking and drafting   54
       Writing the essay   63
       Revising and producing the essay   65
       The learning process   66

Part II   Studying literature in practice

4   Thinking about language   *John Williams*   71
       Rebuilding Babel: Making sense of language   71
       Prescriptivism and descriptivism   72
       Phonology   76
       Grammar (syntax and morphology)   76
       Semantics   79
       Language and society   81
       Pragmatics   84
       Language and literature   86

5   Reading literary texts   *Chris Walsh*   95
       Introduction: The self-conscious reader   95
       Reading literary texts: Practical considerations   97
       Basic reading   99
       Critical reading   101
       Reading the writer   102
       Reading the text   103
       Reading the reader   104
       Reading the context   107
       Reading the language   109
       The questioning reader   109
       Reading and evaluation   110
       Reading in practice   111
       Conclusion: Reading freely   116

6   Reading poetry   *Glyn Turton*   119
       Poetry, pleasure and the dutiful mob   119
       What is poetry?   121
       What is a poem?   129
       The language of the poem   135
       How poetry works   139

7 Reading prose fiction *Susan Watkins*   150
   Introduction: What is prose fiction?   150
   A short story   151
   Reading prose fiction: Significant features   155
   Characterisation   156
   Narration   159
   Language   166
   Reader response   169
   Conclusion   172

8 Reading plays *Graham Atkin*   176
   The theatrical medium   176
   Theatre of the mind   178
   Dialogue and character   181
   Semiotics of drama   184
   Structure and time   187
   Performance   190

9 Practising criticism and theory *Katherine A. Armstrong* 196
   Introduction: Criticism and theory   196
   What are criticism and theory?   197
   Why do we read criticism and theory?   199
   The uses of criticism and theory   201
   How do we read criticism and theory?   209
   Practising criticism and theory   211

Conclusion   221
Index   224

List of contributors

Katherine A. Armstrong took her first degree and her doctorate at Oxford University, and is a specialist in eighteenth-century literature. She is a lecturer in English literature at Chester College; she has also taught at Oxford, Stanford and Manchester Universities, and tutors for the WEA. She is currently writing a book on Daniel Defoe.

Graham Atkin took his first degree at the University of East Anglia (Norwich) and his masters at Liverpool University. He is a lecturer in English literature at Chester College; previously he taught at Liverpool City College. His interests include modern drama and American literature, though his specialism is Renaissance literature. He is currently undertaking doctoral research on Spenser.

Bill Hughes gained both his degrees from the University of Wales. He is a principal lecturer in English literature at Chester College. His specialisms are in nineteenth- and twentieth-century poetry and contemporary drama. He has a particular interest in teaching methods at undergraduate level, and is a former literary editor of *Education for Teaching*.

Merritt Moseley took his first degree at Huntingdon College and his masters and doctorate at the University of North Carolina at Chapel Hill. He is currently Professor and Head of the Department of Literature at the University of North Carolina at Asheville. He has twice been a visiting lecturer at Chester College. He is the author of *David Lodge* (Borgo Press) and *Understanding Kingsley Amis* (University of South Carolina Press).

Jo Pryke took her first degree at Durham University and holds higher degrees from Liverpool University. She is a senior lecturer in English literature at Chester College; previously she taught for the Open University, Liverpool University Institute of Extension Studies, and what is now Liverpool John Moores University. Her specialist area is Victorian studies, and she has a particular interest in the work of Elizabeth Gaskell.

Glyn Turton took his first degree at Oxford University and his masters and doctorate at Warwick University. He is Dean of Arts and Humanities at Chester College; previously he taught at what is now the University of Central England in Birmingham. His areas of specialist expertise are nineteenth-century literature, contemporary fiction and modern poetry. He is the author of *Turgenev and the Context of English Literature 1850–1890* (Routledge).

Chris Walsh took his first degree at Lancaster University and his doctorate at Oxford University. He is Head of English at Chester College; previously he taught at St Mary's College, Strawberry Hill. He has written articles and reviews on a wide range of subjects, but his specialism is Victorian literature. He is currently writing two books on the history and theory of the novel.

Susan Watkins took her first degree at Liverpool University and has a doctorate from Sheffield University. She is a lecturer in English literature at Chester College; previously she taught part-time at the University of Sheffield and at Sheffield Hallam University. Her specialisms are nineteenth- and twentieth-century literature, women's writing and literary theory.

John Williams has masters degrees from Sheffield and Manchester Universities. He is a senior lecturer in English language and professional studies at Chester College. He has also worked as a teacher and as an education adviser. Currently, he is undertaking doctoral research in theoretical linguistics.

Preface

This book has been written with the needs of first-year undergraduate students of literature in mind. Typically, such students may well find themselves following some kind of foundation course or introductory module in literary studies as they start their degree programme at college or university. The help provided with the basics of studying literature at this level will vary in kind and extent from institution to institution. Some user-friendly departments put on courses tailored specifically to the requirements of their students; these courses really are foundational in nature, offering plenty of formal explicit guidance as to what is expected of literature students, perhaps supported by more informal tutorials to assist students individually. But many departments, for one reason or another, operate on a 'sink or swim' basis. In such cases students may find themselves plunged straight into a course such as 'Literature 1575–1660', and waters which to some might feel refreshing and invigorating, to others might seem choppy and icy. Where are such students to find help? However sympathetic the tutor there is a limit to the amount of help she can give; there are only so many hours in the day, and tutors have many responsibilities and duties (including research, administration and course development) over and above what appears on their teaching timetables. But in any case the overworked and underpaid tutor might reasonably expect the student to fend for herself at this level. Or the student might not feel inclined to approach her busy tutor for counselling on a matter which she regards as fairly elementary, her

difficulties notwithstanding. What then? For this is not an unusual situation. Despite the government's repeated attempts to encourage more
students to opt for the sciences, engineering and other vocational courses
at university, the fact remains that the arts and humanities in general, and
English literature in particular (and its near-synonyms and variants:
Literary/Cultural/Media/Communications Studies), continue to be the
most popular area/subject at this level; and the demand shows no sign of
diminishing. As the numbers entering higher education continue to expand and as literature departments are driven to find ever more ingenious
ways of mounting quality courses while having to cope with very high
intakes (with larger and larger classes bearing the brunt of expansion), the
forlorn student left to her own devices is in danger of becoming a common phenomenon.

Where should she seek help if not from her lecturers? The college
library? Libraries, in common with every other resource in higher education, have also come under severe pressure as student numbers have
soared, as college budgets have been slashed and as students have been
expected to become more independent as learners. If you are one of two
hundred students trying to track down a book of which there are only
four copies (and all of those on restricted loan) then you are likely to be
disappointed. What about the college bookshop? Here the situation is
scarcely better: the prices of many books have become prohibitive for
someone struggling on a (shrinking) student grant. So where is there left
to go for help?

This book has been designed to provide for that need. Planning it grew
out of the actual experience of teaching a foundation course in literature
to successive substantial intakes of first-year undergraduate students
from very varied backgrounds and with widely differing expectations and
abilities. Although most of the students who come to Chester College of
Higher Education to study literature (normally as part of a combined
studies degree) are standard literature 'A'-level entrants, there are many
students who have taken instead the language 'A' level, or who have
studied only a small amount of literature to date, including hardly any
pre-twentieth-century texts and no poetry to speak of; then there are the
mature 'access' students whose backgrounds in the subject vary enormously. More particularly, the book arose out of a programme of mass
'core' lectures in which members of the Department of English Literature endeavour to cover the fundamentals of degree-level literary study,
in an attempt to give all literature students the kind of help, advice,
encouragement and information that they so patently need. This book

tries to deal comprehensively and effectively with all of the appropriate issues and key topics and is, therefore, suitable not only as a set text on first-year undergraduate literature courses, but also as a handbook for students to use by themselves as they follow their programmes of study.

It is aimed at undergraduate students of literature in English (though much of the guidance given will also apply to those studying other literatures) especially those just entering higher education, whether at university or college. It is intended that students should read the book before they embark on a degree course, but the idea is that they should continue to make use of it throughout their first year (if not beyond). It may also be of some interest to those sixth-form and other students (and perhaps to their teachers) who are considering whether or not to study literature in higher education. It has been deliberately pitched at a realistic level: while some chapters may be more challenging to read than others, every attempt has been made in the book as a whole to be lucid, lively and accessible, without in any way talking down to the reader. Moreover, although the ground covered is substantial the book is reasonably concise. Above all, it is intended to be useful.

The book has also been designed to bridge a gap between skills-based publications and overtly theoretical studies. Thus the book starts by dealing with the practical skills required to study literature at this level. It then moves on to consider various aspects of studying literature in practice. Some fundamental issues of criticism and theory are examined towards the end. Where applicable further reading is suggested in brief, annotated bibliographies at the end of each chapter.

The book, then, combines academic rigour with pragmatism. The contributors, all of whom have experience of teaching in a busy English Department, are concerned throughout to offer practical guidance and helpful suggestions so that students are encouraged to think for themselves right from the start, thereby ensuring that they are well placed to progress further with, and succeed in, their literary studies. Each chapter has been written to be self-contained, though there are occasional cross-references between chapters. The whole book may, of course, be read straight through, in which case the alert reader will no doubt notice the differences of emphasis and approach of the nine contributors (though when it comes to practical advice the reader should not find that she is being counselled to do contradictory things). The guidelines offered here should apply wherever a student is studying literature in higher education though there will obviously always be slight variations in recommended good practice from place to place: readers should ask their tutors if in doubt.

In the case of the end-of-chapter notes, subsequent references to a text already cited are given within the chapter itself.

Throughout, personal pronouns are given in the feminine gender when referring to the reader, the student, the tutor. We adopt this convention simply because the overwhelming majority of people involved in the study of literature at this level are not men but women.

Finally, the editors would like to thank the various people who helped to make this book possible, including many colleagues and students, past and present, both at Chester and elsewhere. Chapter 2, in particular, could not have been written without the co-operation of several students, including: Corrine Adams, Peter Bursnell, Beryl Campbell, Mark Cox, Judith Crooks, Enys Davies, Christopher Goodwin, Julia Hatten, Lesley Hughes, Kate Lewis, Kerry Marsh, Thomas Plunkett, Annette Rubery, Martin Shaw, Adrian Smith, Caroline Wilson and Louise Woolmer. Jen Mawson's deftness with different word-processors proved to be invaluable. Finally, Jackie Jones, erstwhile of Harvester, is also owed a debt of gratitude for her support and advice in the early stages of the project.

Graham Atkin
Chris Walsh
Susan Watkins

Acknowledgements

The editors and publisher wish to thank the following for permission to reproduce copyright material: Faber and Faber Ltd for 'The Metaphor Now Standing at Platform 8' from *Kid* (1992) by Simon Armitage (copyright Simon Armitage 1992); Penguin Books Ltd for *v.* from *Selected Poems* (1987) by Tony Harrison (copyright Tony Harrison 1987); Victor Gollancz Ltd for 'The Snow Child' from *The Bloody Chamber and Other Stories* (1979) by Angela Carter (copyright Angela Carter 1979).

Introduction

Studying literature: probably no readers need to have the word 'studying' explained to them, though its etymology will be unfamiliar to many – it derives from the Latin *studere*, to be zealous. But what about the second term in the book's title, 'literature'? What *is* literature? Is not this term as straightforward as the first? Actually the question 'what is literature?' is more easily asked than answered and perhaps for this reason is more frequently ignored than squared up to.

All definitions involve setting limits, making decisions about what is to be ruled in and what is to be ruled out. Where trying to define literature is concerned the difficulties make themselves felt at once. 'Imaginative or fictional writing' will not quite do as a definition: biographies, diaries, essays, histories, philosophical works, political speeches, sermons and travel books do not in any obvious way conform to that definition, and yet instances of such texts by (respectively) Boswell, Pepys, Bacon, Gibbon, Mill, Burke, Newman and Hakluyt have traditionally been studied as 'literature' in the past. Moreover, some writings which are clearly fictional, such as Enid Blyton's Noddy books or Mills and Boon romances, are not usually classified as literature, or at least not as 'Literature'. Why is this? Is it because the average Mills and Boon romance is not as good in terms of the quality of its writing or the profundity of its understanding of human nature as the average novel by Austen or Dickens? This line of inquiry seems to be implying that we are dealing here not with measurable, objective criteria but with subjective value-

1

judgements. But whose values are we talking about? Where do these values come from?

Or consider the following list: science fiction, pornographic magazines, car manuals, detective thrillers, children's comic-strip stories, bus-tickets, runic inscriptions, newspaper reports, advertisements, chemistry textbooks, radio plays, legal documents, film-scripts, libretti, cookery books, plays without words, income tax forms, official notices in public parks. Which of these items, if any, would you feel justified in categorising as literature? And what would your reasons be for including or excluding specific items? Does literature have something to do with being non-ephemeral and non-practical (if not non-factual)? But who can say for sure that what we regard as ephemeral and topical today will not be the literature of tomorrow valued for its universal, timeless insights into the human condition?

Perhaps literature is 'creative' writing (thus ruling out bus-tickets anyway) as opposed to more 'utilitarian' writing? But what is meant by this word 'creative'? Is a creative (or 'literary') writer one who uses language in a particularly distinctive or inventive way compared with how most people use 'ordinary' language from day to day? The problem with this approach though is that 'literature' would have to include many adverts and political slogans (because of their obviously rhetorical nature) and would have to exclude certain kinds of factually based stories, the language of which might be wholly naturalistic and unremarkable. Perhaps, in the end, faced with such difficulties we have no option but to concede that to speak of literature as a wholly objective, non-controversial, water-tight category simply does not make much sense: 'literature' is whatever people agree to call literature. Not a very helpful description (certainly not a definition as such) but perhaps as good a description as we are likely to arrive at. Literature, in other words, is what readers such as you sign up to study in colleges and universities every year.

But even this minimalist, pragmatic description glosses over some awkward issues. For example, who decides what literature gets studied on university and college courses? Why is it that in the past some texts have had the seal of approval (the texts in what has become known as 'the canon') while others ('non-canonical' texts) have not? There is not the space here to explore such a question, important as it is.[1] What does matter though is that you register in your mind from the very outset of your literature course that the question 'what is literature?' is not the bland, innocent, uncomplicated question which some people blithely assume it to be. For the phenomenon which you may be about to spend the next few years studying is not something to be taken for granted; on the contrary, as you will soon discover, the essence, in so far as there *is* an essence, of being a student of literature involves asking questions and generally being *critical* about all aspects of the process of (whatever is meant by) 'studying literature'.

The chapters which follow explore various facets of the study of literature at degree level. For convenience they are separated into two parts. The first part, 'Practical Skills for Studying Literature', has three chapters on studying, discussing and writing about literature. The second part, 'Studying Literature in Practice', sees the emphasis switch slightly to the actual process of reading and studying literary texts critically. The six chapters here cover the elements of linguistics, the activity of reading, the main literary genres (poetry, prose fiction, drama) and literary criticism and theory.

Merritt Moseley's opening chapter, 'Studying Literature', offers a wide-ranging and general discussion, the aim being to give the reader a clear sense of what is involved in studying the subject effectively and successfully. The chapter falls into three sections. The first section is on *attitudes*: What are the attitudes which students of literature need in order to study effectively? The second section is on *knowledge and skills*: What kinds of things do students need to know about, and know how to do, in order to succeed as students of literature? The third section is on *behaviour*: What sorts of behaviour make for the successful study of literature? Among the topics discussed in this chapter are time-management, using the library, note-taking and preparing for classes.

Bill Hughes in Chapter 2, 'Discussing Literature', develops this last point. He sets out to give first-year students of literature some basic co-ordinates to do with participating in, and learning from, the various types of classes they may attend in the course of their studies. He puts forward the model of the student as *active learner* rather than as observer and suggests that it is more helpful to think of the group discussion session as process rather than as product. This chapter is mostly devoted to a consideration of the different kinds of classes literature students are likely to encounter and some of the commoner learning and teaching methods used in them. The formal *lecture*, the *seminar*, the *student presentation* and *small group work*, are each discussed in turn and plenty of practical examples are given to illustrate the points made.

In Chapter 3, 'Writing about Literature', Jo Pryke sets out to introduce students to, and guide them through, the process of preparing for, writing and learning from *critical essays* of the kind typically required in literature courses at university. The chapter begins by clarifying the purpose of essay-writing before moving on to discuss the various stages of the writing process, from *planning and drafting* through to *producing* the final version. Questions such as 'How much use should I make of the critics?' and 'How do I build a coherent argument into my essay structure?' are carefully considered. The chapter ends by looking at how to *learn* from the process of writing essays and how to improve from one essay to the next.

John Williams, in 'Thinking about Language' (Chapter 4), aims to heighten the language awareness of the student of literature and to demonstrate some of the ways in which the close careful study of language – apart from being interesting and valid in its own right – can be of considerable help in studying literature. The chapter also sets out to introduce students to a few of the basic terms and concepts of *linguistics* and to acquaint them with some elementary descriptive terms and tools of analysis for their own subsequent use. By the end of the chapter the student to whom language study is relatively unfamiliar should be in a stronger position to explore and analyse the 'raw material' of the literature she is studying.

Chris Walsh's aim in Chapter 5, 'Reading Literary Texts', is to encourage undergraduate students of literature to think about what is involved in the process of reading literary texts critically. The chapter has a theoretical dimension (ideas about the reading process) and a practical aspect (suggestions about how to become a more expert reader). It emphasises and illustrates the importance of reading as the activity upon which success in studying literature is based. It posits two kinds of reading: *basic* reading and *critical* reading. The first is the kind of reading most people do most of the time; the second is more sophisticated, more *self-conscious*, and involves asking certain *questions* about one's response to the text. The questions relate to: the *writer*, the *text*, the *reading process*, the *context* and *language*. The vexed issue of *reading and evaluation* is also briefly discussed. The chapter concludes by emphasising how there is no such thing as a single, fixed, 'correct' reading of a literary text, and by stressing the pleasures of interpretation.

Glyn Turton's subject in Chapter 6 is 'Reading Poetry'. The basic approach of this chapter is to show that *how a poem is read* by somebody depends on what that person thinks poetry is as a linguistic and cultural phenomenon. To this end, the chapter first of all introduces students to selected views or *definitions of poetry* which show how the conception of the genre has changed through time. The purpose of this exercise is essentially a confidence-building one, namely to help students realise that they can enhance their own enjoyment of poetry by giving some thought to what it is. The chapter approaches the question of *what poetry is* by examining *how it works*. The reader is familiarised with the basic elements of poetic discourse by attending to various aspects of the *language of poetry* from rhyme and rhythm to other important rhetorical conventions. The emphasis throughout is on the belief that analysis, properly undertaken, should intensify rather than detract from the pleasure of reading a poem.

Susan Watkins begins Chapter 7, 'Reading Prose Fiction', by posing the question *What is prose fiction?*. Then, using Angela Carter's short story 'The Snow Child' as a starting point, she elaborates several *significant features* of the experience of reading prose fiction. She discusses *characterisation* in novels and short stories, before proceeding to address the different kinds of *narrative method* found in fictional texts; she also explores the *language of fiction* and concludes by considering the *reader's* contribution to the process of reading prose fiction.

Graham Atkin in Chapter 8, 'Reading Plays', begins by examining the ways in which *the theatrical medium* differs from poetry and prose fiction. The unique nature of drama is briefly discussed. However, the emphasis is on the act of *reading a play* as opposed to watching and/or listening to one. The need for the reader to construct a performance in the imaginative *theatre of the mind*, while remaining aware of the different possibilities for actors and directors involved in the performance of a particular text, is explored. The chapter then looks at *dialogue and character*, at what has been termed the *semiotics of drama* and at *structure and time* in plays. It is shown how desirable it is that a reader of a play keep in mind the integrated relationship between writing, reading, analysis, rehearsal, production and reception. The chapter closes with a brief consideration of the nature of the move from page to stage – the art of *performance*.

Katherine Armstrong in Chapter 9, 'Practising Criticism and Theory', makes the case for both criticism and theory, *distinguishing* between them by suggesting that whereas 'theory' defines various methods of reading, 'criticism' applies these methods to particular texts. The discussion then moves on to consider *objections* to criticism and theory; these objections are rebutted by showing how criticism can add to our appreciation of literature, while theory can have potentially revolutionary implications for society. In the next section of the chapter, the question *Why do we read criticism and theory?* is considered. The answer, it is suggested, has to do with how they help us to form our own coherent theoretical and critical stance as interpreters of texts by contesting our assumptions about books and *how we read* them. The stress here is on how much we can learn from critics and theorists, if we read them attentively and discriminatingly (in other words, critically). Criticism and theory, the chapter concludes, should stimulate, not stifle or replace, the student's own ideas.

But this is to anticipate. 'Ideas' are mental abstractions from the experience of phenomena. The phenomenon in question for our purposes is whatever is meant by the term 'literature', which we discussed briefly at the beginning of this introduction. Whatever the difficulties of defining literature, there is no denying its existence in the real world: ideas and theories require an object (an 'about', you might say) just as they need a subject (the human person) to 'think' them. What follows is an attempt to bring object and subject into relation with each other. What is involved when someone studies literature? What are literary studies *about?* And *how* should you go about studying literature? If you want some answers to these questions, read on.

Note

1. For a fuller discussion of this topic, see Terry Eagleton, *Literary Theory: An introduction* (Oxford: Basil Blackwell, 1983), pp. 1–53.

PART I

Practical skills for studying literature

1

Studying literature

Merritt Moseley

If you are reading these words, you have probably already decided that you are interested in studying literature at degree level and would appreciate some ideas on what to expect if you do so. You are probably aware that the study of literature means reading books and other written texts (which often means reading and re-reading), thinking about them, talking about them and writing about them. Other chapters in this book address the specific tasks of reading different kinds of literature, of the organised varieties of 'discussing literature' expected of literature students, and the writing tasks you will face. This chapter aims to provide an introduction to the attitudes, skills, knowledge and behaviour which will make your study of literature as rewarding as possible, beginning with *attitudes* – those traits of mind and personality which will be most useful to the literature student.

Attitudes

The appropriate stance for the ideal reader has been summed up in the phrase 'passionate attention'.[1] Both terms are important: attention not only suggests that readers need to 'pay attention' – surely a crucial practice in any kind of reading – but, in its secondary, more French meaning, asks them to be patient, to *wait upon*, the texts they attend to.

But what about 'passion'? Surely if the study of literature is like other advanced intellectual undertakings, such as the natural sciences, the practitioner should be dispassionate, cool, objective? *No.* Not only are scientists themselves not the dispassionate objective measurers and recorders of popular myth; but the great attraction of reading literature is its ability to engage all our faculties, our intellects, our imaginations, our emotions, appetites, desires, fears, regrets.

Most people who decide to study literature do so because *they like to read.* This is not the dirty little secret of literary study; it is the essential beginning. One of the chief qualifications for a good literature student is the capacity for enjoyment. This should not be overstated however: pleasure is by no means the only desirable outcome of reading, and those who erect their own enjoyment into an unarguable critical standard have less to contribute to, and possibly little to derive from, the formal study of literature.

But Anglo-American critical history, which has a generous amount of Puritan distrust of fun in its pedigree, too easily falls into the habit of distrusting that which is enjoyable. We apologise for reading something that is too obviously pleasurable, explain that we are 'just' reading it for enjoyment. Throughout human history people have read books for *delight.* Cultivate your own delight in reading; work to expand the range of things which you enjoy. Try to recognise the genuine value of books which do not provide you immediately with a simple pleasure. But remember that enjoyment is an important part of being a student of literature.

Studying literature also requires *openness.* The good student brings with her 'a heart/That watches and receives'.[2] Be ready to receive; be willing to have a reaction to what you read. Remember that reading is an activity that involves much more than the retinas. Criticism (the informed discussion of what we read) begins with having a personal reaction. Note that it begins there, not ends; if that reaction remains subjective or visceral, then it is hardly critical at all. But good reading means having a reaction. If, having 'read' a text, your mind contains no response, you have not really read it yet. 'Aesthetic distance' should never mean anaesthesia or frigidity of response.

Another important attitude for the student is *curiosity*, a restless interest in all sorts of things. Vladimir Nabokov, the great Russian novelist, was also a university lecturer, and he insisted on the importance of caring, and knowing, about things like the construction of carriages in nineteenth-century Rouen to help in understanding *Madame Bovary.* Nabokov's own list of desirable traits for a reader includes 'imagination, memory, a dictionary, and some artistic sense'. His repeated admonition to his students was to 'notice and fondle details'.[3] Too quick a recourse to generalisation, too confirmed a conviction that the 'big ideas' or the 'general concepts' or the 'controlling themes' are all-important, the specifics simply a disposable conveyance to get the reader to them – all these habits of thought work against good reading. It is in the details that one poem in praise of the beloved differs from another, just as it is in the details that one person's beloved differs from another; one must be curious, investigative, about these details. These are where the author's choices are available for our inspection. Why is the narrator of Charlotte Brontë's *Villette* (1853) called Lucy Snowe instead of, say, Bella Gay, or Fanny Assingham? We may not always arrive at satisfactory answers to questions of this sort, but we should encourage ourselves to ponder them.

Some questions are not worth posing, much less spending a great deal of time answering, and the decisions you make about which questions to ask are the outcome of another necessary mental trait of the literature student, *careful discrimination*. At all times in your course of study you will need to make choices. You may be asked to choose a passage from a text to read and comment on; you may be asked to choose a topic for a long research project; you will be given a choice of essay questions in an examination and you will often be asked to 'agree or disagree'; you may be faced with a choice of critical approaches or theoretical positions. Even at the mundane level of choosing what to do first when faced by a number of conflicting demands, you will be required to discriminate intelligently, that is, to show good judgement.

Careful discrimination, or good judgement, is not so much a question of outcomes, of whether you end up writing your dissertation on Mary Shelley or Jane Austen, or whether you conclude that the key to interpreting literature is the class struggle or numerology. What matters is how you reach these conclusions, that you follow some sensible process of decision-making. We are all subject to a variety of influences, and it is of course impossible to escape them. Becoming self-aware of our own decision-making procedures is a step toward making good decisions.

One important ingredient in this process is self-confidence. A good literature student should have *appropriate self-confidence*. This (like so many other traits) is a mean between two extremes. One of these extremes is too much self-assurance. One reason why people study literature in groups, at university or college, is to learn from each other; you will be expected to be able to profit from the ideas, beliefs and understandings of your fellow students, of absent others recorded and stored in the library, and of your tutors. None of these exchanges can occur unless you believe that you have something to learn from others.

In fact, excessive self-confidence is rarely the main problem for students embarking on the study of literature; instead they often do not have *enough* confidence in their own knowledge and abilities. It is important not to think that you know nothing, or that what you do know or believe is of little value, or that (for some reason) you are incapable of arriving at sound critical views. Remember that 'education' means to draw out, rather than to put something in; you are not an empty vessel or an erased slate, ready for filling or inscribing. Too much deference to the ideas of others – whether these be your tutors, fellow-students, or critics whose works impress you because they have been published – can be as detrimental to your development as an unwillingness to listen. Disagreement is normal – as you will discover if you listen to any gathering of intellectuals – and is in fact the condition of discovery. That you disagree with received opinion is evidence neither that you are right nor that you are wrong; the important thing is to seek good grounds for your judgements and persuasive arguments to support them.

This raises the whole question of determinate meanings versus subjectivism. If it is true, as many hold, that no interpretation – of a poem or novel or for that matter anything else – is more correct or valid than any other, then it follows that the best interpretation is to be identified by some other criterion than the degree of accuracy of textual references. One such criterion might be novelty – in such a case, because a reading of *Hamlet* which sees it as being about a football game is more unusual than a theory that it is about dynastic and family problems in the Danish royal family, it will be perceived to be superior. Another criterion might be *power*, that is, the best interpretation is the one held by the most powerful reader. In an educational setting, this is usually the tutor, and the conclusion would be that the tutor is right by virtue of her position of power.

There is something appealing about both of these theories, and neither is easy to refute; but this is a practical guide to studying literature, and in your studies you will be expected to make arguments for your own views, to engage in discussion, to read critical essays which differ from your own opinions and from each other – all activities which assume that your interpretation of a literary text is capable of being shared, and that your task as a student is more than simply adopting the views of the most powerful reader in sight.

So what are the attitudes or mental traits which make for the most successful and most satisfying way of studying literature? Enjoyment. Openness. Curiosity. Careful discrimination. And appropriate self-confidence.

Knowledge and skills

In *The Anatomy of Literary Studies: An introduction to the study of English literature*, Marjorie Boulton provides a rather terrifying summary of the sorts of 'background knowledge' which students should possess. Her list includes knowledge of

- Ordinary critical terms.
- English and Ancient History.
- Greek and Roman mythology.
- The Bible and Christian history, including the saints.
- Medieval science.
- The countryside (useful in reading pastoral poetry).
- The history of exploration.
- The history of the theatre.
- General information.
- The history of books, publishing and authorship.
- The history of ideas.[4]

Marjorie Boulton hastens to add that 'no student, and no professor at retirement age, is going to know everything it is desirable to know; but the better our knowledge, the fuller our enjoyment.'[5]

There is no doubt that all the areas of 'background information' listed above are useful for the literature student, in part because background information has a way of being foregrounded. You may think a knowledge of medieval science fairly unimportant, until you read the dialogue between Doctor Faustus and Mephistopheles in Marlowe's *Doctor Faustus* (1604) in which the two discuss the Ptolemaic cosmology, the number of spheres, the nature of the fixed stars, and other standard data of the pre-Copernican universe. Your understanding of the 'cross-dressing' parts in Shakespeare's comedies will be enlarged by some understanding of the use of boy actors in the theatre of the day; and you probably cannot read Aphra Behn's *Oroonoko* (c. 1688) with full appreciation without some awareness of African and Latin American colonisation.

Writers, of whatever period, assume certain kinds of knowledge in their readers. Almost any English-language author writing before the twentieth century felt free to refer to even the most obscure parts of the Bible, on the assumption that readers would be familiar with it; this is as true of a non-believer like Mark Twain as it is of a Christian writer like

Gerard Manley Hopkins. Shakespeare wrote for an audience which fully understood the theory of 'humours'. George Eliot wrote at a time when even city people knew about crops and farm animals, and readers of her books benefit if they know something about them too. One of the sources of richness in literature is *allusion*. But allusion is effective only for readers who, first, know that an allusion has been made and second, recognise the object of the allusion. And readers recognise allusions most surely when they have a breadth of background knowledge and reading themselves.

How can you acquire this impressive store of background knowledge? The answer is: *read*. You will learn English history best by reading histories of England; you can become really familiar with the Bible only by reading the Bible; the best way to provide yourself with the information to recognise Shakespeare's classical allusions is to read an English translation of Ovid's *Metamorphoses*. There are, of course, reference books and you should use them, human life being finite. A good dictionary of classical literature, or a dictionary of the saints, or a biographical encyclopedia can help you with unfamiliar allusions, historical context, or puzzling references. They make interesting browsing, as well. But it cannot hurt to repeat that the best way to be a well-prepared student of literature is to *read*.

Still, though it is broadly true that knowledge is good for the literature student and more knowledge is always preferable to less, there are certain kinds of knowledge which need particular emphasis. Marjorie Boulton places first in her list a knowledge of *critical terms*, and this is an essential shared vocabulary. Without it we cannot have a discourse. Students simply must know what a *narrator* is, what *metaphor, alliteration, scene, irony* and *stanza* refer to. Such terms as these will be used without definition or elaboration in lectures and in critical discussions; they are the language without which literary discussion cannot take place, and the student must know them. The way to learn them is to acquire a good dictionary of literary terms, such as M. H. Abrams's *A Glossary of Literary Terms*.

Literary criticism and theory have increasingly elaborated their own 'jargon', partly in emulation of the natural sciences, and you will undoubtedly come across words you do not recognise, no matter how assiduously you have worked at mastering familiar literary terms. You should not worry if you do not recognise words like *heterodiegesis, jouissance* and *phallogocentric* at first; but do, please, make sure that you are comfortable with *plot* and *lyric* and that you have some knowledge of the fundamentals of English *metre*.

What else is essential knowledge for the literature student? There are two other areas not mentioned yet which are among the most important. The first is *language*. Some theorists argue that literature is defined by its specialised use of language; at any rate it is made up of, and communicated by means of language. To be a good student of literature you should be alive to, and interested in, language. This means, for instance, having an awareness of figurative language – metaphor and metonymy and other tropes; a knowledge of how rhyme and near-rhyme, alliteration and the other special phonic features of literature function; and an understanding of *syntax*. Though analysing grammar may seem tedious, and in fact sometimes is, a good reader of literature possesses an understanding – sometimes perhaps entirely unformulated but felt – of grammatical conventions. To recognise attempts at reproducing dialect through syntactic variation requires a feel for the expected syntax; to recognise stylistic effects based on inversion or reordering requires an awareness of the usual order.

The good student is alert to the sounds of the language, too. Though most reading is ordinarily silent, reading aloud helps in comprehension and in recognising stylistic effects – like careful repetitions. Read this sentence from Margaret Drabble's *The Ice Age* out loud and notice the artful pattern of rhymes and other repeated sounds: 'The hedgerows had never looked so unattractive: bare stalks and withered plants, mudspattered, hung desolately on to a withered life, tattered, bent, spent, spattered.'[6]

Perhaps the most important aspect of language for the student to think about is *meaning*. On the most obvious level, we cannot understand books or poems if we do not know the meanings of the words in them; but the good reader is curious about far more than this. Not only do words change their meanings, so we need to know that 'nice' meant something to Shakespeare, as did 'gossip' to Hawthorne, that these words do not mean today; but every word has a history which includes not only the various denotations it has carried but its connotations as well, and even an archeological sense which is related to its etymology. As Vladimir Nabokov insists, a good reader owns a dictionary. Frequent use of a longer dictionary with full etymologies is recommended, the best being the *Oxford English Dictionary* (OED). The OED entry on 'lord' contains two and a half pages of different shades of meaning, etymology and citations of historical usages, and is illuminating not only on this one word but, if read thoughtfully, on the feudal system and on Christianity, both of which make use of 'lord' in a way which is related to the original word, 'hlafweard' – which means 'bread guardian'. The good student of literature is *curious* about all aspects of language.

One final kind of knowledge the student needs is a knowledge of *literary conventions*. A convention is any kind of agreement, usually unstated, between people, such as the convention among English-speakers that 'hello' is a greeting, or the convention among Americans that 'tire' is the spelling for the word which British people conventionally spell 'tyre'. The relationship between words and their meanings is conventional (this is essentially what is meant by the modern linguistic concept of the *arbitrary nature of the verbal sign*). Specific conventions enabling literature to exist and function, the knowledge of which is part of what is meant by *literary competence*, include the 'fourth-wall convention' by which actors in a naturalistic drama pretend that they are enclosed in a real room and the spectators agree to pretend with them that they are looking through a wall; the division of plays into acts; the traditional plot, with rising action, climax, and falling action; the use of quotation marks or inverted commas to assert that the words within them are exactly those used by another speaker; the use and acceptance of 'omniscient' narrators; free indirect style, and many others. One becomes familiar with the conventions of literature in part through study and through using guides, glossaries and so forth; but the major way of learning one's way around literary convention is by much reading.

The student of literature needs to know the meanings, sounds and history of the words encountered in reading, and the conventions which enable writers and readers to share literature; and all this is in addition to a working knowledge of the Bible, English and American history, the history of exploration, Greek and Roman mythology, and all the other areas of knowledge listed above. This seems, and is, an impossible schedule of material you need to know. But it is broadly true that knowledge is always better than its opposite; the student who knows a great deal will be better able to read and study with appreciation and profit than the student who knows less. Henry James's advice to apprentice writers is good advice for all students: 'Try to be one of the people on whom nothing is lost!'[7] This is not knowledge, but the attitude which leads to its acquisition: the curiosity recommended above is crucial for successful study of literature.

A good literature student needs not only a variety of knowledge but a variety of *skills*. The most important one, as has been indicated already, is *reading*. You can already read, in the sense that you are literate; but this minimal (or *basic*) level of reading, which will permit you to follow a recipe or read a ballot paper, is not the kind which the study of literature requires.

What you will need is a higher-level reading skill which is careful, alert, involved, inquisitive – and aggressive. It is the reading of a person determined to be one of those on whom nothing is lost. (You will learn more about this distinction from Chris Walsh's discussion in Chapter 5.)

Careful, *critical* reading is the kind that is attentive to the meanings, the nuances and patterns, of the language. You cannot insist that language is a transparent medium; literary uses *defamiliarise* reading, *foreground* language, making it, as one writer has explained, a 'roughened' language.[8] This highlights the difference between reading and other activities which may seem superficially similar – most notably watching television or video. It could be argued that watching television is an essentially passive and undemanding activity. Real reading, in comparison, is more active, aggressive, and – though certainly not always difficult – much more challenging. It is also more rewarding. One almost never has to watch television twice, or watch it more slowly, to get the full effect; literature often requires slow reading, or multiple readings. Memory and anticipation are both required and rewarded by reading.

Real reading makes something happen; it produces a reaction. If, when you have finished reading a text, you have no reaction, emotional or intellectual, no resistance, no doubts or enthusiasms – then perhaps you have not read it well enough. A reading ought to arouse reactions; it ought to stimulate the reader to comparisons or contrasts, agreements or disagreements, objections; it ought to raise questions. The best approach to literary study is passionate attention – and the passion is a result of the attention.

An active, involved reading may be assisted by interacting with the text. One way to do this is to mark the book (only if it is your book, but you *should* own the books) – noting points that have struck you, marking important names or phrases or motifs, raising questions to which you will find the answers by further reading in the text or the library or in a conversation or seminar.

Reading is the most important skill for any student of literature. Another is *listening and note-taking*. Again, everyone knows how to listen, in a way, and everyone who can write can, in a sense, take notes. But these skills also work for you only when they are practised sensibly and aggressively. Useful listening is discriminating; and note-taking is largely a matter of choosing the important things to write down, which means discriminating between the serious and the trivial, the central and the peripheral, the general points and the examples. Someone has defined good note-taking as 'taking notes while taking note'. Learning what *not* to take down is the key to effective note-taking, since you cannot write as fast or as copiously as a lecturer can talk. Listen for key words; examples or illustrations are often indicated by phrases like *for example, for instance* and *take*. You may want to write down the example, of course; but you should be aware of the differences between the examples and the more general idea or trait or fact or development which they are being used to exemplify.

Logical connections are revealed by words and phrases like *thus, as a result, therefore, hence, for* and *because*. Following a discourse intelligibly requires the listener to take note of which things are being asserted as causes for which results. Listen for the words which indicate such relations. Contrasts are among the most useful ways in which we organise our thoughts; listen for phrases like *on the other hand, in contrast* and *or* as signposts to contrasts; comparisons – *on the other hand* – are often signalled by language like *similarly, just as* – and *likewise*.

Just as the attentive listener needs to be able to discriminate between the general and the particular, a careful listener must detect *irony* (statements which mean something different from, or even opposite to, what they explicitly declare), jokes and throwaway lines. The student who writes down the lecturer's drolleries, takes straightforwardly remarks meant to be interpreted ironically, and perhaps carefully records some idiosyncratic biographical detail, while overlooking the major points and the overall structure of the lecture is 'taking notes', more or less, but not to much purpose. If your lecture notes are rich in anecdotes about Keats's arterial blood but do not seem to have recorded anything about his poetry, then you are not listening with sufficient discrimination and writing down the most important parts of the lecture. (Some of these points will obviously apply in a modified sense to taking notes from printed critical sources – books and articles.)

Reading, listening and note-taking are skills students of literature make use of acquisitively, in learning; there is another set of skills they make use of dispersively, in sharing their learning with others. The most important of these are *speaking* and *writing*, each of which will be treated more fully in the next two chapters of this book.

Behaviour

In addition to certain desirable attitudes for the literature student, and some knowledge and skills, the possession of which makes for the effective and rewarding study of literature, there are some kinds of ideal *behaviour*, some things which the aspiring student should *do*. Some of these are peculiar to the study of literature; others are important attainments for any sort of student and for life itself.

For instance, you should be conscientious in *time management*. Being a student in a college or university is a life unlike most others, in one way at least: very few of the hours in your week are actually timetabled for presence in class, or 'contact hours'. Compared with the worker in a 40-hour-week position, you have much more 'free time'. This freedom is of course one of the attractions of higher education; but it is a challenge as well, because, as you will soon learn, it is not really free time. It is time for you to use constructively. You need not be a recluse. But you must use your time well.

This means planning both your days and your terms. It might be useful, particularly if time management is not your strength, to make a daily schedule for yourself. Assign enough time for eating, exercise, relaxation and so on; but make sure that you have a real time for reading and writing. You might want to adopt the schedule Benjamin Franklin, the eighteenth-century American inventor and diplomat, created to prevent himself wasting time:

a.m.	5-7	Rise, wash, pray, study, eat breakfast
	8-11	Work
	12-1	Read and dine
p.m.	2-5	Work
	6-9	Put Things in their Places, Supper, Musick, or Diversion, or Conversation
	10-4	Sleep[9]

Perhaps Franklin's schedule is not *quite* the one for you; but, seriously, it is a good plan to have one and to follow it – not slavishly but conscientiously. *Regular* study is the key. Two or three hours every day is worth far more than twice as many hours crammed into the last few weeks of a course.

You need a schedule for your term, as well. As students often point out, tutors do not always consult each other about the timing of assignments; and even when they do, there are certain points in a term, notably towards the end of it, when you are likely to have a lot of work to do. You cannot plan ahead for illnesses or family emergencies, but you can anticipate when you have a long essay to write, when you have an oral presentation, when a long novel to read. A master schedule including all these things, if you use it properly, should provide you with time to do your work properly.

Preparation is always important. You should pay close attention to any syllabus or programme you receive; know what the lectures are about, and do the preliminary reading suggested for them, so that you can understand them. (One cause of difficult and pointless note-taking is that the auditor has no idea what the lecturer is talking about, having failed to do the preliminary reading.) Obviously preparation for examinations is a special topic; but students who prepare for their classes day by day have a far less daunting task when they have to prepare for examinations than those who have neglected their work during the term. Avoid the temptation of concentrating on your strengths at the expense of attending to any weaknesses you may have.

The most important kind of preparation is *reading*. Studying literature is primarily based on reading, including many kinds of texts. *Read all the texts when you are asked to read them.* There are many reasons why you should do this. One is that you will get far more out of lectures and seminars if you have completely and thoughtfully read the text(s) being addressed in them. You cannot understand a class, you cannot take notes on it, you cannot remember what is important in it, on a book you have not read. Another reason for having your reading done on time is that tutors expect intelligent class participation and discussion from students. You cannot discuss a book intelligently if you have not read it. Lecturers appreciate students who come to class prepared to make a contribution. Education is interactive, not simply receptive; you are not an empty vessel transported into a classroom so someone can transfer knowledge into your waiting hull. Your lecturer recognises the signs of blankness and incomprehension, not to mention the student trying to hide behind a larger friend. More importantly, the unprepared student in a class takes from others and gives nothing. (As mentioned in Chapter 2, it is particularly important – the act of a good colleague – to be prepared when other *students* are giving oral presentations.)

Give yourself time to do your reading (here is where your schedule can help). If you find yourself with twenty-four hours left before you must attend a seminar, realising that you must read *Middlemarch* in that time, not to mention eating several meals and getting some sleep if possible, you have not planned ahead or allowed yourself time to read properly. The result is likely to be that you either do not read the book, or at least not completely; or you 'read' it very hastily, skipping parts that look skippable to you. In either event, you will not be prepared when you attend that seminar. You will not get very much out of *Middlemarch*, which, like most texts, asks that you read it deliberately, thinking about what you have read, noticing things; that you read it with close attention, fondling the details. The most likely outcome of poor preparation and inadequate reading is that you will dislike and resent the novel. Deep down, you know that *Middlemarch* did not make you stay up all night; but the fact remains that when we read under intense time pressure, the enjoyment which ought to be a part of our reading is attenuated or banished. You realise of course that the conditions of reading literature in college are special, quite different from those of 'real life' – you are told what to read and given a deadline, unlike George Eliot's original readers, who presumably read *Middlemarch* only if they wanted to and took as long as they liked to finish it. This difference is inherent in your decision to *study* literature. But by sensible planning and time management you can reduce your frustrations.

One more thing about reading: read under the *right conditions*. You should find a quiet, well-lit place, without distractions. Sit in a comfortable chair (though you may find that an overly comfortable seat is too relaxing). Keep the noise to a minimum. People who believe that they can read while listening to music on a personal stereo or watching television are almost always deluding themselves; they may be looking at the words and registering them at some level of consciousness, but they are not doing the kind of critical reading which is required for the effective study of literature.

One good place to do your reading is the library. But even if you have a quiet room with a good light and a cosy chair somewhere else, you should *use the library*. How? To supplement and complement your reactions to, and thinking about, the assigned texts. The library is replete with commentaries on works of literature. Sometimes you will be directed to use them in a research project or scholarly essay. Even when you are not so directed, using the library to help deepen your knowledge and critical awareness is important.

But it is important, too, to remember the distinction between primary and secondary materials. The novels, plays, films, poems and other texts you study are the *primary* objects of study. Biographies, books of literary criticism, encyclopedias, bibliographies, collections of critical essays, reviews – all these are *secondary*. These terms should remind you that primary reading *is* primary – it comes first. You should never substitute the reading of critical commentary for the immediate, deliberate, engaged and thoughtful reading of the text by and for yourself. Have your own reactions before you go looking for other people's. Having read your text carefully and thought about it, only then should you go to the library to see what others have thought about it. And as you do this, remember that different critics and commentators have different ideas; read more than one commentary. Nothing is true or accurate or compelling just because it has been published and shelved in a library. Notice the conflicts and disagreements between critics and draw the right kind of conclusion: not that, since opinions differ, all are equally worthwhile or worthless, but that, since opinions differ, it is no cause for alarm when your own opinion differs from what you have read in a secondary book; and the way to sort out differing opinions is by assessing their comparative persuasiveness or evaluating their ability to account for the details of the text under examination. Neither priority nor recency – nor, for that matter, the prestige of the critic – can guarantee that the critical opinion is one you should adopt. Use your own judgement. Here is where the 'appropriate self-confidence' earlier recommended as part of the equipment of every literature student becomes so important. One way to develop that self-confidence is to read widely in literary criticism and theory. Agree with it, by all means, if it earns your agreement; but do not agree with it because you have heard of the author or because all the other books were checked out of the library.

You should do your utmost to attend all the timetabled sessions which are designated as compulsory. This may seem an obvious or boring suggestion, but it is valuable advice. Not only do students who miss classes miss important announcements and useful information about the reading programme, or future essays, or altered assignment dates, but they miss what is happening in the classroom. Tutors, who almost always know more than their students about the texts, have prepared assiduously and over a long period for their lectures. Learning from them is like using the library for critical enrichment, except that it is more obviously interactive.

This brings us to the final sort of behaviour recommended for the student of literature: *assertiveness*. By no means is this a recommendation that you be pugnacious, rude, obnoxious, or pushy. It does mean, though, that you should take responsibility for your own education, be active, and should not be too easily satisfied with partial knowledge, not to mention ignorance. Ask questions. Be willing to engage in dialogue. Seek out your tutors if you need to speak to them. Do not be too easily discouraged in the library; if you cannot find what you need, ask a member of the library staff for help rather than trudging away empty-handed.

When you finish a seminar, ask yourself, 'What do I wish I had learned today that I did not learn?' Then think about what would have been required for you to learn it: What if you had asked a question? Try to get beyond the fear of appearing foolish. You may think that everybody else in the group knows something and that by asking you will announce your own exceptional ignorance. Even if this is true, what then? Is it more comforting to go on not knowing something just because everybody else knows it? But in most cases your fellow students are wondering the same things as you are. If you ask the question you will prove yourself a benefactor to them all. Be assertive; be prepared; be diligent and organised. These are the kinds of behaviour which make for success in literary study, and, combined with the fund of knowledge and the skills recommended above, with the desirable attitudes of the student of literature, they should help you to success, satisfaction and reward in your higher education.

If there is one piece of summary advice, though, it is this: *do not be satisfied with ignorance or confusion.* Take the steps necessary to eliminate them. No one but you knows fully what you know, what you believe, what you doubt, what you wonder. Take control of your own education; be a seeker; never be complacent or overly diffident; try to be one of those on whom nothing is lost.

Notes

1. The phrase is taken from Richard L. McGuire, *Passionate Attention: An introduction to literary study* (New York and London: Norton, 1973).
2. William Wordsworth, 'The Tables Turned', from *The Poetical Works of William Wordsworth*, ed. E. de Selincourt and H. Darbishire, vol. 4 (Oxford: Clarendon Press, 1947), p. 57.
3. Vladimir Nabokov, *Lectures on Literature*, ed. Fredson Bowers (Fort Worth, Tex.: Harcourt Brace Jovanovich, 1980), pp. 3, 1.
4. Marjorie Boulton, *The Anatomy of Literary Studies: An introduction to the study of English literature* (London and New York: Routledge, 1980), pp. 123–35. The quoted passage comes from p. 135.
5. Ibid., p. 135.
6. Margaret Drabble, *The Ice Age* (New York: Knopf, 1977), p. 115.

7. Henry James, 'The Art of Fiction,' from *Literary Criticism: Essays on literature, American writers, English writers* (New York: Library of America, 1984), p. 53.

8. Victor Shklovsky, 'Art as Technique', trans. L. Lemon and M. Reis, from *Modern Criticism and Theory: A reader*, ed. David Lodge (London and New York: Longman, 1988), p. 27.

9. Benjamin Franklin, *The Autobiography of Benjamin Franklin* (New York: The Modern Library, 1950), pp. 98–9.

Further reading

Elliott, H., *The Effective Student: A constructive method of study* (New York and London: Harper & Row, 1966). (Techniques for mastering examinations, essays, note-taking, study aids, etc.)

Gibbs, J., *Dancing With Your Books: The Zen way of studying* (London and New York: Penguin, 1990). (Focused on attitudes, mental preparations, and techniques for relaxation. A different approach.)

Groccia, J., *The College Success Book: A whole-student approach to academic excellence* (Lakewood, Col.: Glenbridge, 1992). (Much the same; includes a 'general formula for academic success'.)

Jensen, E., *Student Success Secrets* (New York and London: Barron's, 1982). (Advice on studying, using library, writing essays; one chapter specifically addressed to the literature student.)

Manlove, C., *Critical Thinking: A guide to interpreting literary texts* (New York: St. Martin's, 1989). (A manual of thinking and reading approaches for the literature student.)

Morgan, C. and Deese. J., *How to Study* (New York and London: McGraw-Hill, 1957). (Advice on the usual topics: examinations, writing, effective reading, making best use of time.)

Preston, R. and Botel, M., *How to Study* (Chicago and Henley-on-Thames: Science Research Associates, 1981). (Suggestions for improving study habits; includes practice materials.)

Protherough, R., *Students of English* (London and New York: Routledge, 1989). (Unlike the other books listed here, this is a description of students of English, including what they study, why and how: an overview of undergraduate literary study.)

Voeks, V., *On Becoming an Educated Person: The university and college* (Philadelphia and London: W. B. Saunders, 1964). (Some philosophical material and positive suggestions.)

2

Discussing literature

Bill Hughes

Talking and listening

A good deal of your time as a student of literature will be spent talking and listening. The exchange of views between tutor and student, and student and student, lies at the heart of the process of understanding and responding to literary texts. Opportunities for discussion and dialogue will occur throughout your course in a number of contexts. This chapter is concerned with the ways in which you can make the most of such opportunities.

The active participation of students in discussion is important for two reasons. The first has to do with the nature of works of literature. Like any work of art, a literary work functions properly only when it is being experienced by an individual. A novel or play or poem needs the reader to complete the circuit. An unread Dickens novel may make a good door-stop, but it is not functioning as a novel.

However, as later chapters in the book will emphasise, each reader has a different background, a different set of beliefs, kinds of knowledge, emotional make-up, insights and so on. Every student in the class brings to each work a different perspective, registers different aspects as particularly important, and supplies different associations. A physical object can be described most clearly when it is seen from different angles: we would walk round a statue before coming to an opinion about it. In the same way a poem is likely to be more completely grasped when described by different students from different points of view.

This does not mean that all views are equally valid, or equally percep-tive. Some viewers have better eyesight; some have better vantage points from which they can see more clearly; some have more experience in knowing what to look for. But the process of sharing viewpoints can be an illuminating one particularly if, as students and teachers, we are flexible enough to be able to change our views in the light of the evidence of other readers.

The second reason that dialogue and discussion forms a central part of degree-level literature classes is concerned more with the personal de-velopment of each student. You will notice from the results of the ques-tionnaire on participating in classes, printed as Appendix A at the end of this chapter, that students consider that one aim of a degree course in literature should be to improve your ability to express yourself. The process of saying what we think and feel about works of literature is not always easy, even when we are discussing a work that has moved or provoked us. As we go through this process (sometimes a painful one) we can be made aware of what T. S. Eliot, in 'East Coker', calls 'the intoler-able wrestle with words and meanings'.[1] This struggle for articulacy is often difficult enough in an essay, when we have time for reflection and we are struggling in private. It can be more difficult when we are thinking as we speak, and other students are listening. In 'Burnt Norton' Eliot describes what can happen to language in the struggle for clear and coherent expression:

> Words strain,
> Crack and sometimes break, under the burden,
> Under the tension, slip, slide, perish,
> Decay with imprecision, will not stay in place,
> Will not stay still.
>
> (lines 149–53)

Of course Eliot is concerned here particularly with the *poet's* struggle for clarity of meaning, but students are asked to go through the same process in their own way. The process of struggling is important, not simply the outcome; we can discover what we mean only by listening to what we say.

This chapter then is concerned with your active participation in the various activities timetabled into a normal degree-level course in litera-ture. These will include formal lectures, seminars and small discussion groups. Reading literature is usually a private affair; in fact we often need to be by ourselves, or at least undisturbed by conversation, to read effectively. But once we have read the novel or the play or the poem, most of us enjoy the process of discussing it with someone who has shared the experience. This is a natural human characteristic. Whether the shared experience is a film, a wedding, a football match or a lecture we often come away talking about it. The study of literature formalises this process, and provides regular, structured opportunities for such discussion, or the exchange of views. In the large formal lecture such opportunities may be restricted to a few questions at the end. In the seminar there will be far more opportunities for you to put your point of view. And group work will normally be devoted exclusively to this activity. Other methods, such as student papers or presentations, or, occasionally, a one-to-one tutorial, will provide additional opportunities.

The main aim of the chapter is practical: to suggest some ways in which you can make the most of this oral aspect of your course. In particular it will explore ways in which you might overcome some of the difficulties of self-expression or of asking questions in what are sometimes perceived by students as daunting circumstances. If you find the early stages of this process difficult you may be comforted by the answer to question 7 on the questionnaire. Most students strongly agree that expressing their views becomes easier the more they do it.

The lecture

The lecture is the teaching method least likely to allow students to participate in the process of learning. But there will be opportunities and you should be ready to take advantage of them. First, the process of listening, as Chapter 1 has pointed out, is an active one. Few lectures in literature are concerned solely with the imparting of information. The lecturer will be offering opinions, judgements, points of view; she may even choose to offer deliberately provocative statements in the hope of gaining a response from the audience. You should be willing to respond actively to the material in the lecture; questions to the lecturer are the most obvious way in which this can be done.

Lecturers like questions. If nothing else they are a sign that someone in the audience has been listening. It will usually be made clear whether questions are welcome during the lecture, or merely at the end. Even if the speaker allows no opportunity for questions during the timetabled session, there may be an opportunity privately immediately after it. Failing that, you may be able to return to a particular issue in a subsequent seminar with the same tutor. In whatever circumstances you ask the question your first task is to respond inquisitively to the content of the lecture. In many lectures you will be offered a summary of the main points in a handout, leaving you more time to reflect critically on the content, and to note points that you would like to raise. Get into the habit of jotting down possible questions as they occur, particularly if this is early on in the lecture; as the lecturer proceeds to other points, you might well forget the question you had intended to ask.

There are several different categories of questions. You may find yourself jotting down points that you would like clarified. Lecturers often try to cover a good deal of ground in a lecture with a resulting compression of argument. You might like an amplification of the argument or simply a restatement of it in different terms. This might well apply where the argument appears to be a central one in the lecture. Difficulties can be caused by lecturers taking a piece of knowledge for granted, or using a term which is unfamiliar. They are accustomed to the special terminology of literary criticism and may use descriptions such as 'Pre-Raphaelite', or 'Modernist', or 'Surrealist' or 'Gothic' which you would like explained. So questions seeking clarification constitute one important category.

Questions which ask for examples or additional information form another category. A request for an example of a Pre-Raphaelite poet, a Modernist writer, a Surrealist play or a Gothic novel might help to clarify the description, and encourage the lecturer to give more information. If you have some knowledge of the topic the question might come in the form of a suggestion: 'Would you consider Joseph Conrad a Modernist novelist?' or 'When you mentioned surrealist drama, were you thinking of a play like *Rosencrantz and Guildenstern are Dead*?' Students are often more willing to ask this second form of question because it enables them to demonstrate some knowledge while seeking more.

Probably the most difficult questions to ask are those in which you are implicitly offering a view of your own, or even challenging the view of the lecturer. 'Isn't Modernism an odd title to give to a literary movement that you tell us began nearly one hundred years ago?' demonstrates that the questioner has listened attentively, but has also reflected intelligently. Direct challenges to a view expressed in the lecture are rare, but exciting when they do appear. 'Isn't your statement that the Gothic has disappeared as a form of popular culture challenged by the best-selling *Bat out of Hell* album?'

Once the question has been formulated, it still has to be asked. Not surprisingly, the questionnaire shows that students feel more reluctant to ask questions in large lectures than in smaller groups. There is something about the presence of two or thee hundred listeners that inhibits the asking of a question even when we feel it is a good one. Few students will interrupt a lecturer in full flow even if they have been invited to do so, but if you have the nerve to do this then it is best to raise your hand clearly to catch the lecturer's eye before embarking on your question.

A direct invitation to ask questions at the end of the lecture makes the process easier, but still not easy. There are all kinds of psychological factors urging you to keep your question to yourself rather than raising your voice to break the silence. Try to ignore them. Your first question will be the hardest to ask, and once you have asked it it will never be quite as difficult again. However, if you do suffer from starter's block – and many first-year students do – you may want to do something positive about it. It may help if you avoid sitting at the back of the lecture theatre, with all the added difficulties that this would give you. It might also help to have your question clearly worded, in your head if not on paper, and to keep it brief. At least the question will then be precise and clear. It may also help to begin with a non-challenging question, a simple request for clarification or information. If the lecture session closes without time for a question that you would like to have posed, then your timetable system may provide for a follow-up seminar or tutorial. In this case ensure that you keep a note of the points that you would like to raise at that later meeting.

The seminar

The seminar has been a standard teaching and learning format for the study of literature in higher education for some time. The group size varies from institution to institution, but will commonly be between ten and thirty-five. It can be flexibly used to accommodate some input from the tutor, which may vary from a mini-lecture to an informal introduction to a topic. It will sometimes include a student presentation, or small group work, both of which will be discussed later in the chapter. But it will certainly include whole group (or 'plenary') discussion led by the tutor. It is this process, and the student's role in it, that we turn to now.

Participation in seminar discussion is, for many students, the most difficult part of their course. In large lectures individual students can avoid speaking for an entire three years if they are so inclined; in seminar groups this is hardly possible. Yet the size of the seminar group will probably still make many students apprehensive about contributing. As

the questionnaire shows, it is not until small group discussion that virtually all students feel entirely happy about contributing. Fortunately
you can do a great deal to make the talking process less stressful. Getting
to know your fellow students is an important first step.

Preparation for the seminar is even more crucial. In most cases you will
know beforehand what the topic of the seminar is to be. It will often be
related to a specific text, or even a specific aspect of, or extract from, a
text. Your first objective is to be as familiar as you can be with whatever is
to be discussed. The better you know the text, the more you will have to
say about it. You will also understand other students' observations more
easily and be able to respond to them. If, for instance, the seminar is on
Catch 22 (1962) then those students who know that the novel concerns
Yossarian's battle for sanity and survival and is set in Italy in the Second
World War are in a position to make a start on discussion. Those who are
able to cite details of his encounters with Major Major or Milo Minder-
binder, and have reflected on their significance, are able to go further.
Those who have been moved by the chapter 'The Eternal City' to the
extent of having already discussed it with a friend are able to go further
still. Of course there is a limit to the preparation that you can do in the
time available, and the sheer number of texts to be studied can be daunting for students coming fresh from the more leisurely pace of 'A' levels,
or other comparable courses. But planning your reading so that you are
familiar with texts before they are discussed is certainly the first rule for
effectively contributing to the discussion.

Some seminars will begin with an invitation from your tutor to offer
observations on any aspect of the chosen text that you have found of
interest or significance. This is a useful strategy for tutors to employ in
the early stages of discussion since it begins with the student's perceptions of a text rather than the tutor's. It is non-threatening, since students
are merely being asked to offer personal responses rather than critical
judgements. In these circumstances it is helpful to arrive for the seminar
armed with one or two such observations. These need not necessarily be
observations about the text as a whole; many texts can be approached by
looking at details. A recent seminar discussion on Arthur Miller's play
The Crucible (1953) produced the following comment, not on plot or
character or political significance but on stage directions: 'Act Four begins "in darkness but for the moonlight seeping through the bars" but
ends "with the new sun pouring in upon Elizabeth's face" '. Perhaps
understandably the comment was from a student doing a joint degree in
English and Drama, and therefore more aware of aspects of staging. But

this comment on a detail opened up a fruitful discussion of a major aspect of the play, that is, the ways in which Miller dramatises the clashes between good and evil. At this early stage of general discussion, comments may be phrased as questions, or at least presented as speculative opinions. 'Do you think the title *The Crucible* suggests that the characters change like a chemical reaction under intense heat?' adopts this tentative form. In this way a student can sidestep the pressure of offering a dogmatic critical judgement. The formula is also more likely to encourage a response from other members of the group.

Even though you may have done whatever preparatory work may be necessary you may still find it difficult to play a full part in seminar discussion. In the questionnaire, the responses to the statement 'I sometimes have something to say but lack the confidence to say it' are evidence of this. However, there are some positive steps that more retiring students can take to make the process of participation easier, in addition to ensuring that they are properly prepared.

First, you should recognise that the discussion process is central to the success of your course and not an optional extra. You may be working within a system that actually rewards active participation in discussion as part of your continuous assessment. In such circumstances, an awareness that you are being given credit for your contributions to discussion may well provide the necessary motivation to overcome starter's block. Such a practice, however, is by no means common to all colleges and universities.

In a new group try to get to know the names of as many students as you can, and use them when appropriate. The better you know people the more easily you can talk to them. It may be that commenting on a friend's observation is the easiest way of getting started. A response to the comment on *The Crucible* quoted above might have been: 'Does Rachel's point about stage directions mean that we have to treat them as an essential part of the text of a play?' You certainly should not feel obliged to wait for the tutor's response before offering your own.

Listen carefully to the discussion once it starts. Many discussions alternate student contributions with tutor responses. Arguably the most successful seminars consist of students carrying the discussion themselves with the tutor playing merely a supporting role. Listening attentively provides you with opportunities to support, or challenge, or modify what other students are saying. Remember that the longer you stay silent in the group the greater the difficulty of eventually speaking will become. Settling for some non-controversial statement, or even a simple question, in the first week will ease the way into subsequent, possibly more challenging, observations.

The previous paragraphs have been suggesting ways of overcoming natural shyness in order to play a full part in discussion. Many of you will not need such advice. Indeed if you have a sympathetic tutor who uses appropriate strategies to make you feel at ease almost all members of the group will be able to contribute comfortably. At times the opposite difficulty occurs. A student may begin to dominate a discussion, and continue to do so week after week. She may not even realise that she is doing this, or even think that she is doing the rest of the group and the tutor a service. The tutor is primarily responsible for dealing with this situation, but needs the co-operation of the rest of the group. The tutor can hardly suggest that the offending student curtails her contributions if the result is that discussion ceases entirely. The situation is always best resolved by the group as a whole showing that all its members are both capable of contributing and keen to do so.

We have so far been concerned with seminar discussion based on a topic or a text notified in advance. Though this is the commonest practice, you will sometimes be faced with a text that you have not seen before and to which you are asked to respond there and then. This procedure might at first sight seem a more testing one, but in some ways it can be easier. You are not expected to bring any previous knowledge with you; the tutor and the rest of the group know that your comments are immediate reactions. In this situation you will be thinking out loud, using talk as a means of clarifying what you think. Here, more clearly than in any other situation, you will be experiencing Eliot's wrestle with words and meanings. A discussion of Gertrude Stein's one-line poem 'Rose is a rose is a rose is a rose'[2] produced the following initial comments:

- Why does it stop there?
- It seems a difficult poem and a simple poem.
- Does it have something to do with love?
- The poet obviously had his mind on something else at the time; it's just a doodle.
- I think it's trying to say something about language, about how language is inadequate to express how beautiful things are – well, a rose is, or Rose is.

Even though the 'ums' and 'ers' and little pauses have been removed from the observations the language of the comments is recognisably tentative. Two are framed as questions, a technique mentioned earlier. All make use of words and phrases that feel their way towards meaning ('something', 'seems', 'I think'). Here the first steps are being taken around the poem as the members of the group approach it from different angles, expressing their own perceptions and preconceptions. With each one we get a fresh point of view. Since they are initial, almost instinctive reactions, they are not expected to be carefully phrased. There is a sense of students thinking as they speak, a characteristic that will appear even more strongly in the extracts from small group discussions that appear later in the chapter.

One of the advantages of spoken as opposed to written comment is that it can be quickly revised. It can even be withdrawn completely if it is seen to be inappropriate or a misjudgement. The student who observed that the poem was 'just a doodle' later volunteered the amended observation that the poem '*seemed* just like a doodle'. But her initial view had expressed her immediate and genuine reaction, and it was certainly a reaction that was shared by other students in the group. It was therefore important to express it, since whatever view of a work we eventually hold, it is with our genuine first reactions that we must begin.

Not all discussions in seminars take the form that we have so far considered. You may be given a chance to exchange ideas with a neighbour for a short while before a more general discussion begins. This has three advantages: several students can express their views at the same time; the views are more considered; and it is easier to voice to the whole group (and your tutor) views that you have already been sharing with another student. Your tutor may direct your attention to a number of specific issues by means of a worksheet, and give you an opportunity to think things through individually before open discussion begins. In both these cases you will need to make a note of your ideas so that they can be easily recalled when the plenary discussion begins.

You should also remember that most seminars will contain a significant input from your tutor. In the less formal setting of the seminar as compared to the lecture you will find it easier to put questions, to ask for clarification, amplification or examples. Tutors have time to communicate to you only a very small part of the knowledge they have and the views they hold. They select from this knowledge material appropriate to what they consider to be your needs as a student. But some of those needs will be apparent only to you. For really effective teaching and learning your tutors must know what these needs are. If you do not voice them they may well go unmet.

The student presentation

The student presentation has been a common feature in higher education teaching programmes for some time. Traditionally the standard method for a student to express her considered views has been the written essay, which is the subject of Chapter 3. This is usually seen only by the student and her tutor. The essay has also been the principal way for a tutor to assess a student's progress on a course. The student presentation is, however, more and more widely used for these purposes alongside the essay, and it is unlikely that you will go through an undergraduate programme in literature without being involved in the procedure. It can take a variety of forms, but essentially it involves students presenting ideas in spoken rather than written form, and to other students, rather than simply the tutor.

Its increasing popularity reflects two developments in our thinking about appropriate ways of teaching and learning at degree level. They are the need for students to be active rather than passive, and the need to give students greater confidence in expressing themselves in front of an audience. The first derives partly from the maxim that there is no better motivation for learning something than the prospect of having to teach it (and no better sign that you have learned it thoroughly than the fact that you have explained it clearly). The second derives from the growing concern that students should acquire skills that will be useful in employment after graduation. Confidence, clarity and fluency in spoken English, particularly in public, are seen as important transferable skills of this kind. Whatever the precise nature of the presentation you are required to deliver, the guidelines that follow should help you to get the most out of the method.

Though you may be challenged occasionally in seminars to give your views there and then, you will not be asked to give a presentation without reasonable notice. It will, after all, take place in timetabled time and be part of the learning process for the whole group to which it is to be given. If you write an ill-prepared and poorly expressed essay the painful consequences are limited to you as the writer and your tutor as the reader. A poor presentation will have to be endured by the rest of the group as well. Both you and your tutor therefore have a vested interest in ensuring that presentations are as carefully planned as possible.

The *planning process* is particularly important if you are working with one or more partners. You may have to decide on a precise topic for the presentation that suits you all. If the general topic is already fixed by the tutor you will need to establish a precise focus; to decide on an equitable sharing of the work in the early stages of reading; to select appropriate material; to give some thought to how the delivery of the presentation is to be split between you; and to discuss whether the presentation is to be solely talk-based, or to be supported by audio-visual aids or other materials and devices. Try to avoid producing two or three mini-presentations loosely tagged together, usually the sign of inadequate planning and discussion. The process of working with a partner is supposed to give you practice in co-operation, so you should be prepared to compromise in the interests of a successful end-product. The number of meetings that you will need will vary, but it is unlikely that you will achieve a satisfactory product in fewer than three. A record of meetings is sometimes required, so that tutors can see evidence of the planning process, and students can reflect on its effectiveness. The particular form shown in Appendix B was completed as part of a first-year presentation after only six weeks in college. It asks the student to assess briefly the success of the presentation as well as record the planning process. It is not an untypical example. You will notice that the planning process took some time, and went through different stages of optimism and pessimism. There were some late changes to the format of the presentation, and a general feeling that, apart from the lack of questions at the end, it had been successful. We shall return to it in the section on the form of presentations.

The *content* of your presentation will be very much governed by the time you have available. You will often be given certain upper and lower time limits for it; if you are, ensure that you stay within them. This will mean running the presentation through in the exact form in which you intend to deliver it, and pruning if necessary. Most presentations will be relatively short; ten to fifteen minutes might be a typical length. This means that you will have to ensure a clear focus. Establish what is essential to get across, and ensure that you convey this. A sharp focus, a small number of key points clearly conveyed, will be particularly necessary if you are dealing with a large topic, or a substantial text. Remember that you will not be expected to cover everything, and an attempt to do so will result only in confusing your audience. Presentations entitled 'Tennyson: A Survey' or 'Charles Dickens: An Introduction' would give cause for concern. They would not necessarily be unsuccessful – no doubt you can say something worthwhile on such massive topics in fifteen minutes – but they would probably be rapid and indigestible surveys. Either the amount of material covered would need to be reduced, or the topic narrowed to something more precise, or both.

'Tennyson's view of women' would be more manageable; 'Tennyson's view of women in *The Princess*' would be even more so.

Highly successful presentations can often be based on close consideration of single poems, or extracts from novels or plays. In such cases the focus is clear and the presenters could either offer a detailed analysis of the material or move outwards from it to illustrate typical characteristics of the author or the work. Beginnings and endings of novels can often be profitably analysed in this way; so can single scenes from a play, or even briefer passages of dialogue. You may well be given guidelines about the relative importance of the presentation's content as opposed to its form. It is sufficient to say here that the more thoughtful, perceptive, organised and clear the content is, the better the presentation will be. The precise form in which you present that content can certainly make a difference to its impact on your listeners, but no amount of showmanship can make up for content that is inherently weak.

One of the delights of presentations, for students and tutor alike, is that they can be greatly varied in *form*. At one extreme they may appear to be little more than essays read in public. This approach would be limited and unimaginative, but if the content were good and the reading convincing this form of presentation could be successful, though probably not memorable. At the other extreme they can make use of audio- and videotape, slides, overhead projectors, pictures and posters. They can employ dramatised reconstructions, imagined conversations between long-dead writers and the delivery of the presentation in the style of the work being discussed. They can involve distributing grapes to the audience, the singing of 'The Croppy Boy' and the close inspection of real and plastic daffodils. The examples draw only on recent presentations I have seen, but they are typical of the kind of inventive and imaginative approaches that some students bring to this method of assessment.

The record of presentation meetings sheet describes the preparation for a presentation on Virginia Woolf's short story 'The Legacy' (written 1940, published 1985). Three students co-operated on the piece and discussed and rejected a number of ways of tackling the story before deciding on a dramatised conversation between three people: Virginia Woolf herself, an unnamed critic and Gilbert Clandon, the central character in the story. This imaginative approach enabled them to present three different views of the work. At one stage the character interrupted the author to correct her view of him, an interruption which raised some interesting points about the nature of literary works, the function of authors and the status of fictional characters! The imaginative form of this presentation did not guarantee its success; that depended heavily on what thoughts were expressed by the three dramatised characters, and what light they threw on the nature of the short story. But there is no doubt that the presentation was listened to more attentively and stayed longer in the memory.

Using *audio-visual aids* is the most obvious way of supporting and enlivening your presentation. They can help to sharpen your spoken comments, to reinforce a point, or produce an unexpected effect. Some topics immediately suggest visual reinforcement: William Blake's own illustrations of his poems; Pre-Raphaelite illustrations to Keats or Tennyson; Gustave Doré's illustrations for 'The Ancient Mariner'. Others suggest the use of music: Beethoven's fifth symphony in *Howards End* (1910); Benjamin Britten's settings of Wilfred Owen's poems in *The War Requiem;* Paul Simon's 'Hearts and Bones' for *Educating Rita* (1980).[3] You will find it helpful to check your library catalogue for non-book media on the topic you have chosen. There are a growing number of audio- and videotapes available. Try, however, to ensure that the technical aids serve a real purpose, and are not being used merely to demonstrate your skill with them.

When you have decided what equipment is appropriate, and acquired it, check that it works. If you can get into the room a little time before the presentation is due to start this will enable you to set up whatever you need as well as giving it a final check. If circumstances allow it you should run through your presentation at this stage, using the audio-visual aids. Few things can destroy the presenters' confidence more quickly than discovering that they are playing the wrong side of a tape or that a slide is upside down.

Other ways of graphically reinforcing your spoken comments will no doubt occur to you, many of which can be provided simply, without technical help. You may feel, for instance, that it is helpful to give your audience a summary of your key points. This could be done using an overhead projector (OHP), or a duplicated handout which provides a more permanent record of your views. A large clear wall chart can also be useful and inexpensive. If your presentation does include supportive written material try to ensure that your audience is not tempted to copy it down instead of listening to you. This means deciding on the most appropriate time to distribute such material. Take the same care in producing and checking it that you would with an essay.

Good content will always be enhanced by good *delivery*. A poorly delivered presentation will have its effectiveness reduced in the same way as a poorly written essay. Having gone to the trouble of producing interesting and helpful views and information you should communicate them as effectively as you can. Audibility is the first criterion. This should not be difficult to achieve, but if you are not sure whether you can be heard clearly, then get another member of your group to listen to you. Speak more slowly than you normally would. This will not only improve audibility but it will allow your audience to take in what you are saying and give them a chance to make notes. Remember that they, unlike you, are hearing the material for the first time.

You may have the choice of working either from a full script, written out as you would an essay, or from notes. The former ensures fluency and is a safety net for those who fear they may be lost for words at crucial moments. The danger is that the presentation will simply sound like an essay read out. Try to avoid this by looking at your audience as often as possible, and varying your delivery, in pitch and speed. Not all parts of your presentation will be of equal significance, so stress what needs to be stressed. Working from notes is usually more effective, so long as you know your material well. This method is also a more useful transferable skill.

Presentations are usually a valuable learning experience for the whole group. As a member of the audience your first task is to have done any preliminary reading on which the presentation depends. If you arrive for a presentation which you know to be on 'The Love Song of J. Alfred Prufrock' (1917) without having read Eliot's poem then you will not benefit fully from the work your fellow students have put in.

Your second task is to give them your complete *attention*. You will, after all, have to go through the process at some point yourself, and you will welcome an attentive and sympathetic audience. Paying attention is, in any case, in your own interest. Students find the views of other students interesting, and presentations usually offer careful and considered views.

Your third task is to be prepared to ask questions. By doing so you can make the most effective use of the knowledge gained by the presenters, not all of which has necessarily been communicated in the presentation. Asking questions is also supportive of the presenters' efforts. As you can see from the final comments on the record of presentation meetings sheet, presenters sometimes assume that an absence of questions from their audience indicates an absence of interest.

Your course tutors will no doubt provide you with specific instructions for your presentations. Ensure that you know what they are and that you follow them. This is particularly important if the presentation is part of your continuous assessment. The general guidelines suggested above might be summarised as follows:

- Allow enough time for thorough preparation.
- Establish a clear focus for the content.
- Decide on a suitable format and structure.
- Consider what audio-visual aids or supportive material will enhance the presentation.
- Check that equipment is available and that it works.
- Rehearse the complete presentation and time it.

Small group work

The typical seminar group described above may often be broken down into a number of smaller groups (this may even happen occasionally in large lectures). These small groups may operate within the seminar session – reporting back after a short period of discussion to the seminar group as a whole – or they maybe timetabled independently, and allocated a longer period of time. Whatever the precise method employed, the small group has opportunities, and problems, that are different from the seminar group. It is to these that we turn now.

The smaller your discussion group, the harder you have to work. In a seminar group of twenty-five there is much less pressure on individuals to contribute than in a discussion group of five. And since the tutor is not usually part of the group there is no one to fill in the gaps or to control the direction of the discussion; that is no one except the members of the group who must take responsibility for its success or failure. Playing a full part in the group's activities is therefore your first obligation. Where a group is operating without a tutor, and where there is a relatively long discussion period, some drifting into irrelevance is unavoidable. It will not invalidate the rest of the discussion, and can be very enjoyable. However, if you find yourselves spending ten minutes recalling last weekend's party or last night's film then it is time to refocus your attention. As with any discussion individuals will contribute in different proportions. But if you have a group in which one member is reluctant to make any contribution then you might try asking her directly for comments; this may overcome the shyness or laziness.

Though you will have to raise your work-rate for the small group, other things will be easier. The absence of the tutor should be a liberating factor. You will not have to consider what she may think of your comments, and you will be much less worried about confessing ignorance or venturing an opinion. The size of the group will also make discussion easier. The questionnaire shows that it is only when discussion takes place in a small group that virtually all students feel happy to contribute. Again, make sure you know each other's names before discussion begins.

In many cases the tutor will have already provided a structure for your deliberations in the form of a worksheet; this may suggest certain topics to explore, or pose particular questions to be answered. The following worksheet, for first-year groups, on Jeanette Winterson's novel *Sexing the Cherry* (1989) mixes general questions about the novel with instructions to look at specific passages from it:

Sexing the Cherry: initial discussion
Please spend forty minutes on the worksheet below. Make brief notes of your conclusions to report back to the seminar group.

- Devise three or four sentences which summarise the settings and narrative content of the novel.
- What features of the novel's structure can you identify? What use does it make of chapters, sections or smaller units to organise the narrative?
- How is the story told to the reader? What happens to the narrative structure on page 113?
- What do you take to be the function of the banana and pineapple symbols in the novel? Comment particularly on pages 113 and 121.
- Discuss the significance of the title in the light of the Marvell poem attached, and page 79 of the novel.
- Are you aware of repeated phrases in the novel? Do any of them suggest certain issues with which the novel is particularly concerned?

Members of a group using a discussion sheet like this would have to decide only when to move from one point to another in order to complete their discussion in the time available.

In other cases the tutor may want the discussion to be much more open and may therefore be much less specific in the brief given to the group. This strategy may be commonly used when a text is being approached for the first time. The extracts that follow, taken from three separate discussion groups (with four, or five, students in each group), illustrate some of the ways in which students can work together to share insights and solve problems. They are working on 'Spring and Fall; to a Young Child' by Gerard Manley Hopkins:

Margaret, are you grieving
Over Goldengrove unleaving?
Leaves, like the things of man, you
With your fresh thoughts, care for, can you?
Ah! as the heart grows older   5
It will come to such sights colder
By and by, nor spare a sigh
Though worlds of wanwood leafmeal lie;
And yet you *will* weep, and know why.
Now no matter, child, the name: 10
Sorrow's springs are the same.
Nor mouth had, no nor mind, expressed
What heart heard of, ghost guessed:
It is the blight man was born for,
It is Margaret you mourn for.[4]   15

The students have come to the poem fresh, knowing neither the author nor the date of the poem. They have been asked to spend five minutes studying the poem privately, and then each of the students is to read the poem aloud to the others. The remaining twenty minutes are to be spent discussing and recording whatever aspects of the poem they find interesting.

The extracts show clearly how small group discussion can be a co-operative process in which students will happily air, modify or abandon opinions, but that the process almost always moves towards a solution of difficulties and a clearer or richer view of the poem. In the first extract group one is struggling with the opening couplet:

Student A: What's Goldengrove? Is it a place? We don't expect 'unleaving' you expect 'leaving', you know what I mean. I had to look at that again.
Student B: Well, children sort of, the seasons are more meaningful; we get more blasé when we get older, I mean spring, summer and autumn comes and goes but I think probably a child is more observant, and there is a sort of sorrow when you see the leaves tumbling down, and so he's questioning her grief over Goldengrove . . . sort of autumn of life, you know he's saying you're going to meet these . . .
Student C: In the future she's possibly going to come across worse sights . . .
Student B: I just see it as observing her sort of sorrow that autumn has arrived and all the leaves are falling off the trees.

The struggle can be clearly seen in the tentative phraseology. The extracts are punctuated with such expressions as 'if you know what I mean', 'sort of ', 'probably' and 'possibly'. Even though the many pauses and 'ums' and 'ers' have been removed in the transcripts, there is still a strong sense that the students are feeling their way towards saying what they mean. Students in these groups where the tutor is absent also seem happy to ask each other questions. Here, in group two, a student asks a question and has it answered:

> Student G: Why is it 'over Goldengrove unleaving'?
> Student H: It's like another reference to autumn isn't it?
> Student G: Oh, I see, yes . . .
> Student F: It's like the trees unburdening themselves of their leaves.

Here the participants in the discussion help each other towards a more appropriate reading of the poem. This co-operation is seen in the following extract . Earlier in the discussion, group two had agreed that 'sorrow's springs' referred to springs of water. Now they return to reconsider that phrase:

> Student G: 'Sorrow's springs'? Are we convinced that they are springs of water? Or the actual spring season . . . with each spring comes a new sorrow?
> Student F: Well it says, 'Now no matter, child, the name: Sorrow's springs are the same'. Well what I . . .
> Student I: 'From where sorrow springs', you could say.
> Student F: Yes, as you say don't worry about naming it, it'll . . .
> Student I : The source is the same but it comes with different names.

Throughout the discussions participants seem happy to interrupt and be interrupted, and, more importantly, to relinquish opinions they have expressed in the light of the views of other students. This process is particularly important in dealing with passages of obvious difficulty. All the groups express initial bewilderment over lines 13 and 14. But by the end of their discussion group three have come to terms with its compressed syntax, and the student who asks the question supplies her own answer moments later:

> Student J: What did the heart hear of?
> Student K: I suppose it's perhaps inly felt. You don't actually know it; you can't see it outside . . . you can't see it physically . . . mouth . . . your mind hasn't registered it, but in your heart you feel it when you're young; it's only as you grow older and your perceptions change that your heart feels it and then . . .

Student J: Or is it also this sorrow that the girl's feeling; you can't describe it or you can't analyse it in your head but you can feel it and it's like an inexpressible sorrow.

Remember that there is no input from a tutor in discussions like these; the students make progress merely by having thirty minutes in which to read and reflect, and then offering their different perspectives on the couplet. Usually those perspectives which are helpful and enrich the poem are taken up, while those that are limiting, or arise from misconceptions, are abandoned.

It is surprising how often different groups will reach similar conclusions. In the following extracts all three groups have been considering the title of the poem and its implications. All are aware of the two principal associations of 'Fall', but their comments are also similar in the way in which they link 'blight' (line 14) with the title. The extract from group one that follows shows the link being made in the simplest way. One student draws attention to the religious associations of 'Fall' and is interrupted by two others who quote line 14 simultaneously:

Student B: You could take it as Spring and Fall, literally as spring and autumn, but you could also take it as spring and the fall of Man . . . Well I think the fall of Man comes in you know . . .
Students A and D: 'It's the blight man was born for'.

Group three arrive at the association in by a slightly longer route. The first speaker notices the physical connection between a child springing and the possible resulting fall. Then the second speaker builds on that, moving from the literal to the metaphorical and thence to line 14:

Student K: The title chimes in well really; he links the spring to like the seasonal aspect but it also brings in the idea of the child springing, jumping around full of vitality . . . and then the fall's like the poet saying, 'It's not like this, this is what the world's really like'.
Student L: I suppose the fall links in sort of with the fall of Man, perhaps, I don't know, 'this is the blight man was born for' . . . I suppose he means mankind rather than just man, but it doesn't fit in with the rhyme.

Group two arrive at the same association, only they start with a comment on the meaning of 'blight' and then go back to the title. The final comment even sees the tree at the start of the poem as having religious associations:

Student H: Blight's a disease, isn't it?
Student F: It's to do with vegetation as well . . . and maybe, you know you
    said about 'Spring and Fall' being very American, maybe it's to do with
    the fall of Man as well . . .
Student G: Yes, the Tree of Knowledge.

The specific extracts quoted above have been chosen to illustrate certain points about the ways in which such groups work, but they are not untypical extracts. It is clear that where students are prepared to look carefully at literary works and to contribute fully and honestly to a discussion of them, they can make huge strides towards a richer understanding, and greater enjoyment. Of course not all small group discussions work smoothly, but when they do they are probably the most rewarding form of literary study. The students in the discussion groups quoted above had the advantage of knowing each other quite well, and so seem happy to interrupt and disagree. You may not have this advantage, but if the discussion goes well one result will be that you know each other better, as well as the literature.

Discussion groups like the ones above can be self-contained, but it is more likely that you will be asked to report the results of your discussion to a larger group, or in some cases to your tutor. This makes the process of recording the discussion an important one. Where discussion has been based on a detailed worksheet (such as the one based on *Sexing the Cherry* above) it will be obvious what information or opinions need to be recorded. Where the discussion has been more open-ended it is usually necessary to record only the conclusions reached, noting dissenting opinions where they occur. A reporter should be appointed before the discussion begins, though other group members may find it helpful to make their own notes.

Conclusion: The active learner

This chapter has been concerned with discussing literature in class. It has stressed the importance of your active contribution to the process of learning about, and responding to, works of literature. Principally this has been illustrated by examples of the questioning and discussion process in lectures, seminars and small groups, and in the student presentation.

However, you may well come across other teaching techniques which require an input from you. Much can be learned from reading a poem aloud as a prelude to studying it, or comparing different readings. Extracts from plays can profitably be recreated, even in an unpromising lecture-room setting. Role-play, in which students are asked to take on the role of a character and explore it by responding to questions, or improvisation, provides an imaginative way into some texts. Different tutors will have their own variations on 'buzz' groups or 'brainstorming' or 'syndicates'. And of course individual tutorials with a tutor will provide occasional opportunities to explore quite specific issues relating to your own work. But whatever the precise methods employed, the object is the same: to bring literature off the page by establishing a connection with readers who are active not passive, involved not inert. For this process to work well you should be:

- Prepared to contribute, even if this means overcoming natural shyness.
- Willing to ask questions and seek clarification.
- Honest in expressing your feelings and opinions.
- Ready to reconsider your judgements in the light of further evidence.
- Familiar with the work you are studying.

The rewards of approaching classes in this way are considerable. The classes themselves will be much more enjoyable; the texts you are studying will be revealed in a richer and more significant way; and you will emerge from a degree course in literature more articulate and more confident in your ability to express yourself.

Notes

1. T. S. Eliot, *Four Quartets* (London: Faber and Faber, 1959), p. 26.
2. Gertrude Stein, *Geography and Plays* (New York: Something Else Press, 1968), p. 187.
3. Russell refers to the track 'Train in the Distance' when asked about the central theme of *Educating Rita* and other of his plays.
4. *The Poems of Gerard Manley Hopkins*, ed. W. H. Gardner and N. H. MacKenzie, 4th. edn (London: Oxford U.P., 1967), p. 88.

Appendix A: Student questionnaire

Two hundred second- and third-year students at Chester College were asked to respond to a number of statements about contributing to discussion, and self-expression in literature classes. Their responses are given below. (SA = strongly agree; A = agree; N = neither agree nor disagree; D = disagree; SD = strongly disagree.)

	SA	A	N	D	SD
I find it easy to ask questions in the large lecture situation.	3	14	45	99	39
I find it easy to contribute to discussion in seminar groups of twenty-five.	26	56	61	44	13
I find it easy to contribute to discussion in groups of four or five.	40	98	40	15	7
I find it easier to contribute to discussion with students I know.	43	104	48	4	1
I find it easier to discuss literary texts when I know them well.	36	136	22	6	0
I rarely gain anything from listening to the observations of other students.	0	8	27	119	46
Expressing your views becomes easier the more you do it.	44	101	31	23	1
One aim of a degree course in literature is to improve your ability to express yourself.	11	106	51	28	4
Giving presentations does not improve your ability to express yourself.	4	21	61	84	30
I sometimes have something to say but lack the confidence to say it.	24	42	95	28	11

Appendix B: Record of presentation meetings

Title of presentation: 'The Legacy', Virginia Woolf
Names of presenters: Julia, Kate and Lesley
First meeting: 19 October, 1.45 p.m. At this first meeting we discussed individual ideas on how the presentation should be organised. We agreed to go away and bring back written ideas on three basic areas: Virginia Woolf and her writings (Lesley); the narrative of the story (Kate); and the structure (Julia).
We agreed to have an overhead and a duplicated handout.
Second meeting: 26 October, 7.00 p.m. Each of us presented our findings. We discussed the form of the presentation, and agreed to present

the story in a dramatic scene with three characters: Woolf (Lesley); a critic (Kate) and Gilbert, the story's main character (Julia). We felt that this would give us a lot of scope for information. We started on the script.

Third meeting: 31 October, 7.00 p.m. We worked on a critical analysis of the text – lots of discussion. We felt as a group that we worked well and respected one another's opinions. We ran through the script which was a bit short; decided to add a section on the context and language of the story.

Fourth meeting: 1 November, 6.30 p.m. Rehearsed the script – made some final adjustments. Decided to photocopy a script for each of our characters, since we weren't what you'd call word perfect! Kate drew a stage plan. Julia had typed the handout (made some small adjustments). Made sure we were clear about terms such as 'ironic stance' and 'satire' in case we were questioned about them.

Self-assessment of presentation: We enjoyed giving the presentation, which is something we thought we wouldn't do! We felt that our hard work had paid off, and that we were pleased with it as our first presentation in College.

Though we felt the 'audience' paid attention, we were disappointed at the small number of questions – we'd prepared ourselves to answer a lot! We enjoyed working together.

3

Writing about literature

Jo Pryke

Writing critical essays

Why write about literature at all? The only answer you yourself would perhaps feel like giving, at the moment anyway, is 'Because I've got to (or will have to), in order to gain a mark which goes towards my final grade'. Initially, fulfilling course requirements is probably the main imperative for most students, accompanied in varying degrees by the desire to do so as well as possible. Most tutors accept that, and indeed I would add a further utilitarian point: writing is one of the best ways of learning, so that a good piece of written work is an excellent piece of preparation for the end-of-course exam. I will therefore leave to the end of the chapter points on what, apart from a good mark, you may have gained from this rather tightly disciplined exercise, as well as working out how to do better next time. The larger questions of the function of the traditional, formal essay within modern literary studies, and the rationale behind it, are interesting and valid. However, since most literature departments do still use it as the main method of assessment (in both course work and exams) the question to consider here is 'how to do it'. Moreover, while questions do sometimes come in new disguises, the truth is that innovative forms of assignment for literature students will almost certainly demand the same careful attention to the agenda being set, the same personal understanding and judgement of the texts, and awareness of the critical issues raised by them, not to mention the same care with appropriate and correct language and presentation, as do more conventional essay questions.

What follows is therefore overtly addressed to the successful accomplishment of that much more common task.

First, then, what exactly are you being asked to produce? A critical essay is a piece of writing about a literary text, or texts, which addresses a specific question within (normally) 1500 to 2000 words. The 'question' is usually in fact more of an instruction: to discuss, consider, or say how far you agree with a given proposition. A critical essay uses a certain kind of English, is presented in a certain way, and must meet criteria which are almost universally applied by tutors marking them. These are:

- Relevance.
- Logical structure.
- Personal response and evaluation.
- Use of the text(s) and critics.

In first-year degree work use of critics may not be required. (Check on this.) In addition, an essay may have to demonstrate an awareness of the context, both literary and social, within which a text has been produced. All these criteria will be defined and explained at appropriate points in the chapter.

'The most important thing is to think.' That one piece of advice about writing essays, given to my daughter by a third-year student when she started college is, she says, the most useful she ever had. (She did well.) If you really take it to heart, you need not bother to read the rest of this chapter. Making oneself really think is, however, one of the hardest things to do. So, as with any daunting task, the job of writing a critical essay is best tackled on the 'next step' basis. What follows is not, of course, to be taken as an absolute blueprint for anyone, for we all work out our own variations on how to do anything. The stages in the process are:

- Preparatory work (organising enough time; choosing and defining the topic, selecting your texts).
- Reading, note-taking, and drafting.
- Writing the essay.
- Revising and producing the essay.
- The learning process.

If this sounds dreary and daunting, what will keep you going? Surely it is the delight – yes, delight – yielded by the texts themselves, which is the reason for becoming a student of literature in the first place, but which can get lost to sight. Don't let it.

Preparatory work

First, how much *time* should you spend writing a critical essay? Essays do get produced, from start to finish, in the twenty-four (or even twelve) hours preceding the deadline. They show it. So does time taken to mull over your topic, and to think about what you are doing, as you go along. Scraping a pass mark with a rushed job is possible – and rather pointless. Getting a really good mark for a literature essay does demand the kind of 'passionate attention' that Merritt Moseley talks about above in Chapter 1. That in turn demands time, the management of which he also discusses. How much? Several days at least, perhaps a week in some cases. You know your own schedule and pace of work. Remember that a submission date is the *last* date for submission, not the first. How much time do you need for each stage? This is an individual matter, so a rough plan is useful: some people are quicker readers, some quicker writers than others. Another severely practical point is the availability of books, if you are using critics: tutors tend to respond to, 'I need an extension because I've had a terrible problem finding anything on . . .' with the heartless question, 'When did you start looking?'

Next, *choosing and defining the topic* of the essay. This needs careful thought. Since relevance – seeing the point of a question and sticking to it – is a major criterion of a good essay, it is obviously important to choose a topic with which you really want to get involved. This does not necessarily mean a question about texts you love; something you hate might get your adrenalin going better. 'The fascination of what's difficult' (W. B. Yeats's phrase, in the less mundane context of his famous poem by that name) could be a useful challenge, especially if there is something you really need to sort out, but have not yet managed to do so. A further practical consideration, but one which could be enough to concentrate the mind, is the value of doing a substantial piece of work on something which is sure to come up in end-of-course exams.

Given the priority of relevance, the enormous importance of reading, understanding and analysing a question for its hidden agenda is clear. What do I mean by the sinister-sounding 'hidden agenda'? Questions are not plucked from the air, but designed to encourage careful thought about specific aspects of the texts you have been studying with the tutor and your fellow-students. In other words, the essay is not a separate, stand-alone part of the course, but integral to it – or it should be. Thus each question in fact contains it own agenda – that is, a list of things to be done; however, such is the academic mind that this is not always spelt out, but wrapped up in an elegant quotation or deliberately provocative statement. Incidentally, if you have tried to analyse a question, and are still not sure what it is really getting at, it would be a rare tutor who would refuse to discuss it with you.

The most common form of question consists of a quotation, opinion or statement, attached to which there will usually be one explicit instruction or question. Find that and underline it. There are not many variations on the basic terms: 'examine', 'consider', 'compare', 'contrast', 'make the case for – or against', 'how far do you agree that . . .' or 'discuss'. Whichever it is, that is what you have to do, and nothing else.

Just what it involves, however, requires a little more thought: to 'compare' two things will in fact mean distinguishing the ways in which they differ as well as the ways in which they are alike, and to 'contrast' them inevitably means registering their similarities as well as their differences. To 'examine' something means alertly noticing everything about it that is relevant to your purposes, so it means analysing, not just describing. To 'consider how far you agree with' a statement about a text involves a very careful examination of it, in the light of the critical issues raised by the question, in order to provide a convincing statement of the *extent* of your agreement. To 'make a case for or against' a given position, you have to show understanding of both sides of the argument, in order to support your case. In one way or another you are always being asked to 'discuss'. That useful word, the most commonly used of all rubrics, encompasses analysis, comparison and understanding, both of *what* a text is saying and of *how* it is saying it. What you are being asked to do, in writing a critical essay, is to exercise those skills of 'critical reading' described by Chris Walsh in Chapter 5, but to do so from a particular, prescribed point of view. The skill you have to develop here, in finding the hidden agenda, is that of recognising the key words in a question and, having done that, understanding what key issues they raise. A health warning: no question set in a university-level literature course will ever require you, overtly or covertly, to tell the story or describe the characters, or in any other way simply *paraphrase* a text, for what could be more pointless for you, or more boring for the tutor? If you find yourself deciding that this is the nice, easy agenda set by a question, stop and think again.

Let us decode a sample question. (Do not skip this because you do not know anything about Elizabeth Gaskell: it is simply a demonstration of how to tackle the analysis of any question, and contains a fundamentally important point.)

'In a Gaskell novel individual growth and development are shown
to be inseparable from social influences.' Discuss.

Having underlined 'Discuss', you might wonder what on earth to do
next. A preliminary point, about all questions which contain quotations,
is that just because something is between quotation marks you do not
have to agree with it. In practice, to 'discuss' means to consider the
validity of a statement, to think out, and assess, points in favour and
points against. You therefore proceed with this one in the same way as for
all types of question, by underlining what seem to be the other key words.
This takes considerable thought at first, but with practice you will develop the skill. The point here is to develop careful, precise reading – just
what your whole literature course is about. My candidates for underlining here would be 'a', 'shown' and 'inseparable' – as well as 'Gaskell', of
course.

The 'a', which of course means 'any', raises the preliminary question,
which comes up in relation to any critical essay, of the *selection of texts* for
consideration. What an airy generalisation this question offers! You cannot possibly be expected to read all of Gaskell's novels, that is obvious,
but how many should you cover in order to make safe generalisations?
The problem can be tackled in the light of the practicalities of the
situation: the normal first-year essay of 1500 to 2000 words is not that
long; it is better to show good knowledge and understanding of a couple
of novels than to offer sketchy and superficial observations on several. As
long as you make clear at the start of your essay how many texts you are
using, your reasons for your choice, and your awareness of the limitations
of your generalisations, everyone will be happy. The point here is that the
question of range of material is one you need to consider when tackling
any question. Tutors will usually give guidance on this matter. It is an
important one, especially when you are writing not about novels but
poetry, or drama, where there will be much less reading time. Merely
using a few poems already discussed in class will not go down well, but an
encyclopedic knowledge of a poet's work will not be expected either: a
sensibly representative selection, chosen in the light of the issues raised
by the question, will do. The Gaskell question, quoted above, would
probably be set if you were already studying one novel obviously in the
'individual and society' mode, such as *North and South* (1854–5). The
choice of a second text to go with it would need to be made carefully, and
in accordance with your overall response to the assumption being made in
the question.

But to continue with my other 'key' words. You may have been surprised that these were 'shown' and 'inseparable', *not* 'individual growth and development' and 'social influences'. In such a brief, succinct statement, almost all the words may seem 'key'. This is where our *thinking* starts: what is the statement *really* saying? Is it simply saying, 'All Gaskell's novels *are about* individual growth and development and social influences?' No, because that would be a topic merely requiring paraphrase in response, a GCSE-level kind of question. The statement is, of course, more challenging than that, for it is a sweeping generalisation, and as nature abhors a vacuum, so does the academic mind abhor sweeping statements. The good critical essay, such as this question is designed to elicit, is not one-sided, though it does usually end up taking a view. What you are actually being asked to discuss here is whether something which (the statement assumes) Gaskell's novels are always about – individual growth and development – is *shown* to be *inseparable* from something else assumed to be the invariable subject matter – social influences. Of course the assumption here, that Gaskell's work always *is* about these things, would be noted in the opening paragraph of a good answer, and qualified assent or dissent indicated. The choice of texts would be explained in the light of this. But the main point here is that careful thought reveals the question to be not so much about the subject matter (nice and easy to focus on), as about the *method* of a Gaskell novel – considerably harder, but much more interesting, to answer. The 'agenda' being set is, in fact, to consider Gaskell's didactic form of realism.

Why do I say that? Here is the train of thought which leads to that conclusion. First, we need to define the word 'shown' as used in this context: just what does it mean? Thinking about this makes us focus, in the first place, on the nature of a Gaskell text as a piece of realist writing. (This is not the place to go into the tricky topic of the meaning of literary realism, though you would be well advised to do so to *some* extent in putting together a satisfactory answer to this particular question.) Proceeding, then, purely on the basis of carefully working things out for oneself, it becomes clear that 'shown' can mean two things here, which together constitute a description of Gaskell's kind of realism. In one sense, if something is 'shown' to you, it means that you are 'watching'. If you 'watch', you see things happen, noting the order in which they do so, and the importance assigned to them. And at one level, this is what a realist text asks you to do. Taking this sense, you would need to examine a Gaskell narrative to see whether, in fact, the crucial things that happen, in the 'growth and development' of its central figures, *do* occur entirely and inevitably as a result of 'social influences' – in other words that they *are* 'inseparable' from them. This would involve examination of plot development and, more widely, narrative structure (neither of which means re-telling the story).

In another sense, however, 'shown' means 'demonstrated', or 'proved'. If read that way, the statement is saying that a Gaskell text is a very didactic one, *proving* the determinist case that character ('individual growth and development') is entirely determined by ('inseparable from') environment ('social influences'). In other words, it is being suggested that a particular philosophical position is always being argued in a Gaskell text. Now that directs our attention to the degree to which guidance *is* being given to the reader in her response to what is being 'shown' in the first sense. Are interpretation and commentary woven into the narrative, whether in a direct or indirect way? If so, what kind of commentary? Are we being guided to see characters as helpless victims of their environments, or, on the contrary, urged to judge them as moral agents with free will? How effective is the commentary? What tone does it take? Again, therefore, we have got to pay attention to *method*. The analysis we are being asked to conduct is of the blend of the modes of social realism and moral tale which is found in the mid-nineteenth-century English realist novel of which Gaskell was a notable exponent.

I would like to pause here to emphasise how fundamentally important it is to recognise the distinction between 'what' and 'how' which was brought out by this brief discussion of a sample question. To underline the point in the most basic possible terms: in my experience, students like to write about *what* a text says, rather than – what critical essay questions predominantly require – about *how* it says it. Doing the former gets you a mediocre mark at best; trying to do the latter, even if not very successfully, receives a warm welcome. You may object that you cannot, in the last analysis, separate form and content in this way: fine! Being able to make – and sustain – that objection is in itself the mark of the good student, who will herself successfully see and handle the distinction for the purposes of discussion.

Reading, note-taking and drafting

This is the best bit! This is where you begin to create something that is your own. Having absorbed the excellent advice in the two preceding chapters on the skills of studying literature, and using class time to maximum advantage, you can now focus them 'like a laser' on your chosen topic. The time you have for this stage will, however, be most profitably spent if you initially review, and then try to keep well in mind, the normal criteria for a good essay, which I summarised earlier as: *relevance, logical structure, personal response and evaluation, use of the text and critics* and *use of context*. Just what, you may be asking, do they really mean?

Relevance we have already dealt with when considering how to choose and define the topic, and if you have kept the points made there well in mind, it should not be a problem by this stage. So let us take next the requirement of *logical structure*. This is not quite as simple as it may at first appear, for there are two levels on which an essay can meet this criterion. The first is simply that of orderly arrangement: the points made follow one another in a recognisable and clearly signalled order of priority. Such an order might, for example, be simple chronology: texts are discussed, in relation to the question, in order of their dates of composition. In this way matters of development in a writer's work can be considered with maximum clarity. Where discussion text by text is not appropriate, numbering of points, in order of importance – 'First', 'Secondly' and so on – is perhaps not exciting, but it can be very helpful to the reader. On whatever basis you decide to arrange the points of your discussion, it is sensible to make it clear at the outset – and then to stick to it. It is a sadly familiar experience for a tutor to register with pleasure the helpful announcement in an essay's opening paragraph of the order in which topics are to be discussed, only to find herself in a state of disappointed confusion half-way through, when all promises seem to have been forgotten.

However, while clarity of sequence is the most basic level at which an essay's 'logical structure' is judged, there is a second level of coherence which a good essay achieves, and that is the level of *argument*. As we have seen, many essay questions ask you in one way or another to decide the extent of your agreement with a given statement about a text or writer; in other words, you have got to present *your* case with reasons for, on balance, agreeing or disagreeing. Note the phrase, 'on balance'. As I said with regard to sweeping generalisations, the academic approach is essentially to see objections to any given position. A useful standard formula, for an essay offering an argument, which fits well into the normal required length, is 'Two Nos and a Yes, or Two Yeses and a No'. However, given the nature of academic discussion (never mind the complexity and indeterminacy of literary texts) that needs to be re-phrased as, 'Two

Qualified Nos and a Qualified Yes, or Two Qualified Yeses and a
Qualified No'. You may think this rather a mechanistic formula, but
given the limitation on length for your essay, it could usefully make you
sort and prioritise your points, cutting out non-essential considerations.

How could this be applied to our sample question on Gaskell? Taking
the first approach (Two Qualified Nos . . ., etc.), an answer could show
that: (1) a close connection between 'individual growth and development'
and 'social influences' is more obviously embodied in the narrative of one
novel than of another, but that in neither are the two presented as
inseparable (= Qualified No); (2) there is in both novels a considerable
amount of explicitly judgemental language, establishing a view of individuals as autonomous agents who do not simply react to their environment, though there are distinctions to be made as to the subtlety and
sophistication with which this is done (= Qualified No); (3) nevertheless,
the overall effect of Gaskell's realist method, which places individuals
within a mesh of family and social relationships, and within a densely
realised physical and economic environment, mediated by an insistently
explanatory tone, is to suggest strongly that it is difficult, if not impossible,
to conceive of 'individual growth and development' *without* 'social
influences' (= Qualified Yes).

Alternatively, of course, you might want to argue all one way. Then
the pattern would be the statement of a *proposition*, followed by a logically
arranged and clearly signalled set of *proofs*.

Moving on to *personal response and evaluation*, the first point is that
'response' does not just mean feelings, though you should not be afraid to
express them: on the contrary. However, if you do, you must be able to
pinpoint the source of your emotion. For example, a statement such as, 'I
get the feeling that Margaret Hale in *North and South* is an annoyingly
arrogant person', will tend to provoke the irritable question, 'Where
precisely do you get it from?' Moreover, merely providing a quotation to
follow such a statement, though an improvement, is not enough. It needs
to be accompanied by an analytic commentary, which demonstrates how
the text *uses* selected details of bearing and vocabulary to present a
character with a particular social attitude which, from a certain point of
view, could be termed 'arrogant'. 'Personal response', however, means
more than just feelings; it also means a personal, not second-hand, perception of how the text works; it is *your* understanding of matters of
form, tone, point of view, and *your* grasp of the framework of assumptions and ideas within which a text operates that is wanted here. The
great thing to strive for is a confidence that whatever you manage to say

on such matters is based on your own acquaintance with the text, however much assisted by tutors, lectures, or critics. Above all, be wary of making snap *moral* judgements. Of course the text may be passing moral judgements, and then your job as critic is to discern not only what they are, but how they are being conveyed.

What, then, you may ask, of the other part of this criterion: *evaluation*? Evaluation is a tricky business, and should perhaps only be attempted when the question in some way explicitly asks for it. For example, a question such as, 'How, and how successfully, does Dickens offer a critique of industrialism in *Hard Times* (1854)?' would seem clearly to ask for evaluation of Dickens's 'success'. Even here, however, dangers lurk: for example, the risks of sounding absurdly patronising, patting a writer on the back for being 'very successful', or of being facile, condemning a text for being 'boring'. On the other hand, there is a danger of being too overawed by a 'great' text. Always keep in mind your critical reader, who will want to see precise reasons, based on a close reading of the text, for your praise or blame, rather than the evasion of merely using 'hurrah' or 'boo' words.

Next, what does the criterion of *use of the text* mean? It certainly means more than just knowing the text: that is your tutor's assumed bottom line. The whole shape and structure of your answer should arise from your knowledge of the text. The practical questions students often ask, however, are 'How much quotation from the text should an essay include?' and 'How long should quotations be?' The answers are that frequent quotations are less necessary than is often thought, and they should not in most cases be long. The important thing to grasp is that quotations should be *used*, that is, analysed and commented on, in order to demonstrate a point. This shows a student's real grasp of the text. When, however, quotations have just been hunted up and inserted without supporting commentary in order to lend an air of authenticity to an essay which is not, in fact, based on a close knowledge of the text, it tends to show, and does not enhance that part of the grade which relates to 'use of the text'. Since you can assume that your reader already knows the text, a precise reference to make a point can be just as useful and effective as a chunk of quotation.

There are two main points on the criterion of *use of critics*. The first is that all of the above points about making a quotation from the text part of your argument, rather than attaching it without comment, as a kind of decoration, apply to the use of critical works too. Of course, your reader may not know them as well as your primary texts, so actual quotation may be more useful. However, simply quoting a chunk of a critic does not constitute making a point. It is just as necessary to gloss a quotation from a critic, to make clear your understanding of its relevance to, and place in, your argument, as it is when quoting the primary text. It is even better to provide your own paraphrase of a critic's position (properly acknowledged and referenced, of course) as this shows your real understanding of it.

This leads to the most important point to be made about *using critics*: it means just that – *do not let them use you*. If, as a first-year student, you are expected to use critics, this will be a useful beginning on your path to critical maturity. Katherine Armstrong in Chapter 9 deals fully with 'Practising Criticism and Theory'. The practical point here is to remember that critical works are literary texts too: they were written at a certain time, and from a certain point of view. While the facts of being in print, appearing on a reading list, and residing on the shelves of the library give them an impresssive air of authority, they are not, as Merritt Moseley emphasises in Chapter 1, gospels of truth. We have to locate them in their time period, and within their 'school' of criticism. While it is sometimes quite apparent that a critic is grinding a particular axe, another one may write with a convincing air of objectivity. In cases of noted critical controversies, a class tutor or lecturer will probably refer to differences of critical opinion. Some very useful series of short guides to the variety of criticism on specific texts or writers are now being published. The traditional 'Casebook' approach, bringing together a number of pieces on a particular text, in itself makes the point that you always need to discern 'where a critic is coming from', and such collections will usually have a useful introduction, giving an overview of different critical positions.

However, even if a critic's axe-grinding is very obvious, you may find the 'line' very appealing and convincing. Can you therefore accept it and use it in your answer? Yes, certainly, so long as you are yourself convinced that the position being argued really does take account of everything in the text of which you are aware from your own close reading. Surprisingly, it is possible to find a critic arguing a case that takes so little account of some quite important feature of the text that you begin to wonder how carefully she or he has actually read it. On the other hand, it is, as I implied at the head of this paragraph, important not to let yourself be 'taken over' and dominated by critics. At first, an alert awareness of a critic's 'line', using it as seems good to you, is the position to strive for. Taking on and contesting a critical position is a valuable development, which will certainly earn you credit, as long as it is clear that you are doing so in the light of a sound knowledge and understanding of both text and critic.

Finally, what is meant by *context*? The answer is, a great deal more than a bit of 'background' information, for example telling the reader (who already knows) when Charlotte Brontë was born, and where she lived. These kinds of well-worn details should only be used if they are strictly relevant to the question in hand. It is also problematic to assume some kind of direct relationship between the facts of writers' lives and what you find in their fiction, as if the one *explained* the other. However, an essay which shows an intelligent and relevant understanding of contextual matters will certainly gain credit on that score. (For further discussion of context, see the relevant section of Chapter 5 by Chris Walsh.)

Your decoding of the question, and your review of the criteria to which you are working, have now set the agenda and the next stage is to *read and think*. Never do either without a pencil in your hand. Both writing all over and shoving numerous scribbled markers into your own books make them genuinely useful to you. Which books, though, do you read first? Without a doubt, the primary texts themselves. Chapter 9 offers lots of good reasons for reading criticism, and it is very unlikely anyone is going to object if you do. If you are not, however (for whatever reason), using critical works, it is even more important to utilise material gained from class participation, or, of course, to re-read useful lecture notes. *But always return to the text afterwards.* That is the priority. Reading the primary texts with 'passionate attention', and thinking very hard about them *in relation to the topic* set, should absorb the greatest proportion of your time at this stage (just as attention to it should occupy the bulk of your essay, a point we will come to later).

Critical material is usually borrowed from the library, indeed much-used texts are often not even allowed off the premises, from which follow two important points about its use in preparatory work for essays. The first is the obvious importance of taking notes from it, which you can take away with you, rather than causing apoplexy in subsequent readers with your unwanted (and useless) underlinings, and the second is the absolute necessity of recording accurately author, title, and place and date of publication at the head of your notes.

With regard to the first point, there is a further, self-interested reason for recording, as far as possible in your own words, what a critic has to say on the topic in hand. This is that it is a very good test of whether you

have really understood it, for if you have, then you will know how useful
and illuminating you really find it. You will then cite it in your essay only
if it is genuinely relevant, and will be able to comment on it intelligently.
As I have suggested above, it is necessary to do both these things in order
to gain any credit for using a critic.

With regard to the second point, it is an essential precaution against
committing the academic crime of *plagiarism*. This nasty-sounding word
comes from the Latin *plagiarius*, meaning 'kidnapper', and refers to the
practice of presenting another's words or ideas as if they were your own.
When this is detected on a significant scale it is normal practice for the
piece of work in question to be failed outright, that is, given a zero grade.
Deliberate and substantial dishonesty of this kind is, I am glad to say,
fairly rare.

It is, however, a regrettably familiar experience for a tutor to notice
that an essay suddenly changes style, probably into a rather more sophisticated one, and to realise that she is reading the 'kidnapped' words of an
unacknowledged critic, whom she may well recognise. Normally this only
goes on for a few lines at a time, so it is not usually a matter for the
severest penalty, though it certainly depresses the grade gained, and
attracts adverse comment.

This mild form of plagiarism can occur, in my experience, in the work
of normally honest and law-abiding students. Why? One obvious reason
is the desperation of the poorly prepared student producing an essay at
the last minute; another is extreme lack of confidence. Both inspire the
naive and foolish hope that just lifting someone else's words will not be
noticed. I believe, however, that in many cases neither desperation nor
timidity affect the matter but that, strange though it may seem to the
tutor, it is the *student* who does not notice. This is because, at the
preparation stage, chunks of critical material have been copied out,
perhaps from a number of sources, in a welter of other notes, all without a
record of any of their sources. In the ensuing process of drafting, and
writing up, the said chunks become familiar and necessary, and end up
being incorporated into the essay in semi-unawareness of their foreign
origins. Clearly, this sloppy way of proceeding is undesirable on all
counts, while scholarly precision in noting, at the head of a separate page
for each critical text read, the details necessary for accurate citation and a
page reference by each note made, will ensure the clear – and honest –
presentation of other people's ideas and the credit that is given for that.

Now *drafting*: this is the crucial stage because it is when you are
deciding exactly what your essay is going to say. When should you stop

reading and note-taking, and make a rough draft of your essay? In practical terms, the answer is when time, rolling inexorably onwards to submission day, dictates. However, for the reasons outlined above, it is pointless to start writing until you are thoroughly comfortable with the text. A good test of whether you are ready to answer the question is to see if you can talk lucidly about it for five to ten minutes to someone who has not read the text. If this goes well, you are probably ready to knock out a rough draft. The degree of detail with which you do this will depend on your personal style of working. At all events, you need now to assemble your material, *re-focus on the question*, decide on the structure of your answer, brainstorm (that is, jot down however briefly all points to come in each section), sort, and cut out.

Here are some points to bear in mind when drafting the plan for your essay. First, you do not have to provide an opening paragraph of generalisations about life, the universe and everything, loosely related to the topic in hand. Nor, as I suggested above, does your reader want to be reminded of familiar biographical details of the writer under discussion, or of contemporary historical events, unless these are strictly relevant to the question being tackled, and are appropriate at this point. Some essay-writing advice suggests opening with an eye-catcher, but it is risky to attempt this for its own sake, for it must be relevant and securely based. This is not a piece of journalism, and tutors, with many essays to mark, are probably thankful if you just get down to work right away.

The most useful kind of *first paragraph* contains the essence of your answer, and possibly a summary of the process of defining and decoding to which you have subjected the question. Students who are not good at sticking to the point find it helps to start with a sentence which directly addresses the question. The following example refers to a novel by George Gissing, a late-nineteenth-century English writer, whose novels often take a gloomily deterministic view of people and their lives. In response to the question,

> To what extent is Gissing consistent, in *The Odd Women* (1893), in holding circumstances and environment responsible for producing character and action?

an essay could begin:

> While circumstances and environment are given a major role in the novel it is interesting to find that Gissing is not entirely consistent in this respect,

and that personal quirks and improbable coincidences play an important part, at crucial stages in the plot; this essay will examine the relative importance of these two aspects in both the characterisation and narrative in this novel.

The rest of the paragraph could set out briefly the main characters and events to be examined for the extent to which they display determinism or chance. This sets an agenda to remember and stick to.

Another useful technique is to use the first paragraph to set out the questions to be considered in order to arrive at an answer. To take another sample question, of the type that you could easily be confronted with:

> To what extent, and how, does the text of *The House of Mirth* engage our sympathy for Lily Bart as a victim of society?

The House of Mirth (1905), by the American writer Edith Wharton, tells the story of a young woman, of great charm and beauty but little money, whose attempts to marry into New York high society ultimately fail. The first paragraph of an answer could set out the following questions, in the order in which the rest of the essay would go on to consider them: What is the narrative method of the novel, and does it give special access to Lily's consciousness? What level of society is depicted? What are its main characteristics? What is Lily's position in it? How consistently do the main events of the narrative present Lily in a powerless and vulnerable position? Is there any overt authorial commentary sympathising with Lily and condemning those around her? Here again, a useful frame of reference would be provided for both you and your reader. The essay would go on to answer each question in turn, and, in conclusion, review the evidence for deciding the extent to which the text seems designed to engage our sympathy for Lily 'as a victim of society'.

The *body of the essay*, then, contains the answer, set out in the order announced in the introduction. Again, remember to avoid telling the story or describing the characters: both have been done much better by the author, and are, of course, very familiar to the tutor. As I have constantly (even tediously) emphasised, the points made must consistently relate to the text or texts under consideration, and show that a close reading of them underlies everything that is said. Critics should play a strictly supporting role, if they appear at all.

Your *conclusion* should briefly recapitulate the main points made, and state – or restate – the position arrived at. It is also interesting if you can offer – briefly – some broader reflection or perception stimulated by the topic and your consideration of it.

Writing the essay

What did I mean by saying at the beginning that a critical essay 'uses a certain kind of English'? Every piece of writing has an appropriate *style*. Learning not only to recognise different styles, but also to define their distinguishing characteristics is, indeed, part of the education of a literature student. At the present time the style generally considered appropriate for a critical essay is a fairly formal one. Extensive use of the vernacular or colloquialisms are not acceptable: in other words, writing in the way you normally talk is not appropriate and could well be penalised.

As with all writing, in order to strike the right note, you need to think about its purpose, and who will be reading it. Thus, I am writing this chapter in a style different from that which I would use in an article on Wordsworth in an academic journal. I have been trying (you will judge with what success) to write in a way that is clear, precise and fairly authoritative, but also relatively informal and conversational – addressing the reader as 'you', and so on. This is because this book is intended as a *practical* guide for literature students, primarily those in their first year: people who need clear guidance, but want it in an accessible and non-patronising form. When you write a critical essay, your reader is your tutor, that is, someone possibly sympathetic, friendly and interested in your response, but certainly rather rigorous about precision of thought, and clarity and accuracy of expression, as well as (usually) busy, and probably rather short of time for discerning points wrapped up in woolly expression and arranged in no easily discernible order. The formal English of an academic essay is therefore not pompous or high flown, but it is not everyday speech or journalistic clichés either. Aim to be fluent, but not flowery, lively but not too chatty. Aim for maximum clarity, which usually means simplicity. If you are having difficulty conveying your meaning, use short sentences. If you are unsure how clear you are being, an excellent test is to read a passage aloud to an intelligent, unsympathetic friend: if she cannot understand it, you definitely need to rephrase it.

Clarity and simplicity do not mean a narrow *vocabulary*. As a student of literature, you probably have a love and enjoyment of interesting words which exactly convey a writer's meaning. It is entirely appropriate that at this stage of your career you try to extend and vary your vocabulary, though it is always wise to check on your more experimental usages in a good dictionary, to avoid making a fool of yourself.

Remember that each *paragraph* should have one main point, not several. Moreover it is most helpful to the tutor – as well as good practice for any form of writing – to make clear how each paragraph follows from the last, for example by using link words or phrases such as 'furthermore', 'however', 'this leads to the next question . . .'. Indeed it is a good test of whether you are presenting a coherent set of points to see what link word or phrase is appropriate at the beginning of each paragraph. Do not be afraid of seeming heavy-handed or obvious in doing this; it will almost certainly be welcomed.

Another aspect of clear, coherent presentation of points is the smooth incorporation of *quotations* from texts or critics. The correct method for setting out quotations is important, and will be dealt with in the rules adopted by your institution. However, the main point here is to make sure that when you include a quotation within a sentence the whole thing makes sense, and that you do not have to *alter* the quote to do so. A final point on good practice in the use of quotations: quote them correctly. Reproducing pieces of text with missed words or punctuation, or errors in spelling, denotes a lack of respect for the text, and arouses uneasy suspicions about the essay writer's relationship with it more generally.

Getting the mechanics of writing, that is, *grammar, punctuation* and *spelling* right is important in a critical essay. The fundamental point here is that grammatical incorrectness can seriously obscure meaning and thus impede the tutor's appreciation of your ideas. It is for that kind of reason, and not mere pedantry, that in scholarly work precision and attention to detail are of the essence. The sin of 'sloppiness' is a great academic sin. To take *grammar* first. A particularly important point is that, as a general rule, you must write in sentences; not doing so is a widespread habit among first-year students, but is not popular with tutors. If your grasp of what constitutes a sentence is still shaky, seek help. It is probably wise not to ignore this rule in any context until you are an accomplished writer, and never to ignore it in an academic essay.

As you move now into a more sophisticated kind of writing than perhaps you have engaged in before, it is good to experiment with more varied *punctuation* than the simple comma and full stop, but unwise to make extensive use of colons and semi-colons unless you are confident of being correct: again, the eagle eye of the trained scholar is on your text. The correct use of the widely neglected or misused apostrophe is perhaps becoming the mark of the highly educated: it's essential to understand its correct use, for a student's essay's quality suffers from ignoring the apostrophe's usefulness as a signal of a word's function (did you notice all those?).

Spelling must certainly be correct, especially the spelling of the names of writers and of the characters in their books: nothing so shakes one's confidence in a student's close acquaintance with a text as consistent misspelling in this area. If you cannot even spell a character's name correctly, what else may you have missed about her or him? Since spell-checks on word-processors now so helpfully substitute for dictionaries, tutorly expectations of correct spelling are high.

What did I mean by saying at the outset that a critical essay must be presented in a certain way? Basically this means informing your reader clearly where each reference or quotation comes from in what text, and providing a *bibliography*. This is simply an efficient and helpful way of enabling readers to check on or follow up interesting points. Your department will have a required convention for referencing, setting out quotations, and the format of the bibliography. There are various widely used conventions: the Harvard system, the MLA Handbook rules, the MHRA method, to name the big ones. Find out which one your department requires you to use, master it and stick to it. There is usually a copy of the rules readily available, or guidelines may be given out to all students. The paramount requirements, whichever system is used, are clarity and consistency. It is easy for correct practice to become habit if you use it from the word go. Again, value is attached to careful attention to detail, and marks may well be lost for careless, inconsistent practice.

Revising and producing the essay

All writers revise. If you possibly can, it is best to give yourself a little time to go away and let the essay settle. Then come back and cast a cold eye over it for relevance, coherence and the other criteria of a good essay that I have discussed, but also for the *adequacy* of the finished product as an answer to the question set. As I mentioned at the outset, a critical essay usually has to be of a specified length, or at least to fall within a minimum and a maximum number of words. If your essay is a little thin, or a little overweight, think again carefully about *what the question was really asking for*. This is the key. If you think you have said everything, and yet your essay is markedly short, you probably have not covered the necessary ground; equally, serious obesity in an essay is almost certainly a sign of self-indulgence, and ruthless elimination of irrelevance is in order.

Revision also means combing through for *mechanical errors*, using all the resources of civilisation at your disposal: spell-check, dictionary, long-suffering literate friend or relation. It is essential to do this, for good results. Such is the cast of the academic mind that a tutor will prefer a little untidiness resulting in correct spelling or punctuation to beautifully neat but – to her way of thinking – illiterate work. Such things can influence marks – and why not, since the student of literature should of all people show understanding of language and its correct and appropriate use?

Every literature department will provide its own precise requirements for the *format* in which an essay is to be submitted: whether manuscript is acceptable, whether a typescript should be double-spaced and so on. Find out out what these rules are, and obey them. It is amazing what a different impression is given by a well-presented piece of work, as opposed to a scruffy offering, and hence the influence this can have on a grade. This is possibly regrettable, but it is true. Luckily it is within the power of any student to produce well-presented work, since this is a matter of effort rather than of natural brilliance.

The learning process

A sordid refrain running through this chapter has been what will or will not please the god-like tutor. I hope you have noticed this (since it was meant to be helpful), but thought it perhaps a rather inedquate rationale for the whole exercise of writing a critical essay. However, 'it is a truth universally acknowledged' that students want to know first what mark they have got, and only second what the tutor's comments are. Yet both are matters for reflection, to which you should devote some time before setting to work on your next essay. If the comments are very cryptic you could try asking for more, and you are unlikely to be treated like Oliver Twist by a tutor for whom this is probably an unusual experience: a student who wants to improve sufficiently to take the trouble to hunt down the tutor and arrange for further discussion is fairly rare (in my experience) and so a gratifying and welcome phenomenon. If you are seeking clarification, however, of quite full comments, make sure you have read and thought about them carefully before talking to your tutor.

In any event, *review* your essay, and try to set down a list of points to feel pleased about, and of things to improve on next time. Only if you do this will you gain all the benefit you should from the considerable effort involved in this exercise. For what is the real purpose and value of writing a critical essay? Great claims have been made in the past for the benefits of studying literature, for instance that it is 'the education of the emotions', or 'a moral education', claims easily undercut by evidence of the behaviour of some famous literary critics, not to mention everyday observation of the normal human beings who staff literature departments. I think we can still sustain a claim, however, for the value of writing critical essays, and that is one based, believe it or not, on the more modern (or perhaps very ancient) criterion of *enjoyment*.

The point is that writing an essay is a learning experience, not just a hurdle. Both intellectual development and personal growth can be experienced through the increasingly successful accomplishment of this task (as they are through other activities which are part of your course, and no doubt would be by other forms of assessment, such as medieval disputations, not currently in fashion). There is a unique kind of excitement about intellectual achievement – really understanding something, and making it your own, and creating a piece of writing which embodies that understanding and 'ownership'. For a student of literature, this must also be a source of *delight* – that word I used at the beginning of the chapter, and make no apology for coming back to – for the text which you come in this sense to 'own' will almost always be something moving, or funny, or fascinating for its craftsmanship, or stimulating in its ideas, or indeed several of these things, or more, all at once. You may not experience the excitement of intellectual achievement initially, and no one achieves perfection. It is however amazing (and the source of another kind of delight, to tutors) to see the change that can take place in the work of a committed student even in the space of the first year, let alone the full length of her degree course. In my experience, it is the mark of a committed student that she ponders constantly on her work, mulling over the comments on her essay, worrying at the implications of the question she has decided to tackle next, thinking about the texts she is reading for it, in a word, growing.

Further reading

Pirie, D., *How to Write Critical Essays* (London: Methuen, 1985). (A useful book, specifically on writing about literature. Very full and thorough, and interestingly written.)

Two very useful series of the type mentioned above in the section on *use of critics* are:

Scott, M., General Editor, *The Critics Debate* (London: Macmillan). (Written with students in mind, each short volume surveys and explains the main critical positions that have been taken on the text in question, and offers the writer's own interpretation. There is a growing list of titles, each on a specific text, ranging from *Othello* to *Sons and Lovers*.)

Selden, R., and Smith, S., General Editors, *Longmans Critical Readers* (Harlow: Longman). (Designed for students, this series takes full account of recent and contemporary literary theory. Each volume has a clear, full introduction, and contains pieces by different writers who consider specific texts. The growing list includes volumes on specific schools of criticism, e.g. *Feminist Literary Criticism*, and on specific *genres* and writers, e.g. *Shakespearean Tragedy*.)

The study skills industry generates a steady flow of good advice on thinking and writing, not specifically aimed at the literature student. Examples are:

Hall, J., *Essays and Exams. A Practical Approach for Students* (Cambridge: University of Cambridge Local Examinations Syndicate, 1989). (Very short, very practical.)

Harrison, N., *Successful Writing* (Ely: Peter Francis Publishers, 1987). (Full and thorough on getting right the mechanics of grammar, punctuation, etc.; clearly written in a fairly informal style.)

National Extension College, *Clear Thinking. The Key to Success* (Cambridge: NEC Trust, 1980). (A slim volume which takes a step-by-step approach.)

PART II

Studying literature in practice

4
Thinking about language
John Williams

Rebuilding Babel: Making sense of language

Gentle my lord,
Let me entreat you speak the former language.

Measure for Measure (II.i.140–1)

As students of literature, you may well find that some elements of your degree course are explicitly devoted to the study of language. You may also have studied English Language 'A' level. Whether or not this is the case you should be interested in, and alive to language: to its diversity and complexity, and to the ways in which different writers make use of it. After all, language is what all literary texts are made of. The aims of this chapter are to introduce the main areas of language study, and to discuss some current issues which students of literature will find relevant. The chapter will explain linguistic terminology as a descriptive tool, particularly when applied to literature, and offer opportunities for those who would like to explore further. Language is an emotive issue, and even eminent public figures can speak in a prejudiced and nonsensical way about it. This chapter begins by considering the difficulties in assessing popular and publicly expressed views about language use. Many people only give a thought to language when it annoys them, or when they consider the problems associated with deafness, or aphasia (loss of speech through brain damage), when trying to speak in a foreign tongue, or when language causes bloodshed.

Prescriptivism and descriptivism

To read the letters page of any newspaper is to be aware that other people's 'mistakes' in language, while not a cause of bloodshed, represent a great cause for concern in some quarters. The following letter illustrates this 'tradition of complaint':

> Me, you and I
> Surely that club for the brainy, Mensa, ought to command a working knowledge of English grammar? Its advert (last week) asks 'Can you solve this problem faster than me?'
> Me am sadly disappointed.
>
> T. A. Dalton,
> Carlisle.
>
> *The Guardian*, 23 June 1990, p.6.

Faster than me? Faster than I? Why one and not the other? Opinions as to what constitutes good English are largely matters of conditioning or prejudice. Spoken English differs from written English more sharply than is the case with most languages. In spoken English almost every word that can be omitted usually is, and most of the abbreviations possible are used. The rules of written English are often applied to speech with disappointing results, as we can hear whenever a speaker tries to be dignified or logical. We tend to speak in *utterances*, rarely in *sentences*, which belong to written discourse. Utterances are fragmentary, repetitious and temporary. Sentences take no account of non-linguistic features. The time of day or the age of the person making the utterance is irrelevant in the analysis of the sentence. Written sentences are well-formed, crafted and permanent. The description of sentence structure comes under the discipline of *grammar*. The interpretation of utterances is the field of *pragmatics*.

For over a thousand years, the rules of Latin have been applied to English, with mixed results. The playwright Bernard Shaw once commented that a child would be corrected for missing the 'b' out of 'debt' simply because Caesar spelt it that way. In 1931 H. W. Fowler objected to the word *racial*: 'an ugly word, the strangeness of which is due to our instinctive feeling that the termination "-al" has no business at the end of a word that is not obviously Latin.'[1] For centuries, the split infinitive ('to *boldly* go') was hounded out of the language with great enthusiasm simply because it could not boast a Latin parallel. Similarly, the 'error' of putting the preposition in final position ('something I won't put up *with*') was lampooned by Sir Winston Churchill in his famous remark 'ending a sentence with a preposition is something up with which I will not put'. Today, the split infinitive and the preposition in final position are common in speech. So what do we make of the 'tradition of complaint'? Does it bear serious consideration? Does it claim a long but futile history? Are the objectors of the past merely obstinately clinging to everything that is out of date? It is interesting that after the enormous creativity of Elizabethan English, seventeenth- and eighteenth-century critics deemed the language a mess. To soften the censure, it is worth sharing the feelings of writers from these earlier generations. The seventeenth-century poet, Edmund Waller, wrote:

> Of English Verse
> Poets may boast, as safely vain,
> Their works shall with the world remain;
> Both bound together, live or die,
> Their verses and their prophecy.
>
> But who can hope his lines should long
> Last, in a daily changing tongue?
> While they are new, envy prevails;
> And as that dies, our language fails.[2]

Waller was afraid that the English language was changing so rapidly that future generations would be unable to understand his own poetry. Pope found such problems in understanding the language of Chaucer that he re-wrote *The House of Fame* making it more 'picturesque', even changing its title to *The Temple of Fame*.

Waller, Pope and others saw language as an art form to be cherished for its good taste and fine distinctions. Linguists see language as a *social* phenomenon, as a practical means to a practical end, and they *describe* what they observe: 'First and most important, linguists are descriptive, not prescriptive. A linguist is interested in what *is* said, not what he thinks *ought* to be said. He describes language in all its aspects, but he does not prescribe rules of correctness.'[3]

The 'tradition of complaint' boasts a prestigious pedigree, and represents a fascinating area of study in itself. Linguists can learn from the 'tradition of complaint' how the language has changed over the centuries and how people have felt about it. The tradition focuses, for the most part, on three features: what is new, what is regional and what is informal.

When considering complaints about 'what is new' it is important to note that this tradition is certainly a long-standing one. Jonathan Swift complained incessantly during the first decades of the eighteenth century about changes in the language. In his famous *Proposal for Correcting and Improving the English Tongue* (1712), he wrote:

> How then shall any man, who hath a genius for history equal to the best of the ancients, be able to undertake such a work with spirit and cheerfulness, when he considers that he will be read with pleasure but a very few years, and in an age or two shall hardly be understood without an interpreter?[4]

Swift complained about 'modern terms' such as *sham, banter, mob, bubble, bully, cutting* and *palming* which were entering the language at this time. He condemned all phrases that were 'offensive to good sense and those barbarous mutilations of vowels and syllables' (p. 13). In contrast, in the previous century, Shakespeare was liberal in his attitude towards foreign borrowings. He used: *agile, allurement, armada, barricade, catastrophe, discountenance, emulate, exist, extract, horrid, meditate, prodigious, vast* and hundreds more, all of which were new in the last decades of the sixteenth century. Many words are found in Shakespeare's work for the first time. Arguably, the nearest living speech to the language of Shakespeare is that of America. The Pilgrim Fathers took their dialect to the new world. Three hundred years later, the Talkies brought it back. One of the strongest influences on English in the past century has been Hollywood. In England a visit to the cinema was a language lesson. With an irresistible attraction, the Talkies infiltrated the language with a seductive transatlantic *idiom* and a 'slangy' way of speaking. The 'tradition of complaint' launched its salvoes against these colloquialisms, but was finally defeated in the cinema seats. American words by the hundred infiltrated the language, for example, *maybe, to quit, waterfront* and the shibboleth *different than*, with phrases such as *on a shoestring, ain't* and *I guess*. Little did protesters know that all these were *archaisms* which had been good Shakespearean, but had died out only to be preserved in twentieth-century America. 'I guess', for instance, was Chaucerian: 'Of twenty yeer of age he was, I gesse.'[5] The final establishment of English as the global *lingua franca* is one of the most remarkable social phenomena of the second half of the twentieth century.

Regional aspects of the 'tradition of complaint' are also important. A Wicklow tinker would be unintelligible to a Dorset farmer. It could be argued that such breakdowns hinder progress in our age of instant global communication. The media, however, with its mass networks and state-of-the-art technology, is eager to appoint dialect speakers as newsreaders and maintain solidarity with the *language communities* it serves. Strong arguments are put forward both in favour of and against the use of dialect. When a Geordie says 'we gans back and he gives us threppence' she is speaking in her *dialect* and has adopted the speech of her language community. Linguists would claim that dialect speakers are united by a common *standard*. During the 1950s concern was expressed that dialects might be wiped out by television and radio, that we could expect a gradual decline of regionally marked speech until everyone spoke the deracinated language of the media. The recording of a newsreader from the 1950s sounds very artificial when heard today and represents a non-regionally marked variety of English called *Received Pronunciation* (RP), a dialect which emerged in the nineteenth century from English public schools. Recently, RP has given way to SSB *(Standard Southern British)* as the most prestigious English dialect. Regional speech, far from being 'a lazy way of talking', often requires more effort to pronounce than standard speech. You might consider whether accents and dialects are enjoying a growth or suffering a decline in the locality where you live.

Features of informal speech, such as *United'll be goin' down*; *Wanna go home?*; *Gonna fix a drink*; *Didn't see nothing*; *I ain't got none*; *Dunno*; and *Gotcha* are considered the epitome of laziness and are pounced upon by enthusiastic purists. Linguistic research in the field, however, shows that the less grammatically 'correct' a conversation is the more intimate the relationship is likely to be between the speakers. The reasons for this are not hard to find. They could include the accommodation to one another's personalities, or a marking out of the warmth of the relationship by indicating that formal rules are less applicable. Language is an emotional issue, as parents, friends and lovers know. This is not to say that anything goes. We need to recognise that 'd-o-g' spells dog, and that the intention behind NOTICE TO QUIT is what it says. But 'correct' English is not necessarily 'good' English, as anyone who has encountered a tax form understands. George Orwell commented:

> the defence of the English language . . . has nothing to do . . . with setting up a Standard English which must never be departed from . . . it has nothing to do with grammar and syntax, which are of no importance so long as one makes one's meaning clear.[6]

The argument is not about correctness, but about *clarity*, which is paramount. If we want to be taken seriously in our subject, for example, when writing essays, we must adopt ways of expressing our ideas as clearly and as concisely as possible. And, if we want to share an experience, like the best poets and novelists, we must make the language sing.

Comments on language, whether prescriptive or descriptive, often boil down to three things: observations about sound (*phonology*), structure (*grammar*, comprising *syntax* and *morphology*); and sense (*semantics*). These are the traditional levels of linguistic description.

Phonology

Phonology is the study of how sounds are organised within particular languages, in what positions they occur and what sorts of variants are possible. As far as *Standard English* is concerned, for example, most speakers would find that the pronunciation of Standard English does not correspond exactly to their own. For instance, Cockney has no /h/ and the northern speaker has no /ʌ/. The line between *accent* and *dialect* is not a sure one and is often disputed. Is Trinidadian English an accent or a dialect? Specialists find it hard to decide. Accent is claimed to refer to the sounds of a language, whereas dialect refers not only to its sound system, but also its vocabulary and grammar. By using the term *language variety*, linguists try to avoid the accent–dialect distinction. Sociolinguists tend to talk of *codes* to avoid committing themselves to such terms as dialect, language or variety. A roll-call of English literature shows that Wordsworth pronounced *matter* and *water* as perfect rhymes in Cumbrian, Keats spoke Cockney, Dr Johnson had a Midlands burr and Shakespeare brought his Warwickshire dialect with him to the stage, rhyming *tiger* with *bigger*.

Grammar (syntax and morphology)

Comments about word order or the structure of a phrase are observations about the syntax. Comments about the structure of a word are observations about its morphology. In English, the *subject* (the person or thing performing the action) precedes the *verb* (the word expressing the action), for instance: *Charlie Brown* (subject) *kissed* (verb). It would be ridiculous to think that the word order of English is superior to or more logical than that of Gaelic where the verb comes first. Neither is the word order directly conditioned by 'the real world'. In short, if we want to make accurate descriptions, we cannot begin by making value-judgements. In English, word order happens to be important. Consider the following two sentences:

> *Charlie Brown kissed Lucy.*
> *Lucy kissed Charlie Brown.*

In the first, Charlie Brown did the kissing and Lucy received the kiss; in the second sentence, Lucy did the kissing and Charlie Brown received the kiss. The two sentences contain the same words, but differing word orders signal different relations among the words. Clearly, word order in a sentence is an important clue to the relations among the words, and hence to meaning.

It is our learning of grammar that provides what has been called 'our rule-governed creativity'. Masterminding this epoch-making event is the American linguist, Noam Chomsky, who focuses on the ability of all speakers to understand and construct sentences that they have not met previously in the language. We know that language is not learned solely by imitation, because a child generates utterances such as 'I *do can* walk' and 'I thought*ed* it was Patrick's' which adults never say. What is happening is that the rules of grammar are generating new sentences, but the child is over-generalising and applying the rules indiscriminately.

Grammatical theory took a different turn after Chomsky published his *Syntactic Structures* in 1957, and has been seen since as comprising various components. The underlying or *deep structures* of syntax and semantics form one component; the *surface syntactic structure* forms another; the *surface phonetic structure* forms yet another. Consider the following sentences:

> *The car was repaired by a new method.*
> *The car was repaired by a mechanic.*

In the first sentence we do not know who repaired the car, but we know it was repaired by a new technique. In the second we do not know how the car was repaired, but we know who did it: a mechanic. The mechanic is actually the *underlying subject* of the sentence, as we can show by turning the sentence round: *The mechanic repaired the car*. If we perform the same operation with the first sentence we produce nonsense: *A new method*

repaired the car. This supports our intuition that *method* is not the underlying subject of the sentence, but the agent who performed the operation.
Deep structure, then, may be defined as the underlying relations among
the words of a sentence.

Discussion about the changes in a language tends to concentrate on
vocabulary: its origin, nature and change. In these days of mass communication, English is well ahead in the race to rebuild Babel and
become the global human medium. Not only is it the language of
America, England and the former dominions, it is the *lingua franca* of
the major powers, and the external linguistic vehicle of thousands of
minority communities whose native speech has no general currency.
The widespread use of English means that it exists in many more
varieties than Spanish or Chinese. It is subject to many more foreign
influences and this raises the problem of the relation of its speakers to a
hypothetical *standard*. In simple terms, English has become extremely
successful in adapting to new contexts. Most of these contexts have
offered new words to the language, especially *lexical* items: nouns,
verbs, adjectives and adverbs. Words have been imported from every
country where English has been used, and perpetually enrich the language available to writers. By the same token, other languages have
imported words from English. French families enjoy *le week-end*, Japanese enjoy a *pikunikka*, the Poles switch on the *telewizja* and Liberia
has *holiholi* (hold it!hold it!) for bus. The list shows vitality and flexibility in the way languages respond to a changing world. English, for
instance, has nothing to match *glasnost*, *steppe* and *vodka* in Russian;
balcony, *duet*, *spaghetti* and *umbrella* in Italian; *jasmine*, *paradise*, *check* or
lemon in Persian, words which represent vast geographical contacts
spanning the globe. By contrast, little words such as *the*, *a*, *an*, *in*, *at*, *to*,
are more resistant to change. Known as *function words*, they glue the
lexical words together and serve as useful but not infallible signals of
what is coming next. To test this, try to fill in the function words
missing from the following paragraph from *The New York Times*:

> _____ crack _____ _____ rifle volley cut _____ suddenly still
> air. It appeared _____ go on, _____ _____ solid volley, _____
> perhaps _____ full minute _____ _____ little longer.[7]

It is reasonably easy to supply the function words in this example. We
create part of the *surface structure* from our understanding of Chomsky's
deep structures.

Semantics

'When I use a word', Humpty Dumpty said in a rather scornful tone, 'it means what I choose it to mean – neither more nor less.'[8]

In the above quotation, some complex notions are outlined for us. Behind the simple comment that words mean what Humpty Dumpty wants them to mean lies the area of *semantics*. When a dictionary is published, it is scrutinised by a 'usage committee', a group of scholars, broadcasters and well-known writers who are asked their views on the usage of particular words. For instance, how acceptable are these: *biffing, boffing, brill, flaky, gobsmacked, gutted, naff*? Panels have objected to *finalise, wellness* and *to parent* which are in widespread use. On one panel, 83 per cent of members refused to accept *disinterested* for *uninterested*. Attitudes towards *hopefully* as a sentence adverb (as in *Hopefully, we will arrive soon*) have become progressively more conservative. By comparing results with earlier surveys it is possible to trace these changes in attitudes towards usage.

Humpty Dumpty also prepares us for the *semantic field theory*. This claims that it is no use knowing a word, for example, *king*, without knowing the semantic field in which the word *king* operates: kingdom, ruler, country and so forth. This is what is meant by saying that knowing a meaning of a word is knowing how to use it. Humpty Dumpty also illustrates the area of *lexical semantics* – the meanings of words, particularly the *sense* of words, as opposed to the meaning of sentences or utterances. We should also draw a distinction between *sentence meaning* and *utterance meaning*. Sentence meaning falls within the field of semantics. Utterance meaning comes under *pragmatics*. A speaker may use the sentence 'it's too cold in here', to mean something different from, or in addition to, what it characteristically means: for instance 'close the window'. If I come home late at night and ask my wife, 'Is there any food?' she may say with a sigh, 'I've cleared the table'. The extra meaning here ('you're too late') is not part of the lexical or grammatical content. If my wife asks 'Have you washed up and cleared the table?' I can say, 'I've cleared the table'. The extra meaning here (I have not washed up) is not part of the surface structure. So the sentence 'I've cleared the table' can mean at least two different things: *you're too late;* and *I have washed up*. These meanings are known as *implicatures*.

A fascinating dimension of semantics can be seen in cases when grammar and phonology change, but the meaning remains the same. In

Trinidadian English, for instance, the past tense of 'gave' was replaced by the present form 'give', and therefore the form 'do give' was introduced to distinguish present from the past; instead of 'I give/I gave', the same system is realised as 'I do give/I give'. Hence, while change takes place at the phonological and grammatical levels, the semantic content remains unaltered.

Language changes constantly. It ceases to change only when it dies – like Latin, Classical Greek and ancient Egyptian. Change is responsible for much of the vitality of the language. However, the causes of change are complex, and are oversimplified by prescriptive commentators taking easy swipes at convenient agencies, from fashion, fads and foreigners to misrule, modernism and moral decline. E. B. White, the essayist, commented bitterly on the language of advertising: 'with deliberate infractions of grammatical rules and its cross-breeding of the parts of speech, it profoundly influences the tongue and pens of children and adults . . . It is the language of mutilation'.[9] Ironically, the language of advertising is among the most carefully crafted in the world. Standard English accents are used to sell insurance, ready meals, expensive liqueurs and bleach. Regional accents sell beer, cider, holidays at inclement British coastal resorts and 'bootiful turkeys from Norfolk'. Advertisers are acutely aware that the accents which overlay many current television commercials betray some fundamental British social attitudes towards accent variation. Enormous amounts of time and effort are expended, along with millions of pounds, as advertisers colonise the community with consumers. The language of advertising is indeed 'the language of persuasion'.

To recap on some of the ideas covered so far in this chapter, you might like to consider the following questions:

- In what different ways do news broadcasts on Radio 1 and on BBC1 use language to inform and persuade? Are these differences mainly phonological, gramatical/lexical or semantic?
- What are your own views about 'correct' and 'incorrect' language? John Locke, writing in 1700, claimed that 'usage is the sole arbiter and norm'. Examine your own prescriptive tendencies. Do you have good grounds for your views?
- Advertising language has been described as having 'no short sentences, no negatives and no past'. Is this an adequate description of the particular features of advertising language? How do the adverts which appeal to you manipulate through language?

Language and society

A great deal of the first part of this chapter was concerned with attitudes to language. This section introduces the field of *sociolinguistics*, which examines those factors, for example, age, social class, religion, ethnic group, race, gender and social network, which are involved in language change. A sociolinguistic study might focus on language as it changes over time (*diachronic* study), or language at a particular point in time (*synchronic* study).

No single theory can adequately explain why language changes. The founder of modern linguistics, Ferdinand de Saussure, was so puzzled by this question that he divided the study of language into two areas: one concerned with the study of *langue* (the overall language system), and one concerned with *parole* (specific instances of individual language use).[10] His preference for the synchronic study of language over the diachronic, led to an idealised view of language, which removed it from its social and historical context. The field of sociolinguistics developed in reaction to this, and partly under the influence of disciplines outside linguistics, such as anthropology and sociology.

Language in society is studied in order to identify what matters to a culture and how that culture is structured. In Malay, for instance, the language encodes whether a person is old or young. Some Apache Indians welcome strangers with silence. Japanese has no native swear words. In English, arguments are conceptualised in terms of warfare: he 'defended' his view, she 'won' the point. In Aborigine Dyirbal the moon, storms and rainbows are classed with men, while the sun, stars and birds are classed with women.[11] Language is a *social* phenomenon, bound up with social structures and value systems, and different varieties are valued differently. While Standard English may be imbued with a prestige other English varieties lack, from a linguistic point of view, it cannot be considered better than any other.

What makes the notion of accent so important sociolinguistically is that members of a language community often react in the same way to tiny contrasts of sounds (*phonemes*) which act as indicators of a speaker's regional and social origins. These tiny *phonemic contrasts* can be said to be socially meaningful. Try it yourself and see when you listen to a range of accents. William Labov, the American sociolinguist, showed how people's accents and dialects vary systematically with the formality and informality of the situation in which they find themselves.[12] You might like to give some thought to the ways your own speech varies in different contexts, between, say, an interview for a job compared with a cosy chat in a pub.

Sociolinguistics deals with four areas of language study: *variation*, *national languages*, *attitude* and *interaction*. Variation studies looks at how linguistic changes are initiated, and how they are best measured and interpreted. Traditionally, it has been customary to focus on sound changes and grammatical changes and distinguish between 'internal' and 'external' factors which have caused change. Often words are borrowed from another language, and this process is classified as an 'external' influence (*banana* and *guitar* entered the language from abroad). At the same time, sound rules are adjusting in relationship to each other all the time, and these are counted as 'internal' influences. Look, for instance, at the way a particular pronunciation of a word catches on. In some social contexts, a new Cockney pronunciation of 'sad' has been adopted, which no longer rhymes in final position with 'dad'. In the phrase '*his dad is sad*', the word *sad* becomes a dipthong; the vowel undergoes a glide to rhyme with *fade*. A list of such changes represents a fascinating opportunity to explore *rules of realisation* in the phonology (i.e. principles governing the production of sounds). A researcher exploring how language varies between groups would look at gender, age or regionally based differences and might focus on the occurrence of a particular word or phrase. 'Cheers' is used when drinking and to express gratitude for a small favour. It has also been used more recently when parting and represents 'a small goodbye'. Linguists would claim that it originates from men's conversations in pubs and that it is differentiated by age (young) and sex (male). The transfer of usage from a pub to a term for 'goodbye' does not occur arbitrarily. It is not *free variation*. Sociolinguistics studies the speech of one individual (or idiolect) as she or he moves from one context to another.

National language studies makes up another area within sociolinguistics. England is an unusual country; the majority of people speak only one language. Many countries have bilingual communities where it is easy to demonstrate how languages change when they rub along together.[13] National language studies explore the relationship between these *languages in contact*. Such studies involve an understanding of how many individual language varieties have undergone significant restructuring. They might consider whether a language fits the definition of a *pidgin* or *creole*. Pidgin is a makeshift that is worked out for trade purposes and then may be used so often that children learn it more and more as a native language thereby 'creolising' it. Many hundreds of pidgins and creoles have been born from Portuguese, French, German, Dutch and Spanish – from any country, in fact, which developed a trading empire. English has its own fascinating varieties, from Tok Pisin, a *lingua franca* serving almost eight hundred indigenous languages in New Guinea, and Eskimo Trade Jargon on the whaling coast of the Bering Strait, to Pitcairnese, the language spoken by the descendants of the British sailors who mutinied on the *Bounty* in 1789.[14] An estimated forty-five speakers of Pitcairnese remained in 1983. Immigration from the Commonwealth West Indies to Great Britain since the 1950s has led to the emergence of several new varieties of British Black English. Most young black Britons have some competence in 'Jamaican', regardless of their parents' island of origin. They seem to use *code-switching* (changing from English to Jamaican) in informal situations to mark solidarity. What follows is an example of London English and London Jamaican text.[15] Italics indicate London Jamaican; / / indicates a pause:

> Come on you can't use that *raas niem* that is the *niem* of *Dievid* Black them sound *jimafia* – solomonic 'ow can you *tiif* someone's *niem* like that man . . . no *tell mi no bulshit about huu finish and huu no finish rait* / / you can't *tiifman di niem.*

Recognising contexts where 'Jamaican' is appropriate requires sensitivity and judgement. White adolescents may use it, but under extremely restricted conditions. On a larger scale, national language studies explores language and political power, such as the status of Basque in Spain, French and Flemish in Belgium, French and English in Canada, and English and Welsh in Wales. There are also areas where different varieties of the same language are spoken, such as Demotiki (low) and Karethevousa (high) in Greece. Sociolinguists describe this situation as one involving *diglossia*.

Attitude studies examines the perceptions of attitudes to other people's language usage and judgements made about them. This area also looks at how society's attitudes are reflected in their language forms; it might explore the range of varieties of English, and the establishment and maintenance of prestige dialects. Public statements about language always refer to language use, and never make the distinction between *system* and *usage*.

Interaction studies examines how people interact linguistically. Such studies have a lot to say about the structural features which produce various styles of speech – those appropriate to an interview, reading aloud and so on, which are clearly marked off by different sets of constraints and incentives. Judgements of language inadequacy are frequently based not on objective measures of linguistic ability, but on prescriptions about a particular *communicative competence*. Interaction studies focuses on those formal and informal social relationships of which any human society is composed – our *social networks* – as distinguished by language use. Recent studies of West Indian immigrants have shown that speakers, far from abandoning low-status *creole*, are actually extending it for social purposes. Not only do black adolescents use creole with black friends, but white adolescents use it with close black friends. If a white speaker uses creole to indicate friendliness, he or she risks hostility. A knowledge of when and when not to use creole in such a context requires great sensitivity.

As a follow-up to the ground covered under 'Language and society', you might like to think through the following topics:

- Compare the ways men and women refer to one another. Can you find any differences in the 'naming patterns' (for example, 'mate', 'pal', 'love', 'pet', 'kid') used by men and women? To what do you attribute the differences?
- In her book *You Just Don't Understand*, Deborah Tannen suggests men and women contribute to conversations in different ways.[16] What are your views?
- Make a collection of words which could be reckoned to be 'insider' language with reference to the theatre, rock music, or student life.

Pragmatics

According to the first issue of the *Journal of Pragmatics*, pragmatics is 'the science of language use'. It avoids focusing on the sociolinguistic territory of social conventions, examining instead strategies adopted to achieve individual *conversational goals* or *intentions*. If we listen to any conversation, we can try to identify the 'rules' of exchange. For example, how do we know it is our turn to speak? How are we made aware of what to say? How do we know when one topic has finished and a new one has begun? The following snippet of conversation was recorded between an infant (aged 2 years 8 months) and a woman while they were standing in a queue outside a post office:

Woman: What's your name, then? [She bends down to speak to the child.]
Infant: What's that? [He points to a poster on the wall.]
Woman: What's your name, then? Is it Jonathan?

Why does the adult ignore the child's question? Does she not understand him? Why is she so concerned about her own question that she repeats it? Is answering the child so difficult? Or is asking a name such an important social event that it takes overriding prominence in the conversation? These are the kinds of question a researcher might ask about such an encounter in order to identify the dynamics of *conversational exchanges*.

H. P. Grice claims that conversations are able to occur only because people obey the *co-operative principle*; they make a relevant contribution by accepted means and at the stage at when it is required.[17] This might sound amazingly obvious, but conversations are extremely complex structures. Alan Bell shows how conversations are managed by negotiating the powerful role of 'speaker'.[18] The 'audience', in contrast, plays a more passive role in the negotiation of meaning. You might consider this next time you buy a drink, or telephone home. Sperber and Wilson in *relevance theory* develop Grice's co-operative principle and suggest that the most important property of a discourse is its relevance to the topic under discussion.[19]

Recent criticism in drama, for example, has focused on the meanings behind the words the characters speak, which are often made apparent to the audience in a theatre by use of gesture, tone of voice and so forth. We can see Shakespeare exploiting the co-operative principle in *Romeo and Juliet* where Gregory and Sampson are picking a quarrel with Abraham and Balthazar:

Abraham: Do you bite your thumb at us, sir?
Sampson: I do bite my thumb.
Romeo and Juliet (I.i.43–4)

Sampson breaks the co-operative principle here by offering Abraham information he already possesses, and establishes very quickly the state of near war between the Capulets and Montagues. In other texts characters might claim not to understand one another's contribution. Here is an example from a Harold Pinter play:

[They stare at an envelope on the floor.]
Ben: Pick it up.
Gus: What d'you mean?
Ben: Pick it up!
The Dumb Waiter (line 208)

This exchange reflects a battling for control of the conversation. Sometimes the meaning lies elsewhere than in the utterance exchanged. These implicatures are common in everyday conversation. In the opening of *Hamlet*, the meaning is darkly glimpsed beneath the surface when Francisco says, 'You come most carefully upon your hour'. The utterance carries the implicature that you don't usually come so promptly (i.e. why are you so punctual?) and this is important in a scene otherwise short on detailed information. Scholars are beginning to view language as part of a larger whole: as a system that participates in and is influenced by systems larger than itself. Hence the interest in features such as implicature and relevance which call upon meanings over and above those at the surface level.

Particularly important in this area of meanings beyond the literal, is the principle of the *speech act* which developed out of the work of the philosophers Austin, Searle and Grice.[20] Concerned with defining the properties of speech acts such as requests, promises, threats, warnings and so on, the principle explores the relationship between the forms of utterances and the speech acts which they can convey. For example, if someone said, 'Have some cake', it is most likely to be interpreted as an offer and not a command. Austin argues that in producing a speech act a speaker performs three kinds of act simultaneously:

- Locutionary act (the act of saying something).
- Illocutionary act (the act performed by saying something, i.e. making a request, a declaration).
- Perlocutionary act (the effect on the hearer of the illocutionary act, e.g. frightening, persuading, etc.).

Speech-act theory has been related to literature by Mary Pratt, who claims that works of literature represent different kinds of speech act and belong to a class where utterances are addressed to an audience.[21] Her views contrast with those of Henry Widdowson in *Practical Stylistics* (1993), who claims that literature, and poetry in particular, has unique linguistic features.

Language and literature

The touchstone is emotion, not reason. We judge a work of art by its effect on our sincere and vital emotion, and nothing else.[22]

In criticism critics must speak about their own understanding – and this understanding includes an experiential dimension. Critical techniques of linguistic analysis and stylistics have been accused of ignoring the meaning of the literary text. But a simple word-count of Jane Austen's first hundred sentences in *Pride and Prejudice* compared with Sterne's in *Tristram Shandy* must be related to patterns of meaning and our overall response if linguistics is to be a helpful tool at all. A purely structural analysis of a text, removed from the author's intention, the reader's response and depth of feeling, leaves the text cold. We might consider Hamlet's crushing reply to Polonius:

> Polonius: What do you read, my lord?
> Hamlet: Words, words, words.
> *Hamlet* (II.ii.190–1)

Everyone knows that poetry, plays and novels are easily distinguishable. Poetry often follows conventions of rhyme and rhythmical structure. Plays use realistic speech between characters on a stage. Novels, by contrast, are fiction and are read silently. Close scrutiny, however, shows that it becomes difficult to say where one genre ends and another begins. The term *dramatic*, for example, can be applied to the poetry of Chaucer, which has basic resemblances to drama and fiction, but also to lyric poetry, which is often thought of as being quite different from these forms. Shakespearean drama, for instance, often achieves its depth and range of feeling by means of poetry, but at the same time exploits the extended range of the novel. At a moment of intense realisation in *King Lear*, the King confesses to his daughter, Cordelia:

> You do me wrong to take me out o' th' grave.
> Thou art a soul in bliss, but I am bound
> Upon a wheel of fire, that mine own tears
> Do scald like molten lead.
> *King Lear* (1V.v.38–41)

Here is language at its most articulate and ceremonious: the King expresses the torment of despair as Cordelia's love redeems him. The language is *metaphorical*, and contributes to the scene by involving the audience physically in the spiritual and emotional suffering of the old King. The imagery is therefore *functional* and has the potential to generate *symbolic meaning*. *Metaphor* shows that two unlike notions (the suffering of the King, and 'a wheel of fire') are implicitly related to suggest an identity between them. The *simile*, 'my tears do scald like molten lead', shows two things explicitly compared, 'tears' and 'molten lead', using a marker such as 'like' or 'as'. The difference between simile and metaphor is not just a grammatical one, depending on the use of 'like' or 'as'. A simile joins two separate images or ideas, while a metaphor is more complex and creates new meanings as a result. Metaphor, in particular, is considered by some analysts to be at the core of linguistic (and especially poetic) creativity. Traditional views would point to poetry's characteristic range of figurative language. Some of these *figures of speech* deserve mention because they are found extensively in literature.

John Keats's celebrated 'Ode on a Grecian Urn' begins:

> Thou still unravish'd bride of quietness,
> Thou foster-child of silence and slow time[23]

Again, one thing (an urn) is expressed in terms of another (a bride and a foster-child). The urn is represented in human terms using a particular type of metaphor called *personification*.

Poetry also makes use of *paradox*, a statement that is contradictory or absurd, and demands a search for deeper meaning. Andrew Marvell's 'The Definition of Love' builds on the fact that his love cannot be consummated, which somehow makes it more rare and precious than a love that can be fulfilled, and may become routine:

> My Love is of a birth so rare
> As 'tis for object strange and high:
> It was begotten by Despair
> Upon Impossibility.
>
> Magnanimous Despair alone
> Could show me so divine a thing,
> Where feeble hope could ne're have flown
> But vainly flapped its tinsel wing.[24]

Despair is not dreadful, but magnanimous here. It is a startling paradox and helps the reader understand the complexity of the poet's attitude.

The figure of speech which substitutes something closely associated with the thing for the thing itself is known as *metonymy*. Shakespeare makes such a substitution for 'sovereign' when he writes 'The crown will find an heir.' In Collins's 'Ode Written in the Beginning of the Year 1746', the soldiers are not named directly:

> How sleep the brave, who sink to rest
> By all their country's wishes blest![25]

'The brave' refers to a larger concept (all those who died in battle). We also speak of *Shakespeare* for his works, *the stage* for the theatrical profession, *the ring* for the sport of boxing and *the bench* for the judiciary. When two contradictory expressions are brought together, they produce a figure of speech known as an *oxymoron*. When Macduff asks Macbeth to wake the King, he says, 'I know this is a joyful trouble to you' (*Macbeth*, II.iii.48). 'Joyful' does not normally *premodify* 'trouble' – the oxymoron forces non-literal interpretation. A famous example which has come into the language is Milton's 'living death'.

Structural linguistics focuses on the function of various elements in the text. Poetry, for example, enjoys a flexibility of word order and grammatical structure that is rarely possible in other kinds of texts. Blake's 'Ah, Sun-flower', for example, carries no main verb:

> Ah, Sun-flower, weary of time,
> Who countest the steps of the Sun,
> Seeking after that sweet golden clime
> Where the traveller's journey is done:
>
> Where the Youth pined away with desire,
> And the pale Virgin shrouded in snow
> Arise from their graves and aspire
> Where my sun-flower wishes to go.[26]

The poem is merely an expansion of the statement 'Ah! Sunflower' and avoids the grammatical completeness which would be carried by a main verb. Structurally, the effect is achieved through a series of *postmodifications*, 'who . . . seeking . . . where . . . where' which are stacked to create an impression of simultaneity and timelessness. Postmodification has attracted attention in the past. Robert Bridges claimed that Milton's Adam first shows symptoms of his fall through slipshod use of *relative pronouns* ('who', 'whom', 'which', 'that').[27]

Poetry can also change one class of word so that it functions as another. e. e. cummings wrote, 'anyone lived in a pretty how town'. The line dislocates our expectations by dislocating the grammar. The word 'how'

changes its class to function as an *adjective*. It has been suggested that the
design of *abnormal usage* is seldom found in everyday speech. In the next
day or so, you might listen for any abnormal usages in your conversations
and try to decide what functions they serve.

All these features can occur in any piece of language, and contribute
to the cohesion of the text, a statement which implies that sentences
carry some mutual dependence. *Cohesion* is relevant to the way texts are
persuasive, present arguments or construct narrative. It carries importance in plays, where the audience is exposed temporarily to the language and where there is almost no place for description. Through this
affinity with everyday conversation drama claims to be the most 'natural' of all literary varieties. Yet in a play such as *Hamlet* the action and
dialogue are clearly highly cohesive in ways which real-life dialogue
almost never achieves. In general, drama works by characters acting out
a situation themselves instead of merely viewing it. In contrast, a work
of prose fiction can describe both the inner world of the mind and the
outer world of things. The ability to shift easily from present to past
means that novels have a variety of resources to take a trivial situation
and give it a richer meaning. They can take a difference of attitude
which appears in a casual conversation and give it dramatic substance.
Drama lacks these devices and must present the differences of attitude
in a clash of characters, where language is not merely descriptive, but
becomes an accompaniment of action.

There are three questions we cannot help asking about a story:

- What is happening?
- Who does it?
- What does it all mean?

The questions are natural because they represent the fundamental aspects
of any story, aspects that in technical language are labelled *plot*, *character*
and *theme*. The unity arising from such a fusion of elements we can grasp
as an image of life. The novelist calls upon the wide scope of human
experience, exploiting the full range of linguistic resources, whether it be
the descriptive language of place and setting, the discursive language of
argument and deduction, or the language of intimacy. Above all, it is
through their everyday speech that the novelist creates her or his characters. The novelist also takes care to describe the way characters respond:
'he exclaimed', 'he gloated', 'she whimpered', 'she demanded'. These
techniques of characterisation are completely absent in everyday speech.

Few novelists try to convey dialect accurately, leaving it to the reader's imagination to create the full effect. When The Mellstock Choir is 'going the rounds' in *Under The Greenwood Tree* (1872) Thomas Hardy skilfully suggests a Dorset dialect without strictly adhering to it:

> 'Robert Penny, you was right,' broke in the eldest Dewy. 'They should ha'
> stuck to strings. Your brass-man is rafting dog – well and good; your reed
> man is a dab at stirring ye – well and good; your drum-man is a rare bowel-
> shaker – good again. But I don't care who hears me say it, nothing will
> spak to your heart wi' the sweetness o' the man of strings!'[28]

Toni Morrison in *Beloved* (1987) conveys the rhythm and intonation of Black American English:

> 'That better? Lord what a way to die. You gonna die here, you know. Ain't
> no way out of it. Thank your Maker I come along so's you wouldn't have
> to die outside in them weeds. Snake come along he bite you. Bear eat you
> up. Maybe you should of stayed where you was, Lu. I can see by your back
> why you didn't ha ha.'[29]

Many of these issues, which are specific to the study of poetry, prose fiction and plays, will be discussed in more detail in Chapters 6, 7 and 8.

The linguistic choices made in texts reflect and influence relations within society. Studying literature as *social discourse* means focusing on the ways in which varieties of linguistic usage reflect social forces such as power relations. This way of studying literature would argue that there is no special variety of language use which is exclusively and distinctively literary. W. H. Auden's workable definition of poetry as 'memorable speech' suggests that poetry can be found in everyday conversation. The linguistic features of drama and the novel also occur in conversation, in advertisements and in news reports.

It could be argued that we do not need a knowledge of linguistics or an understanding of how language works in order to enjoy and deepen our understanding of literature. Criticism can work convincingly without the descriptive tools of linguistics, as F. R. Leavis and his followers have shown. However, one of the main purposes of linguistics for the literature student is that it can clarify what we are aware of when we do engage with the language of a work of literature, and can provide us with precise and detailed ways of describing how a text creates its particular effects through language. Some modern developments in criticism and theory have been linguistics-based (for example, *structuralism* and *post-structuralism*) and these will be briefly considered in Chapter 9.

Notes

1. H. W. Fowler, *Modern English Usage* (Oxford: Oxford University Press, 1931), p. 242.
2. *The Cavalier Poets*, ed. Robin Skelton (London: Faber and Faber, 1970), pp. 261–2.
3. J. Aitchison, *Linguistics* (Sevenoaks: Hodder and Stoughton, 1978), p. 13.
4. Jonathan Swift, *Proposal for Correcting and Improving the English Tongue*, eds Herbert Davis and Louis Landa (Oxford: Basil Blackwell, 1953), p. 11.
5. *The Works of Geoffrey Chaucer*, ed. F. N. Robinson (Oxford: Oxford U.P., 1957), p.18.
6. George Orwell, 'Politics and the English Language', in *Collected Essays, Journalism, and Letters of George Orwell*, vol. 4, 1945–50, eds Sonia Orwell and Ian Angus (London: Penguin, 1970), pp. 347–8.
7. The original passage: 'The crack of the rifle volley cut the suddenly still air. It appeared to go on, as a solid volley, for perhaps a full minute or a little longer.'
8. Lewis Carrol, *Through the Looking Glass*, in *The Complete Works of Lewis Carroll*, ed. Alexander Woocott (London: The Nonesuch Press, 1957), p. 214.
9. E. B. White, *The Points of my Compass* (London: Hamish Hamilton, 1963), p. 14.
10. F. de Saussure, *A Course in General Linguistics* (New York: Philosophical Library, 1916), p. 59.
11. Annette Schmidt, *Young People's Dyirbal: An example of language death from Australia* (Cambridge: Cambridge U.P., 1974), p. 267.
12. W. Labov, *Sociolinguistic Patterns* (Philadelphia: University of Philadelphia Press and Oxford: Basil Blackwell, 1972), p. 68.
13. R. Appel and P. Muysken, *Language Contact and Bilingualism* (London: Arnold, 1987), p. 38.
14. John Holm, *Pidgins and Creoles* (Cambridge: Cambridge U.P., 1989), vol. II. Reference survey, p. 546.
15. M. Sebba, 'London Jamaican and Black London English', in *The Language of the Black Experience*, ed. D. Sutcliffe and A. Wong (Oxford: Basil Blackwell, 1986), pp. 149–67.
16. Deborah Tannen, *You Just Don't Understand: Women and men in conversation* (London: Virago Press, 1992), p. 25.
17. H. P. Grice, 'Utterer's Meaning, Sentence Meaning and Word Meaning', *Foundations of Language*, 4 (1968), 225–42.

18. Alan Bell, 'Language style as audience design', *Language in Society*, 13 (1984), 145–204.
19. D. Sperber and D. Wilson, *Relevance* (Cambridge: Cambridge U.P., 1986), p. 219.
20. See the following: J. L. Austin, *How to Do Things with Words* (Cambridge, Mass.: Harvard U.P., 1962) and J. Searle, *Speech Acts* (Cambridge: Cambridge U.P., 1969).
21. Mary Pratt, *Towards a Speech Act Theory of Literary Discourse* (Bloomington and London: Indiana U.P., 1977), pp. 1–37.
22. D. H. Lawrence, *Phoenix*, ed. D. Macdonald (London: Heinemann, 1936), p. 539.
23. *The Poems of John Keats*, ed. Miriam Allott (London: Longman, 1970), p. 532.
24. *The Poems of Andrew Marvell*, ed. Hugh Macdonald (London: Routledge and Kegan Paul, 1952), p. 34.
25. *The Poems of Gray, Collins and Goldsmith*, ed. Roger Lonsdale (London: Longmans, 1969), pp. 436–7.
26. *Blake, Complete Writings*, ed. Geoffrey Keynes (London: Oxford U.P., 1966), p. 215.
27. Robert Bridges, *Milton's Prosody*, 2nd edn (London: Oxford U.P., 1921), p. 38.
28. Thomas Hardy, *Under The Greenwood Tree; or, the Mellstock Quire Rehearse*, ed. Geoffrey Grigson (London: Macmillan, 1974), p. 52.
29. Toni Morrison, *Beloved* (London: Chatto and Windus, 1987), p. 79.

Further reading

Austin, J. L., *How to Do Things with Words* (Oxford: Oxford U.P., 1964). (Seminal text for the study of speech-act theory.)

Blakemore, D., *Understanding Utterances* (Oxford: Basil Blackwell, 1992). (A challenging summary and informative introduction.)

Carter, R. and Simpson, P. (eds), *Language Discourse and Literature* (London: Unwin Hyman, 1989). (A challenging collection of essays contrasting with traditional approaches to literary criticism.)

Cruse, A., *Lexical Semantics* (Cambridge: Cambridge U.P., 1986). (A major contribution to the field. Superb introduction to a fascinating study.)

Huddleston, R., *An Introduction to English Transformational Syntax* (Harlow: Longman, 1976). (Advanced grammatical theory.)

Hudson, R. A., *Sociolinguistics* (Cambridge: Cambridge U.P., 1989). (A delightful introduction to this popular branch of linguistics.)

Hyman, L. M., *Phonology: Theory and analysis* (New York: Holt, Rinehart & Wilson, 1975). (Accessible and well-structured.)

Levinson, S., *Pragmatics* (Cambridge: Cambridge U.P., 1985). (An accessible approach from a major contributor to this recent area of study.)

Milroy, L., *Language and Social Networks* (Oxford: Basil Blackwell, 1980). (A sharply focused account of sociolinguistic fieldwork in Belfast.)

Milroy, J. and Milroy, L., *Authority in Language* (London: Routledge, 1985). (A magnificent summary of the prescriptive/descriptive debate. This book is essential reading.)

Widdowson, H., *Practical Stylistics* (Oxford: Oxford U.P., 1993.) (Persuasive and well-structured. Widdowson's ideas on the language of literature contrast with those of speech-act theorists.)

5

Reading literary texts

Chris Walsh

Reading itself is extraordinarily hard work. It does not occur all that often. Clearheaded reflection on what really happens in an act of reading is even more difficult and rare. It is an event traces of which are found here and there in written form, like those tracks left in a bubble-chamber by the passage of a particle from outer space.[1]

Introduction: The self-conscious reader

What does the process of reading literary texts actually involve? To begin to answer this question it might be useful to consider briefly the experience of Dickens's first readers. While each of his novels was in the throes of serial publication Dickens apparently derived great pleasure from the elementary notion that his readers were being kept in a state of suspense from one episode to the next. 'Make 'em laugh, make 'em weep, make 'em wait!' was the formula of his friend and collaborator Wilkie Collins.[2] And Dickens, it is clear, operated along similar lines. Here is a typical example of a cliff-hanging conclusion to the twenty-seventh number of *Great Expectations*, a novel published in weekly instalments in 1860–1:

> 'Here's a note, sir. The messenger that brought it, said would you be so good as read it by my lantern?'
> Much surprised by the request, I took the note. It was directed to Philip Pip, Esquire, and on the top of the superscription were the words,

'PLEASE READ THIS, HERE.' I opened it, the watchman holding up
his light, and read inside, in Wemmick's writing:
    'DON'T GO HOME.'[3]

It is plain that Dickens savoured such moments, with the crucial words
('DON'T GO HOME') delayed to the very end of the number. Dickens's original readers would have had to wait a whole week for Chapters
45 and 46 to have their – by then aching – curiosity satisfied. Today's
readers are unlikely to pause in the same way. It has been pointed out
often enough that we live in a postmodernist world where instant satisfaction is routinely and impatiently demanded by the consumer. And a
week is a long time in the world of television serials; most soaps, for
example, appear at least two or three times weekly. For us, reading
Victorian novels is a rather different affair than it was for the reading
public of the 1860s. None the less Pip's very deliberate reading of Wemmick's dramatic communication can be read instructively for our purposes. It reminds us, like the quotation from Hillis Miller at the head of
this chapter, that reading is an activity which it is very easy to take for
granted. Indeed unless faced with a particularly difficult book most literate people find that reading quickly and unreflectingly is easier than
reading slowly and self-consciously. (Reading in the latter way would feel
alien as well as arduous.) But for a student embarking on a degree course
involving the study of literature perhaps the single most important point
to grasp is that good critical reading – the kind of reading required at this
level – is slow, patient, careful, thoughtful and (ineluctably) self-
conscious. In this sense Pip, in the above extract, can be taken as something of a model reader as he works his way, word by word, through
Wemmick's missive, aware as he reads that he *is* reading – reading by the
light of the watchman's lantern, watching and being watched in turn.

The method throughout this chapter will be to place the reader in the
limelight, to see what can be helpfully observed. The aim may be summarised simply: to encourage degree-level students of literature to think,
from the very outset of their course, about what exactly is entailed in the
process of reading literature critically. In other words, the aim is to lay
the foundations for a truly productive, critical practice as literature
students.

It is surprising how easy it is to take the activity of reading for granted
and not to bother reflecting on:

● What we actually do when we read.

- I Iow wc read in practice.
- Why we read in one way rather than in another.

It is important to develop an enhanced self-consciousness as readers and students of literature, because without some sense of the fundamentals involved in reading it is difficult to improve by developing the good habits and eliminating the bad ones. It is worth noting at this stage that the emphasis is not so much on what, or how much, you *know* about the literary texts you are reading; rather, the stress is on heightening your awareness of what you *do* as you read. As was pointed out in Chapter 1, you should find this reassuring. For one thing, as students beginning to follow a degree programme in literature you are already reasonably good at what you do – reading literary texts – or you would not have reached this stage! You certainly possess the *basic* reading skills needed; and most of you will already have picked up some of the more advanced *critical* skills as well. This chapter will look at both kinds of skills in turn, but will focus in greater detail on the more purely 'critical' reading skills as these are the key skills students of literature need to acquire and sharpen early on in their studies. (A critic, incidentally, is only a kind of reader – 'an experienced and expert reader' would be one definition.) The chapter will look critically at the reading process in action, offering illustrative examples where appropriate. But ideas about reading and what constitutes *good* reading will be to the fore throughout; so the chapter will have a theoretical dimension also.

Reading literary texts: Practical considerations

To begin with, here are a few general practical points about the business of reading literature for a degree.

To start by reiterating an obvious but significant claim (made in Chapter 1): reading is the single most important thing that students of literature do. Wherever you do it, and whenever you do it, you cannot do too much of it. Because everything, but everything, in your studies depends on it. Lectures, seminars and essays, for example, all mean very little without it. Reading is not only an integral part of your studies: it is the very foundation on which every act of talking and writing about literature has to be based.

So, as Merritt Moseley pointed out earlier, it is extremely important that you organise your time to allow for lengthy periods of uninterrupted reading in circumstances where you can be relaxed and comfortable. (Admittedly this is easier said than done in some circumstances but the point remains.) You must plan and manage your time so that you have plenty of it in which to read the primary set texts. You should also make time to re-read the set texts (in whole or in part as appropriate) and to do some supportive secondary reading of critical materials.

A few words of advice first. It makes sense to obtain your own paper-back copies of the set texts, copies with which you can become physically familiar and find your way around in easily. In literary study you will often have to go back to find something you perhaps half-noted, the significance of which only dawns on you many pages later. It is surprising how much one's study is eased by familiarity with the layout, print-face and thickness of a particular edition.

And the text should be thought of as a tool. It is something to be used. Annotate your text in pencil as you read. (You might note that this does not apply to library books!) 'In pencil' because first impressions often need revising in the light of subsequent discoveries. You might limit yourself initially to underlining or marking in the margin those passages you find significant or interesting or puzzling. Aim to get to know the text fairly thoroughly. Your reading of a novel such as E. M. Forster's *Howards End* (1910), for example, will not sound convincing if it is obvious that you are not familiar with the basic facts of the story.

So read! read! read! But read slowly. Take your time. Cultivate the unfashionable virtue of patience. Some people find it easier reading in concentrated intensive bursts punctuated by mini-breaks (for example, reading for forty minutes followed by a five-minute rest, then reading again for another forty-minute spell before taking another break). Avoid skim-reading primary texts. Resist the temptation to go too fast. (This is especially important for poetry which should never be rushed.) In other words, try not to run before you can walk.

It might be helpful here to distinguish between the two different kinds or levels of reading. The first we might term 'basic reading' – the kind of 'ordinary' reading most people do most of the time (irrespective of what they are actually reading). The second we might term 'critical reading' – a rather more self-conscious, reflective, analytical kind of reading as practised by professional and academic critics of literature. The distinction is by no means watertight: in practice the two kinds of reading will often spill over into each other for the student of literature; but for now the distinction may be of some use.

Basic reading

To begin with let us focus on basic reading; or 'consumer' reading. Neither term is meant pejoratively. When we read in a fairly attentive, observant way what *happens* to us whilst we are reading? And what kinds of things do we *do*? (Assume that we are considering the process of reading a novel such as Jane Austen's *Emma* (1816) in this instance.)

First, what happens to us as we read? The following points suggest themselves:

- We are entertained (or bored) by what we read.
- We experience various emotions.
- We learn new things.
- We are reminded of things we already know.
- We want to know 'what happens next'.

Secondly, what do we do during the reading process? This time the list might read as follows:

- We try to make sense of the words on the page.
- We ask ourselves questions.
- We formulate hypotheses or tentative answers to those questions.
- We probably form mental images of the setting and characters (in 'the mind's eye').
- We may identify imaginatively with one or more of the characters in the novel (reading 'as if' Emma, say).
- We fill in gaps ('reading between the lines').

This list is by no means exhaustive, of course; it will not apply to reading all novels; and the responses of individual readers will vary enormously in certain respects. Much of the above may be thought of as 'common sense' and 'obvious'. Of course this is what readers do because that is what reading is! But perhaps we should pause here and reflect further on this 'common' (if not 'natural') process.

Notice that there is a fair amount of information-processing going on in this kind of reading. We are working out what is happening, what we

are being told, whose is the voice addressing us, who the different characters are, what their relationship is to each other, what the setting is in
time and place, what the novel seems to be about and so on.

You might also note that even though we are engaged in these activities we may not be aware as we read that we *are reading*: we may be
completely lost, disbelief suspended, in the 'virtual reality' of *Emma*,
gripped by the events unfolding before us – rather like watching the
latest box-office success at the cinema.

The point to grasp is this. Reading in this quite ordinary way provides
the starting-point for all subsequent critical investigations. It gives us the
data, the raw material as it were, for us to process. And there is no
adequate substitute for it; there are no short cuts worth taking. Even
where these exist – for example, being able to look up the plot summary
of *Emma* in a standard reference book such as *The Oxford Companion to
English Literature* – they do not give us the sense of what it is like to read
Austen's novel for ourselves.

There are a couple of features to notice about this kind of fundamental
reading. First, to read in this way I have to draw on my own personal
'repertoire' (the experience, knowledge, beliefs and values I have acquired thus far in life, together with the linguistic and literary skills I
have built up over the years): no repertoire, no reading. The nature of the
repertoire will dictate up to a point what the reading experience will be
like. It is partly because no two individuals have exactly the same repertoire that no two readings of a literary text exactly coincide.

Secondly, an intelligent, sensitive, perceptive reader will be responding to the text not merely intellectually but emotionally, imaginatively
and morally. Reading literature is not simply a matter of information-
processing though it does include this. It also involves relating experien-
tially and psychologically to the text; this is partly what gives literature its
complexity; it also goes some way to explaining why we take literature so
seriously. You might call this dimension of reading 'making the text your
own'. It is a matter of living with the text for a while, giving it a chance to
make a difference to your life. For reading a book *can* change your life if
you open yourself to that risk. Reading certain books can make you think
of yourself, of others, of the reality of which we are all a part, differently.
As students just starting a degree or part-degree in literature you have a
lot of reading in front of you: some books you may not get on with, but
you should be prepared to give every book a chance whatever your initial
reservations and prejudices concerning particular books may be. An open
mind, a positive attitude, a readiness to enjoy reading: these are not

exactly preconditions for reading literature effectively but they certainly help.

Critical reading

This kind of reading is somewhat more sophisticated. As was pointed out earlier it has been separated, for clarity of analysis, from basic reading. In practice it tends to accompany or overlap with the first kind of reading: because of time pressures it is not always possible to have a straight basic reading of (say) George Eliot's *Middlemarch* (1871–2) followed by a second critical reading of it. This kind of reading involves stepping back from the text itself and from one's initial subjective response to it and trying to gain a wider perspective on both text and response. It involves asking certain kinds of questions about one's response to the text. What *is* my considered personal response to the poem or play or novel in question? What do I really think of it? What is it about the text which produces such a response in me?

If these strike you as tough questions then be reassured. They are not. To reiterate a point made earlier: what you are being advised to get to know about is something you already know about, in a sense, because it is something you do: reading.

Critical reading may be best thought of in the context of an elementary model of literary communication:

CONTEXT
WRITER TEXT READER
LANGUAGE

Each of the components relates to each of the others, with some relationships being clearly more important than others. A reader reads a text written by a writer within a specific context and in a particular language. For my reading of *Persuasion* (1818), for example, the diagram would be as follows:

BRITAIN/1818
JANE AUSTEN *PERSUASION* CHRIS WALSH
ENGLISH

Critical reading has *five* dimensions, each dimension relating to a component in the above model. For each dimension we can formulate a main question. To make matters clearer, each dimension will be considered in turn.

Reading the writer

First, is the writer. The question to ask here is: What view of reality is inherent in the text? Or to put it slightly differently: What ideology informs the text?

To begin with, the main thing is simply to note what subjects the writer writes about. What seems to interest Austen? What issues does she raise in *Persuasion*? What ideas are explored and what attitudes are expressed in her novel? What understanding or vision of life emerges from a reading of it? In rather more traditional terms this would be described as a matter of attending to the literary work's 'content'. With this approach it is important to guard against oversimplifying a complex phenomenon (a literary text) by coming up with a crude paraphrase of some 'message' or 'theme' we think the writer is somehow 'trying to get across'. A literary text means more than it merely says. We should certainly be extremely wary of assuming that every statement in a text somehow has the author's own seal of approval; and authors can be wholly identified with their own characters very rarely. In any case a text's meaning cannot be adequately summed up by plucking from it the ideas, beliefs, values and arguments embedded in it. That would be to reduce and distort textual meaning by giving a partial account of it. Part of what a text means is not reducible to ideas and words; the meaning of *Persuasion* for its readers is partly a matter of what and how they *feel* as they read it – a point to which we shall return later.

But there is another point which needs to be made here. A text is layered: it consists of surface and depth (or depths). It has a conscious and an unconscious. It can be read 'with the grain' or 'against the grain'. To put all this another way, a text can be read not merely in order to understand its ostensible meaning but in order to grasp its unwitting self-exposure of the ideological contradictions which necessarily inform it. For a text has silences which, once detected by the reader, can be seen to be profoundly revealing of a society's assumptions and ways of thinking (in a word, its ideology). That the author may have been blithely unaware of the ideological contradictions which can be uncovered in the text is beside the point. Samuel Richardson's *Pamela* (1740), for example, is, in Terry Eagleton's words, 'a sickly celebration of male ruling-class power', but the novel is also, he continues, 'a fierce polemic against the prejudice that the most inconspicuous serving maid cannot be as humanly valuable as her social superiors'.[4]

We have to realise that in any given text what we are presented with is artifice, a *construct* of reality. One of the most common tasks students are given in class is to try to work out what the text's perspective on reality in effect amounts to. What assumptions are built into it? What conclusions appear to be drawn by the writer? What we have in the text, though, is a writer's ideological *interpretation* of reality – which we in turn attempt to interpret. Looked at in this way, what we as critical readers are doing is *interpreting interpreting*. Or to put it slightly differently, in so far as what we are reading is a critique of life, society, reality, we are *criticising criticising*. This cannot be stressed too much: all there *is*, strictly speaking, is inter-pretation, in the sense that nothing is uninterpreted. All we can talk or write about, therefore, is *our* interpretation of (for example) the 'interpreta-tion' we know as *Waiting for Godot* (1956) by Samuel Beckett. This realisa-tion should give us pause and hold us back from proceeding with undue haste to offer glib summaries of 'Beckett's philosophy in *Waiting for Godot*'. Both Beckett himself and the play itself are too complex to be reduced to pithy (or not so pithy) aphorisms in this way. But that should not deter us as readers (as critics) for posing questions and attempting to come up with answers which do some justice to the subject. We might take a leaf from Stanley Fish's book: he writes about how he 'stopped worrying and learned to love interpretation' – a useful habit of mind to acquire; for as Fish reminds us, 'interpretation is the only game in town'.[5]

Reading the text

Secondly, there is the text. The attention here is not to the text's subject-matter but to its form. The question we should pose under this heading is: What kind of text is this? Or put another way: How does this text function?

A helpful parallel might be between an initial critical reading of a text and meeting a person for the first time. In the latter situation we take note not just of who someone is and what she says, but how she looks, how she is dressed and how she behaves and speaks. In other words, we attend not merely to *who* and *what* but to *how*. We are back to information-processing again, but in the case of the literary text the information being processed has to do with style, method, structure and technique.

Actually we practise reading the formal features of aspects of reality all the time. In a sense, just as all there is is interpretation, so too everything can be thought of as a text – and that applies not merely to books and documents, but to people, buildings, vehicles, landscapes, kitchen utensils . . . the list is endless. So when we approach reading a poem or a play or a novel critically it is largely a matter of processing the text in question in a (broadly) similar way.

The question 'What kind of text?' can be further broken down into a series of sub-questions relating to aspects of the text's literary features. Thus in the case of a novel we might ask the following questions:

- Does it belong to one or more particular sub-genres? (Is it a romance? Is it a social-problem novel?)
- How complex is its plot? (Is there perhaps more than one plot?)
- What is its structure? (Is the novel subdivided into books, sections, chapters? How is the material organised? Is there a linear chronological scheme?)
- How is the narrative delivered? (How many narrators are there? Is it told in the first or third person?)
- What is the main point of view throughout? (Do we see events largely through the eyes of the central character?)
- How are the characters presented to the reader? (Are they mostly presented dramatically or discursively?)
- What is the function of setting in the novel? (Is the novel set back in the past? Are there frequent changes of locale? Note that 'setting' is not to be confused with the text's 'context', discussed below.)
- How much use is made of patterns of imagery and symbolism? (Are there motifs running through the entire novel perhaps?)

(Some of these questions will be explored further by Susan Watkins in Chapter 7, 'Reading Prose Fiction'.) Other genres would have a rather different set of questions to be asked.

Reading the reader

Thirdly, there is the reading process. When we talk about a novel what we are really talking about is our reading of a novel. That is all we *can* talk about. The only access I have to Jeanette Winterson's experimental novel *Sexing the Cherry* (1989) is through myself – principally through my own reading of it. This may seem obvious but it is often overlooked. When we talk about texts we are essentially reporting back on how we interacted with texts. Texts do not have somehow magically built into them a meaning which is there independently of the reader. Texts can only mean something to someone – the reader, usually. ('Usually' because texts can mean something to people who have heard about them even though they may not have read them for themselves.)

So the relevant question here in relation to the reader is: What exactly happens when I read? And moving on from this: How do I explain what happens?

A critical reading should attempt, among other things, to account for what we can term 'the production of response'. To account for how a response is produced it is vital to appreciate the contribution made by *both* elements in the dynamic interactive process: the text *and* the reader. This involves attending to the fact that we read *in time*, with various thoughts and emotions succeeding one another as the process unfolds. It involves working on the basis that we co-operate gradually with the text to make meaning: we, as readers, are active and constructive, not mere passive recipients. (We are 'writerly', not merely 'readerly', would be another way of making this point.) For the text to make any sense at all we have to be there, reading attentively and filling in the many gaps which the text presents.

Consider the process of reading the opening lines of Emily Brontë's only novel *Wuthering Heights* (1847):

> 1801. – I have just returned from a visit to my landlord – the solitary neighbour that I shall be troubled with. This is certainly, a beautiful country! In all England, I do not believe that I could have fixed on a situation so completely removed from the stir of society. A perfect mis-anthropist's Heaven – and Mr Heathcliff and I are such a suitable pair to divide the desolation between us. A capital fellow! He little imagined how my heart warmed towards him when I beheld his black eyes withdraw so suspiciously under their brows, as I rode up, and when his fingers sheltered themselves, with a jealous resolution, still further in his waistcoat, as I announced my name.
>
> 'Mr Heathcliff?' I said.
>
> A nod was the answer.
>
> 'Mr Lockwood, your new tenant, sir . . .'[6]

This is a useful passage to illustrate the similarities and the differences between a first basic reading of a literary text and a later critical reading of the same text. For a reader coming to this novel for the first time, totally unfamiliar with even the story-line (neither having seen a version of the novel on film or on television, nor having heard anything about the novel second-hand) the opening presents a number of interesting problems of interpretation, which the reader must at least confront if not actually solve. The experience of reading the opening few lines is likely to involve, initially, a sense of puzzlement: Whose is the voice telling us the 'beginning' (as we are likely to assume it to be) of the story? The date is given (baldly, '1801'), making it sound like a rather vague journal entry. But who is the 'I'? Nothing in the first paragraph even reveals for sure the sex of the narrator (though the phrase 'A capital fellow!', it might be thought, is more likely to be heard from male lips). And what about setting? We may assume from sentences two to four that the 'beautiful country' is a remote sparsely populated area somewhere in England, but that is as much as we are likely to infer (the novel's title will not have been much help). The narrator seems mostly interested in telling us about the land-lord, Mr Heathcliff, who is made to sound intriguing, though quite how his taciturn manner squares with the narrator's emphatically positive assessment of him is far from clear; we may suspect that the narrator, who – we soon gather – has never before met Mr Heathcliff, may be jumping to conclusions about this landlord based (somewhat flimsily) on a self-assessment. At any rate Mr Heathcliff is certainly written about as if he were a kindred spirit in the narrator's eyes and, for the time being, we may feel forced to accept this reading until something better comes along, for the narrator is thus far our only guide. The opening dialogue confirms our impression of Mr Heathcliff's surliness besides giving us the information that the narrator's sex is male and his name Mr Lock-wood. That is perhaps as much as we may reasonably be expected to deduce from a first reading of the novel's opening. The reading process in this case would seem to be largely a matter of puzzling out a number of issues; for most readers it probably involves coming up with rather tentative answers to quite basic questions and then revising those answers in the light of subsequent information. Notice that in order to make much sense of the extract we have to be actively involved in the decoding of the information supplied, and that this active involvement proceeds step by step and includes an element of guesswork, on the understanding that our initial assumptions and expectations may have to be revised later.

A subsequent *re*-reading of the opening would be, on the whole, a quite different experience. Less time would be spent puzzling out the basics of plot, setting and character, and more time would be available for attending critically to the finer points of Lockwood's narrative. For this time round we know that Lockwood is but one narrator of six and that though he has his uses he also has his limitations. Re-reading the opening we can, for example, watch Lockwood pompously making his callow errors of judgement as he misreads himself, his surroundings and his landlord. Our attitude this time is unlikely to involve reading 'as if' Lockwood for we realise that the writing at this stage of the novel is ironic. Lockwood is no misanthropist (as he fondly imagines himself to be); it is he who repeatedly troubles Heathcliff, not the other way round; Heathcliff is far from being a 'capital fellow' ('a capita*list* fellow', perhaps) and his similarities to Lockwood are, to put it mildly, not marked. We realise that the Heathcliff of this opening is not 'exaggeratedly reserved' (Lockwood's phrase later the same page) but a 'perfect misanthropist' (Lockwood's earlier phrase being truer than he realised). Moreover the Heathcliff of 1801 has only about six months left to live, and the bulk of the novel is taken up with a narrative which describes the events of the previous thirty years – a narrative in which Lockwood himself, we now know, hardly features. The process of reading this opening critically, in short, depends for its effectiveness on the nature and extent of our self-reflexive involvement *as readers*: to read this novel productively, we must learn to read (to question, to reflect upon) not just the text itself but our own responses to that text. Any other approach would be incomplete.

Reading the context

Fourthly, there is the context. Just as texts do not exist in a vacuum in the sense that they have to have readers in order for anything to happen, so too their existence in the real world is crucially dependent on their context. A text comes from somewhere. Someone wrote it at a particular time and in a certain place. It is the way that it is because of its context. Texts are not mere consumables – bought and read by their readers; they are products. And, like all products, they can be explained, at least in part, in relation to the society in which they were originally produced – that is to say, written and published (and it is worth noting here that the date of publication can sometimes be many years after the text was written). All texts, in other words, have a history. (So too, incidentally, do readings of a text as the 'Critical Heritage' series illustrates – a point to which we shall shortly return.) And it is one of the tasks of a literary critic or scholar to account for the nature of a text in terms of its historical context(s). So the question to be put on this occasion is: What factors determine the nature of the text as we know it? How do we explain the way it is? The questions, it should be noted, are not optional extras to do with something called 'background'. There is a compelling argument that no text can be properly understood viewed in isolation from its originating context – the writer's life and times. The problem, of course, is gaining an adequate understanding of that context, which in the case of many texts will be remote from the reader's own context. There are many different ways of understanding the relationship of text to context. Marxist theorists and critics especially have produced many contrasting explanations of the complex relationship between the two. It has often been argued, for example, that texts do not simply reflect, mirror-like, the reality which produced them, but that they mediate it in sophisticated ways. So in considering the interaction between a text such as John Milton's *Paradise Lost* (1667) and its context in the wake of the English Civil War, we have to be very careful not to assume a simple one-to-one relationship between literary text and historical event. To put the matter at its crudest: Milton was a Puritan and a supporter of Oliver Cromwell; but that does not necessarily make *Paradise Lost* narrowly denominational in its religious outlook, nor does it inevitably make it revolutionary in its politics.

Two more points need to be made about the issue of context. The first is – notoriously – Derrida's: '*il n'y a pas de hors-texte*' (there is nothing outside the text).[7] The implication being that when we speak of a text's context we have to bear in mind that our access to that context can only be through other texts of one kind or another; context *is* text in this sense and should be considered accordingly. So we have to be careful: we must not assume that there is anything fixed and stable ('the historical context') in relation to which we can understand the text and against which we can measure its historical accuracy. Both text and context share the same characteristics. Another point to bear in mind: just as there is a context for writing so too there is a context for reading. I can only read Richard Brinsley Sheridan's *The School for Scandal* (1777) from my perspective of today (at the time of writing, mid-1990s Britain) which is *my* context. I grasp at the meaning of a play more than two hundred years old from the limited, constrained perspective of the present, my viewpoint being every bit as much a product of my point in history as Sheridan's play is of his. And even a comparatively recent play such as John Osborne's seminal *Look Back in Anger* (1956) can seem, by virtue of its very topicality, remote from the concerns and preoccupations of a reader today. To sum up: to read a text critically its context must be acknowledged; but to read its context will incontestably involve reading other texts; moreover, the act of reading itself takes place within a context and to fail to take that elementary fact into account may be the easiest mistake of all to make.

Reading the language

Finally, there is the language of the literary text. How does what might be termed the text's 'raw material' function? For language is what the text is made of. Words are its building blocks. And they are put together in particular ways. As with context, the reader cannot afford to ignore language if the text is to be adequately understood. *How* something is said crucially affects the reader's response to *what* is said. (In one sense, of course, the words on the page are all there is to go on.)

Another way of looking at this is to see language as the text's code, as the very web of its textuality. It is a sophisticated (but slippery, problematical) medium of communication. A basic reading would hardly attend to the language of a text as such at all; in that mode language is treated as what it is *not* – *un*problematical – as if it really were a clear transparent window onto the text's subject-matter. A critical reading, on the other hand, attends very closely, minutely, to language. No word or punctuation mark should be disregarded in the course of a really detailed critical reading. The apparently straightforward, the seemingly trivial, may turn out to be more significant than previously thought. It pays to take pains over a text's language – its vocabulary, grammar, syntax, spelling, punctuation. And in the case of earlier texts it is sometimes especially important to attend to the etymologies of particular words, for knowledge of what a word commonly means today may be an unreliable basis for understanding what it meant to Shakespeare's audience or Donne's readers. To the critical reader a text's language is itself 'critical' indeed.

The questioning reader

A critical reading, then, involves paying attention to each of the five dimensions of the literary experience listed above. And it involves asking questions about each dimension. The questions need not be asked in any particular order, and in the end they will be seen to relate to each other and – often enough – to overlap. To discuss ideology is, inevitably, to consider context; to ponder the reading process is to reflect on the reader's decoding (and re-encoding) of the text's language; and to grapple with the text's issues and ideas necessarily entails coming to terms with its formal features as well.

The ideal reader is always alive to the complexities and ambiguities of the text in question. Perhaps the most fascinating task to attempt towards the end of a critical study of a text is to work out what the text's contradictions are. To revert to a comparison made earlier: just as no human personality is without contradictions so too with texts without exception, though in some cases the contradictions need to be teased out with great care. But it is a revealing and rewarding business.

A few further thoughts. There is, of course, no such thing as a reading innocent of assumptions and values, and no critical practice without theory – whether or not one is conscious of having a theoretically grounded position as such. Neither is there such a thing as a single, fixed, correct meaning of a text. Texts have multiple, if not infinite, meanings and all the thoughtful reader can realistically hope to achieve is to put together an interpretation or reading of a text which does some justice to the complex, many-faceted nature of the phenomenon of literature. With any luck the matter of putting together a reading of a text will involve not merely taking pains, but taking pleasure in the acts of interpretation as well.

Always try to be clear about what you are setting out to do and why as you approach a critical reading of a text. Be prepared to be explicit and critical not just about the text itself but – where necessary – about your position and approach, and about the positions and approaches of others as well ('others' here referring to your fellow students and to your tutors as well as to published critics). Bear in mind that divergent positions and approaches dictate the different kinds of critical readings that result.

Reading and evaluation

Finally, before pulling the above points together by working through an example in some detail, here are a few thoughts about value and evaluation. The above discussion of critical reading has concentrated exclusively on descriptive and analytical approaches to literary texts. But it might be urged that to the five dimensions listed (with their associated questions) there should be added a sixth: How good is the literary text under discussion? The argument here might be that a genuinely critical reader should be critical and discriminating as to questions of value, in addition to being rigorously probing about ideology, form, language, context and the reading process. Is it not important to define the merits and demerits of one poem relative to the merits and demerits of another? This is a difficult question to answer satisfactorily. The issue of value is always present, of course, in every discussion and in every statement. The mere fact that a particular text is being discussed at all implies something about its interest or significance. And every proposition is loaded to the extent that simply making it involves the assumption that it was worth making it in the first place. A statement altogether innocent of value is inconceivable. But is it tenable to move from this position to the position that 'it is *possible* to make objective judgements about the value of particular literary texts', and (further) to 'it is *desirable* to make objective judgements about the value of particular literary texts'? Most readers are able to say whether they enjoyed reading a particular novel – whether (say) A. S. Byatt's *Possession* (1990) was to their taste or not, and whether they preferred it to John Fowles's earlier neo-Victorian novel, *The French Lieutenant's Woman* (1969). Such readers might also be able to give reasons for why they responded the way they did; they might point to features in Byatt's novel which satisfy certain criteria which, in their view, need to be met for a novel to be described as 'good'. But the give-away phrase here, of course, is 'in their view'. Where do these criteria come from? Whose criteria are they? Is it not the case that all value-judgements and all the criteria upon which they are based are inescapably subjective? To say that '*Possession* is extremely impressive – certainly better than *The French Lieutenant's Woman*', is really tantamount to saying 'I like *Possession* much more than I like *The French Lieutenant's Woman*'. No doubt critics and theorists will continue to disagree about the complex, vexed issue of objectivity in critical judgements. At this stage perhaps all we need do is concede that issues of value permeate all critical statements and be ready to formulate our positions with circumspection, explicitness and honesty.

Reading in practice

What might a typical critical reading involve in practice? By way of illustration, let us consider a reasonably well-known poem – Tennyson's

'Break, break, break' – and see what reading this particular literary text critically entails.

Here is the poem in full.

> Break, break, break,
>   On thy cold gray stones, O Sea!
> And I would that my tongue could utter
>   The thoughts that arise in me.
>
> O well for the fisherman's boy,   5
>   That he shouts with his sister at play!
> O well for the sailor lad,
>   That he sings in his boat on the bay!
>
> And the stately ships go on
>   To their haven under the hill;   10
> But O for the touch of a vanished hand,
>   And the sound of a voice that is still!
>
> Break, break, break,
>   At the foot of thy crags, O Sea!
> But the tender grace of a day that is dead   15
>   Will never come back to me.[8]

What can we say, to begin with, about the process of reading this poem? In one sense it is a relatively straightforward matter to give a report of 'the thoughts that arise in *me*' as *I* read the poem. But it is not so easy to write about 'the reading process' in more general terms. Every reader will have a different response to reading this poem and so to generalise about 'the reader's response' is bound to be somewhat dangerous. Given that caveat, what can be reasonably observed about a reading of 'Break, break, break'? The reader is likely to be struck at first by the harsh-sounding, monosyllabic, heavily stressed words of the first two lines. The poem's persona – the voice apostrophising the sea ('O Sea!') – 'speaks' in an obviously agonised tone, but beyond the stated inability to 'utter' the thoughts preoccupying him no clear indication is given in the first stanza as to what is upsetting the speaker. (I write 'him' here on the premise that the reader knows the poem to be by Tennyson and that as no character or speaker distinct from the poet seems to be presented as thinking or saying the poem's words the likely assumption is that the poem's voice may well be akin to the poet's own.) In so far as the reader tries to work out what the occasion for this painful poetic outburst is the second stanza is unlikely to make matters clearer. What is the

thread of connection between this stanza and the first? In the second
stanza there seem to be feelings of resentment, perhaps even of self-pity,
in the exclamations about 'the fisherman's boy' and 'the sailor lad': they
seem happy and content to the speaker, their situation contrasting with
his own – they 'shout' and 'sing' while the speaker asserts his dumbness
(dumbness of a metaphorical kind the reader probably infers). The
speaker's feelings of being lonely, forlorn, alienated from his surroundings spill over into the third stanza: the reader will grasp that the ships
are envied for their 'stately' progress to a calm, tranquil harbour (*they*
have somewhere to go), while the speaker's anguish erupts violently in
the lines

> But O for the touch of a vanished hand,
> And the sound of a voice that is still!

The reader is likely to conclude at this point that it is the premature
death of a close relative or friend which has provoked the poem's response. The final stanza will be read as confirming this hypothesis: there
is anger, combined with a bitter-sweet nostalgia, regret and (perhaps)
resignation in the final lines as the voice bemoans his loss once more. The
reader may well come to the end of this poem powerfully moved by its
simplicity and the depth of the feelings expressed. Subsequent readings
of the poem – and with a poem of this length many such re-readings
might be practicably attempted – would confirm this initial impression of
the poem, but a surer, fuller sense of its complexities and nuances of
mood and feeling and a greater awareness of its artistic subtleties (its
simplicity is superficial) are likely to emerge as the critical process
unfolds.

At some stage, probably quite early on, the reader is going to need
to switch the emphasis away from the reading process to the object of
attention proper: the text itself. What kind of poem is this? How is it
structured? How does it function? It is a short lyric, elegiac in tone
without being an elegy, and consisting of four quatrains with the even
lines rhyming in each stanza. The metre is basically anapaestic tri-
meter, with irregular iambic and amphibrachic substitution in the case
of some of the feet; two lines (11 and 15) are tetrameters; and the first
and thirteenth lines each consist of three strong unaccompanied
stresses. Thus, in the second stanza, the stress pattern is as follows
(/ = stressed syllable; x = unstressed syllable; | = metrical foot
divisions):

x   / | x   x   / | x   x   /
Ô well for the fisherman's boy,
   x   x   / | x   x /| x   x   /
   That he shouts with his sister at play!
x   / | x   x   /| x   /
Ô well for the sailor lad,
    x   x   / | x   x   / | x   x   /
    That he sings in his boat on the bay!

(For a discussion of the significance of metre in poetry and an explanation of basic technical terms, see Glyn Turton's account in Chapter 6, 'Reading Poetry'.) Rather more than half the lines have alliteration built into them. The combined effect of these features is the creation of a strong, pulsating rhythm aptly conveying the shock, the heartbreak and the yearning of the speaker's miserable bereavement. The rhythmical variations and the pronounced rhymes every other line serve to emphasise his stark predicament further. And the sea's breakers crashing against the cliff's foot are echoed in the very movement of the verse itself – slow, measured, pounding. It is a painfully insistent poem: even the images – of sea, stone and crag, boat and ship, haven and hill (conventional enough in themselves) – resonate in their simplicity. These outward and visible signs are hardly metaphors for the speaker's inner graceless state: rather, they point to the enormity of the gulf between the seen and the unseen, between what is so remorselessly real and what is no less real, though it has no physical shape – the poet's intense grief. The sea, the fisherman's boy, the sailor lad, the stately ships all express in sound and movement their being and existence; the speaker is impotent by comparison.

What view of reality seems to be emerging in this lyric? What is the poem's ideological configuration? Christopher Ricks observes that 'the poem's sense is plain enough; yet – like most of the best poems – it has a riddling quality too'.[9] This is partly a matter of the links between some of the poem's statements being left implicit, rather than spelt out: the 'And' at the beginning of lines 3 and 9, the 'But' at the beginning of lines 11 and 15, are hardly logical connectives – in 'conjuncting' they juxtapose seemingly different elements, so that the reader has some thinking to do to arrive at a satisfactory explanation of the poem's chain of thought. Then there is the paradox of the poem itself taken as a whole. The poet laments being unable to do something in the very act of doing it! Tennyson's pen, if not his tongue, does 'utter' to all intents and purposes the 'thoughts that arise' in him – hence the poem. (Whether the poem fails to do justice to the poet's thoughts, perhaps because of their complexity or because of the inadequacy and imprecision of language as a tool, there is, of course, no way of telling.) The poem makes present once more (*re*-presents) what the poet mourns as permanently absent: 'a vanished hand', 'the sound of a voice that is still', 'the tender grace of a day that is dead'. What is desired by the poet is something negative, destructive, dead: he urges the sea (and his heart?) to 'break' six times; he envies the access of the ships to 'their haven under the hill' (a cross between 'heaven' and 'grave'?); he wants to hear a 'still' voice; he wants to relive 'a day that is dead' knowing how impossible that is. Locked in the prison of his grief the poet reaches out, hopelessly, the outer world of objective reality failing to mirror his inner subjective world of loss, just as the language of the poem fails to mirror his deeply felt loss. Death is both feared and desired; so too is life. The poem, in other words, is replete with contradictions. A poem where the silences speak at least as loudly as the words.

What difference does a knowledge of the context of the poem make to a critical reading of it? Though published in 1842 it was written some years earlier, probably in the spring of 1834 in Lincolnshire. The immediate personal context for the poem was the sudden, tragically early death (at just 22 years old) in September 1833 of Tennyson's close friend Arthur Hallam, of apoplexy, while in Vienna. His body was brought back by ship for burial in England. 'Break, break, break' was one of many poems which show the poet trying to come to terms with his loss, the most notable being the sequence of lyrics written over sixteen years and published in 1850 – the year Tennyson married, and became Poet Laureate in succession to Wordsworth – under the title *In Memoriam A. H. H.* An appreciation of this context clearly provides at least a basic set of co-ordinates with which to map out the poem's referential dimensions. What previously may have been somewhat speculative (as in the interpretative phrase, 'the premature death of a close relative or friend' above) thereby becomes more securely founded. *Hallam's* 'vanished hand' is more readily graspable by the reader (if not by Tennyson – at least in *this* poem). But read in 'intertextual' conjunction with other Tennyson poems dealing with the same theme, 'Break, break, break' also helps to sharpen our sense of the landscape of loss in the nineteenth century more generally; it illuminates our view of the Victorian way of death, which involved hopes and fears in relation to an afterlife, the existence of which, in the wake of the century's geological and biological discoveries, was no longer seen to be as certain as it once had been. Text and context: their relationship should be one of reciprocal enlightenment. 'Break, break, break' is a poignant cry from Tennyson's heart, a poem in which, as one Victorian critic put it, the poet turned 'an ordinary sea-shore landscape into a means of finding a voice indescribably sweet for the dumb spirit of human loss'.[10]

What can be said about the poem's language? Much has already been implied about this feature: to discuss the poem critically while ignoring its language is, of course, an impossibility. But a few further points may be made here. The diction of the poem, like a number of its other features, is deceptively simple. Tennyson's art does not always draw attention to itself. Consider the lexical choice in line 4: 'The thoughts that *arise in* me'. 'The thoughts that *occur to* me' would have done: it is a phrase close enough in meaning, and metrically equivalent. But 'arise in' is better: the phrase suggests that the poet has in mind deeper thoughts than mere passing notions; indeed, 'thoughts' here surely implies 'feelings' – and profound feelings at that. There may even be the suggestion of tears welling up (as in his poem 'Tears, Idle Tears') from somewhere deep inside, the significance of which Tennyson is unable to express, such is the pain. The rising movement may also remind the reader of the swelling and pounding sea of the poem (a motion replicated in the ebb and flow of the poem's rhythm throughout). Tennyson was an accomplished technician when it came to crafting poetic lines: his mastery of word-music is impressive. And his ear for sound (W. H. Auden once claimed Tennyson had the finest ear of any poet[11]) is apparent in this lyric. The harsh-sounding, grating gutturals of the first and last stanzas, for example, convey quite brilliantly the jaundiced, bitter, life-weary perspective of the despondent speaker. Or consider the end of line 11: 'a vanished hand'; the phrase rises and falls away, the fourth vowel sound echoing the second, before dying out. The poem is full of little touches which show Tennyson's dual sense of both the language of poetry and the poetry of language. When T. S. Eliot remarked on Tennyson's 'complete competence' it was, no doubt, the poet's scrupulous attention to detail which impressed him.[12] And, reading 'Break, break, break', it is clear why Eliot was right to be impressed.

Conclusion: Reading freely

Reading a literary text critically in the ways suggested and illustrated above can be a demanding process. In working fairly systematically through Tennyson's poem I have inevitably misrepresented what the average critical reading experience is really like. This was a consequence of trying to exemplify the discrete dimensions of the activity of reading literature critically. In practice, it is to be hoped, few readings will be as mechanical as mine. Most critical readers, I imagine, move quite *freely* from talking about the reading experience, to considering questions of form and technique, to examining a text's ideas, back to an overview of the reading experience and so on. In other words, most people approach a critical reading of the literary text holistically, as something greater than the mere sum of its constituent parts. And that is sensible. In the next few chapters, the points made so far about reading literary texts will be elaborated by considering the critical process in relation to the three main literary genres – poetry, prose fiction and plays – in terms of the specific demands and challenges posed by each kind of writing. And in the final chapter some of the theoretical implications of reading literary texts critically will be explored.

Notes

1. J. Hillis Miller, *The Ethics of Reading: Kant, de Man, Eliot, Trollope, James, and Benjamin* (New York: Columbia U.P., 1987), pp. 3–4.
2. Quoted by Peter Haining in his introduction to *The Best Supernatural Stories of Wilkie Collins* (London: Robert Hale, 1990), p. 17.
3. Charles Dickens, *Great Expectations*, ed. Angus Calder (Harmondsworth: Penguin, 1965), p. 379.
4. Terry Eagleton, *The Rape of Clarissa: Writing, sexuality, and class struggle in Samuel Richardson* (Oxford: Basil Blackwell, 1982), p. 37.
5. Stanley Fish, *Is There a Text in This Class?: The authority of interpretive communities* (Cambridge, Mass. and London: Harvard U.P., 1980), pp. 1, 355.
6. Emily Brontë, *Wuthering Heights*, ed. David Daiches (Harmondsworth: Penguin, 1965), p. 45.
7. Jacques Derrida, *Of Grammatology*, trans. Gayatri Chakravorty Spivak (Baltimore, Md. and London: The Johns Hopkins U.P., 1976), p. 158.
8. *Tennyson: A selected edition*, ed. Christopher Ricks (Harlow: Longman, 1989), p. 165.
9. Christopher Ricks, *Tennyson*, 2nd edn (Basingstoke and London: Macmillan, 1989), p. 133.
10. R. H. Hutton, cited in Ricks, *Tennyson*, p. 134.
11. W. H. Auden, *Forewords and Afterwords*, ed. Edward Mendelson (London: Faber and Faber, 1973), p. 222.
12. T. S. Eliot, *Selected Prose*, ed. Frank Kermode (London: Faber and Faber, 1975), p. 239.

Further reading

Eagleton, T., *Literary Theory: An introduction* (Oxford: Basil Blackwell, 1983). (Chapter 2, 'Phenomenology, Hermeneutics, Reception Theory', offers a witty if unsympathetic account of reader theories.)

Fish, S., *Is There a Text in This Class?: The authority of interpretive communities* (Cambridge, Mass. and London: Harvard U.P., 1980). (Entertaining, polemical collection of essays on reading and interpretation.)

Newton, K. M., *Interpreting the Text: A critical introduction to the theory and practice of literary interpretation* (Hemel Hempstead: Harvester Wheatsheaf, 1990). (Lucid, fair survey of the controversies surrounding literary interpretation.)

Montgomery, M., Durant, A., Fabb, N. and Mills, S., *Ways of Reading: Advanced reading skills for students of English literature* (London and New York: Routledge, 1992). (Wide-ranging coursebook with a theoretical edge; has sections on basic techniques, language, narrative; includes activities at end of each chapter.)

Selden, R., *Practising Theory and Reading Literature: An introduction* (Hemel Hempstead: Harvester Wheatsheaf, 1989). (Concise readings of texts exemplifying specific theory-led approaches; includes exercises.)

McCormick, K., Waller, G. and Flower, L., *Reading Texts: Reading, responding, writing* (Lexington, Mass. and Toronto: D. C. Heath & Co., 1987). (Textbook with plenty of worked examples; theoretically informed; includes glossary of terms.)

6
Reading poetry
Glyn Turton

Poetry, pleasure and the dutiful mob

Poetry has enormous power to delight and to satisfy – by exciting, by consoling, by amusing. And yet anyone attempting to argue for the general importance of poetry in the late twentieth century must feel as if they have their work cut out. Poetry has numerous functions, but foremost among them is that of giving pleasure. If easily accessible pleasures abound, the case for those which may first require some effort is harder to make. Samuel Johnson, the eighteenth-century critic, is said to have observed that 'people in general do not willingly read, if they can have anything else to amuse them'.[1] Johnson's remark seems especially apposite in an age in which stimulation is more often a matter of the visual than the verbal, the ephemeral than the enduring.

Anxiety about the ability of poetry to hold its own in the cultural market-place goes back at least as far as the Renaissance. In fact, attempts to defend it are the starting-point of poetry's ascendancy as a literary form. Sir Philip Sidney's *The Defence of Poesie* (1595) makes the case for poetry against the claims of other forms of discourse (such as history and philosophy) by insisting on its superior capacity to be pleasurable, to put before its readers a 'golden' world, more enjoyable to contemplate than the real one. With the rise of the novel and the growth of mass communication and entertainment, concern that poetry was providing its particular pleasures to a dwindling constituency arose – not least among poets themselves. In 1957 Philip Larkin expressed the view that poetry had lost its voluntary readership and acquired an enforced one – students. This Larkin attributed to a regrettable collusion between poets, literary reviewers and academic critics, at the root of which loss was the poet's neglect of 'the pleasure principle'. '[A]t bottom,' Larkin argued, 'poetry, like all art, is inextricably bound up with giving pleasure, and if a poet loses his pleasure-seeking audience he has lost the only audience worth having, for which the dutiful mob that signs on every September is no substitute.'[2] More recently Frank Kermode has restated the same problem of literature's retreat into the classroom and lecture theatre:

> The ample provision of ephemeral writing for the masses made it more and more obvious that serious writing must be content with its own small audience; the avant-garde took pride in the fact but eventually its products were to be saved by the creation of an artificial class of readers who taught, or were taught, in colleges. The division widened as cinema, radio, and television took over the task of filling people's leisure time; and all the duties of the old Common Reader have now virtually devolved upon professional students of literature.[3]

But while Larkin saw the captive student audience as no substititute for the former 'cash customers' of poetry, Kermode regards it as the challenging responsibility of teachers and critics to turn students into the new common readers. This ambition is more realistic than it might seem. First, the number of students has expanded to the point where thinking of them as constituting a common readership is by no means far-fetched. Secondly, as far as poetry is concerned, Larkin's 'pleasure principle', always supposing that it had become neglected in the first place, is certainly at work in the writing of many contemporary poets. It is probably easier now than it was in the 1950s to demonstrate that poetry answers to the actual concerns of common experience. Since Larkin delivered his strictures against modern poetry and its failure to communicate, many have succeeded in doing what William Wordsworth urged upon his fellow poets nearly two hundred years ago, namely that they should 'descend from [their] supposed height' and '[select] from the real language of men'.[4] In finding ways of composing in the spirit of the real language of men and women, good contemporary poets such as Seamus Heaney, Tony Harrison and Fleur Adcock have made it easier for teachers to introduce their students to 'the pleasure principle'. The sections of this chapter which follow will consider the questions of what poetry is and how it works, in the conviction that pleasure is increased through understanding – and that the 'mob' is not only dutiful when it comes to reading poems, but capable of sustained enthusiasm as well.

What is poetry?

For poetry makes nothing happen: it survives
In the valley of its making where executives
Would never want to tamper, flows on south
From ranches of isolation and the busy griefs,
Raw towns that we believe and die in; it survives,
A way of happening, a mouth.[5]

There are two distinct aspects to this question: the technical one of what specific attributes make a poem a poem; and the wider issue of how poetry has been perceived as a cultural phenomenon. The first of these we can attempt to define – though the definition will not be so watertight as might at first be thought. But before we consider the issue of what a poem is and how it works, it will be useful to explore the more complex issue of how poetry's central function and purpose have been identified in relation to the ways of interpreting reality proposed by religion, philosophy and history. For notions of what poetry is inform our reading in quite involuntary ways. However innocent we may think the eye and ear we bring to poetry, we may be sure that they have been conditioned by ideas about it which often operate as subconscious assumptions.

As I suggested above, it is easier to define a poem by its characteristics and to describe how it works than to state what poetry is in general. The very way in which I have formulated the last sentence – by making a contrastive distinction between what something is and what it does, between doing and being – provides a clue to the cause of this difficulty. One of the most influential insights of modern linguistic and literary theory has been the recognition that, in Western civilisation at least, rational inquiry and speculation have traditionally been governed by an organising principle which is binary (i.e. two-sided) and, therefore, oppositional in nature. We make our meanings in the space between concepts which are polar opposites – light and dark, Heaven and Hell, north and south, male and female and so on. From the earliest theories to the views taken of it in the late twentieth century, poetry has been pulled first this way and then that by what one might call the force fields of just such opposing concepts. But poetry does not easily yield to processes of classification rooted in the principle of diametrical opposition.

Why is this? One important reason is that poetry by its very nature is a highly inclusive, combinative form and therefore not easily susceptible of definition, which, by *its* nature, aims to be exclusive. As the philosopher Imlac says in Samuel Johnson's moral fable *The History of Rasselas* (1759), 'To a poet nothing can be useless'.[6] Poetry is a synthesising art; its very task is to create a new entity out of things which are normally held apart.

It is possible to draw up a long list of antithetical concepts which have been used as reference points for discussion about the nature of poetry. Here are just some of them: *truth and invention; realism and idealism; reason and imagination; classicism and romanticism; history and philosophy; intellect and feeling; universality and particularity; imitation and expression; utility and beauty; magic and science.* Poetry eludes definitive enlistment under any one of the categories in any one of these pairings, but it taps into all of them. The argument about what poetry is, and the energies of poetry itself, have been generated by the creative tension between these opposites. And at different moments in its history, both the theory and the form of poetry have been moved forward by one set of polarities exerting the greater pull.

Today we tend to think of poetry as personal, expressive, concerned with an individual's feelings and thoughts about the relationship between the self and the world. Of course, in one sense, this is what poetry always has been. But it is important to note that this subjective aspect of poetry has assumed its particular prominence only in the last two hundred years. This is because of that important shift in cultural history called Romanticism. This movement, which ran its course roughly between 1770 and 1830, brought about a new emphasis upon the distinctive nature of the poet's individual imagination and its power to reshape reality. This tendency for poetry to be regarded as a form reserved for articulating private concerns and projecting a personal vision was accentuated by the increasingly dominant (and much more social) form of the novel in the Victorian period, and the advent of film and television in the twentieth century. What we have to remember is that poetry has lost its preeminence only in the last hundred years or so; prior to that, it enjoyed great prestige and authority as an art form. That authority stemmed largely from its capacity to represent reality and communicate ideas *through pleasure.* We need to look briefly at how and why it came to be regarded in this way – and how it came to lose some of that self-confidence as other genres and art forms eclipsed it in popularity.

The effective origins of Western European theories of poetry lie in the thought of the major figures of ancient Greek philosophy, notably Plato (427–347 BC) and his pupil Aristotle (384–22 BC). It will be helpful to give some consideration to the thought of these two major figures, since their ideas have had a seminal influence on Western theories of poetic art. In Plato's conception of the properly ordered state, the poet was considered to be a disturbing and undesirable influence, so potentially subversive that he might be banished. Plato's objections to poetry were essentially twofold. He propounded the view that primary reality exists on an ideal, eternal plane, unknowable, directly, to the world of the senses. The known material world he took to be made up of imperfect replicas of ideal, invisible original forms. Since, to Plato, the poet's art was that of *mimesis*, or imitation, of the world which our senses perceive, the products of poetry must be at several removes from primary, eternal truth, and, therefore, a kind of untruth. Moreover, poetry's imaginative power, playing upon the emotions and varying the shape and nature of things, tended, in Plato's opinion, to disturb the rationality upon which a properly ordered world-view depends, making the poet a dangerous 'image-maker, far removed indeed from the truth'.[7]

Plato's judgement of poetry against the yardstick of a hypothetical ideal reality may appear to us as alien in conception as it is remote in time, and if it is taken as the starting-point of poetic theory appears to be a decidedly inauspicious one. Nevertheless, it has had important implications which we need to consider.

First, Plato's distrust of poetry on account of its capacity to stir the human mind and emotions has stood as influential testimony to its power as an alternative mode of communication whenever attempts are made to monopolise language and logic for political ends. This is not to say that poems may not be politically committed; much good poetry has been. What it means is that poetry can easily insinuate itself between those oppositional distinctions which politics, by its inherently adversarial nature, deals in. As poets have been quick to recognise, poetry by itself can work no practical effects in the sphere of history and politics. Yet it has a power of intervention in that word's strict sense of 'coming between'. Distilling thought and feeling into intense and memorable verbal form, it could be seen as transcending the given moment, yet carrying with it the force of momentary experience. By taking time out, it places itself outside history's most fundamental binary pairing, cause and effect. The contemporary poet Seamus Heaney has written eloquently of how poetry cannot affect history, yet operates on its own terms within history:

> Poetry . . . is arbitrary and marks time in every possible sense of that phrase. It does not say to the accusing crowd or to the helpless accused, 'Now a solution will take place', it does not propose to be instrumental or effective. Instead, in the rift between what is going to happen and whatever we would wish to happen, poetry holds attention for a space, functions not as distraction but as pure concentration, a focus where our power to concentrate is concentrated back on ourselves.[8]

What Heaney is claiming for poetry in relation to historical and political forces is the ability to present itself as an alternative voice. By being 'arbitrary' – it may exist, but it need not – it stands outside the chain of necessity (or, as often as not, expediency) which has bound all political orders – from Plato's ideal republic to the regimented dictatorships of the twentieth century.

The second aspect of Plato's thought which has had a profound effect upon the development of the European poetic tradition is his insistence upon there being an extrasensory dimension to reality, a plane within which the immortal soul has its origins and to which it yearns to return. This proposition, fundamental to Plato's thought, has had a great bearing upon both the general course of Western philosophy and the Christian religion. And it has had a powerful effect upon the outlook of poets since the works of Ancient Greek and Roman philosophy became a preoccupation of secular writing during the Renaissance. Ironically, the idea of an invisible reality – to which, Plato contended, the inferior image-making poet has no access – has proved an important stimulus to poetry. The reasons for this are not far to seek. Poetry is the province of the imagination which may be defined as 'the mental faculty which forms images or concepts of external objects not present to the senses' (*The New Shorter Oxford English Dictionary*). Clearly, there can be no greater challenge to the imagination of the poet than to intimate in words that which cannot be verified by the senses. Because of this, the idea of the material world as a veil behind which lies hidden an eternal unifying principle has proved a persistent concern of poetry right down to the twentieth century. A central feature of Romanticism, for example, was the endorsement of poets' individual imaginations and a licensing of their powers of intuition. Since the idea of an invisible sphere of unity and perfection must be an imaginative construct that can only be intuited, not proven, it is not

surprising that some of the major figures in the Romantic tradition –
William Blake, Percy Bysshe Shelley, the twentieth-century Irish poet
W.B. Yeats – have ventured to conceive the inconceivable, to make the
Platonic idea of a transcendental reality central to their imaginative
systems.

With the essentials of Plato's system of thought as a starting-point, I
have tried to suggest the way in which poetry came to be thought of as
having the capacity to negotiate between that which we know to be true
and that which we might suppose or wish to be true. In order to understand how that view of poetry came to be propagated, we need first to
consider the all-important influence of Plato's pupil, Aristotle. For if in
the history of poetry Plato is associated with the abstract and the mysti-
cal, with his conception of the Ideal, arrived at by processes of inference,
Aristotle is the chief source of our thinking about the nature of poetry's
effects and its kinship with other human intellectual activities.

Aristotle's principal work on aesthetics, the *Poetics*, has been the most
important source of all in the development of poetic and dramatic theory
since the Renaissance. Its concern is to classify types of poetry and drama
– the epic, the tragic, the comic; to specify the nature of their proper
concerns; and to describe and recommend the language appropriate for
each kind of literary activity. In doing so, the *Poetics* consistently takes as
its points of reference the *human* determinants of verbal art and its effects
upon human sensibilities. My purpose here is not to summarise the
Poetics since good summaries abound. I wish simply to indicate those
points in Aristotle's thought which describe the scope of the poetic
imagination and locate poetry in relation to the two forms of intellectual
activity which give accounts of the world – philosophy and history.

Aristotle, like Plato before him, holds that the basis of poetry, as of all
art, is *mimesis* or imitation, the representation of that which is held to
exist. He maintains that the pleasure we take in poetry is the pleasure of
being made to 'realise' that which we did not previously understand. But
it is in designating the scope and function of poetry that he produces
formulae which, since their rediscovery at the time of the Renaissance,
have had a profound influence on the theory and practice of poetry.

Aristotle puts forward three cardinal principles concerning poetry: (1)
the poet represents either 'what was or is, what is commonly said and
thought to be the case' or 'what should be the case'; (2) the poet uses
'verbal expression, including dialect terms and metaphor, and many abnormal elements of expression, as these are licences we allow to poets'; (3)
'correctness in poetry is not the same as correctness in morals, nor yet is

it the same as correctness in any other art'.[9] These principles negate the hostility of Plato, by constituting a kind of poet's charter. In the process, they affirm the involvement of poetry in the moral life while at the same time exempting it from judgement on the same terms as common morality.

What is particularly significant is that Aristotle specifies the proper concern of poetry as general or universal patterns of human behaviour and action. For this reason, he insists that the affinities of poetry are more with philosophy than history, contending that 'poetry is at once more like philosophy and more worth while than history, since poetry tends to make general statements, while those of history are particular.'[10]

This view of poetry – as a source of understanding, resembling philosophy in its concern with universal principles, but distinct in its capacity to communicate them through the pleasure-giving medium of emotive language – is where its cultural authority derives from. In its essentials, such a view survives from the late sixteenth century to the nineteenth. Sir Philip Sidney, a leading intellectual figure in Renaissance England, defending poetry against those of his contemporaries who were hostile to imaginative literature, rests his case squarely on Aristotelian principles, arguing that poetry surpasses all other forms in its capacity to instruct while pleasing, calling it a 'speaking picture, with this end to teach and delight'. For Sidney, the poet as a teacher of moral doctrine surpasses the historian, and 'for instructing is well nigh comparable to the philosopher, for moving, leaving him far behind'.[11] Throughout that phase of literary history which we call the neo-classical period – roughly from 1660 to 1780 – this *classical* conception of the function of the poet is perpetuated. John Dryden, the major figure in English poetry of the late seventeenth century in his *Defense of an Essay of Dramatic Poesy* speaks of poetry as that which 'only instructs as it delights'.[12] Samuel Johnson, the foremost English critic of the eighteenth century, has Imlac maintain that the poet must concern himself not with the individual but with the species, and should write 'as the interpreter of nature and the legislator of mankind, and should consider himself as presiding over the thoughts and manners of future generations'.[13]

Although the Romantic movement moved poetry significantly away from one pole towards the other, emphasising its expressive more than its imitative function, it did not depart from that lofty conception of poetry and the poet built up since the Renaissance. On the contrary, the views of Wordsworth, Coleridge and Shelley actively reinforced the conception of the poet as an interpreter of the general laws of the universe and the principles of nature. Shelley, for example, echoed Johnson by speaking of poets in *A Defence of Poetry* as 'the unacknowledged legislators of the world'. Herein lies the tension which, as the nineteenth century progressed, turned itself into a crisis over the nature and function of poetry. A gap had opened up between the theoretical claims of poetry and the actual preoccupations of poets. For while the elevated Aristotelian conception of poetry's public function – its obligation to speak to humanity of humanity's universal concerns – remained one that some poets subscribed to as late as the mid-Victorian period, the final effect of Romanticism, with its emphasis on the expression of personal feelings and thoughts, was to create a climate of introspection in the actual practice of poetry. Add to this the progressive specialisation of the language of poetry and the result was a form seemingly ill-adapted to compete with fiction in the sphere of *mimesis*.

Those nineteenth-century poets and critics who sensed this crisis reacted in different ways. The great Victorian poet Tennyson, torn between public and private realities, drew some of his creative energies from the tensions which his own sense of divided aims generated. Matthew Arnold, Tennyson's contemporary, tried to talk himself into believing that the brooding, introspective side of his poetic preoccupations could be suppressed in favour of the adoption of tragic and heroic themes, drawn from myth and history, in the hope that poetry might function not just as a rival to philosophy but as a substitute for religion. Arnold's claim, on the basis of his attempt to revive the classical, Aristotelian spirit in his own poetry, that 'the future of poetry is immense',[14] does not look altogether convincing in a mid-Victorian cultural context. Arnold's close friend, the poet Arthur Hugh Clough, was perhaps the most realistic of all his generation in acknowledging that poetry must find a way of accommodating the concerns of a society increasingly dominated more by materialism than by myths and metaphysics – or else lose out to the novel:

There is no question that people much prefer *Vanity Fair* and *Bleak House* to poetry. Why so . . .? Poetry should deal more with the actual, palpable things with which our every-day life is concerned; introduce into business and weary task-work a character and soul of purpose and reality; intimate to us relations which, in our unchosen, peremptorily-appointed posts, in our grievously narrow and limited spheres of action, we still, in and through all, retain to some central celestial fact. . . . The novelist does try to build us a real house to be lived in; and this common builder, with no notion of the orders, is more to our purpose than the student of ancient art who proposes to lodge us under an Ionic portico. We are, unhappily, not gods, nor even marble statues.[15]

Clough's remarks are a scarcely veiled reproach to his friend Arnold, who would have poetry turn back to its classical roots. They are a plea for poetry to reorientate itself in the modern world, to find a scope and language appropriate to the times and to match ambitions to real possibilities. That being said, it is significant that Clough the realist (whose own poetic practice ran to satire and humour) still sees poetry as having the function of providing a link with a non-material level of reality – 'some central celestial fact'. That aspiration, while it might not hinge on anything so clearly defined as Plato's transcendental realm of perfect forms, represents an echo of the ancient role of the poet as a mediator between the real and the ideal.

It has been the task of poets and poetic theorists in the period since Clough made these comments to rethink the nature and possibilities of poetry in line with its altered cultural status. I want to conclude this section by citing two twentieth-century poets who, in different ways, have contributed to the twentieth-century debate about the nature of poetry by offering carefully measured judgements about its proper function in the modern world. The Anglo-American poet and critic T. S. Eliot has been a major influence on twentieth-century notions of poetry and its role in the modern world. Eliot attempted to specify exactly what poetry could and could not do when compared to other fields of creative inquiry. In his essay 'Shakespeare and the Stoicism of Seneca' (1927), he sought to distance poetry from philosophy and religion, towards which critics from Aristotle to Arnold had attempted to draw it. 'Poetry', wrote Eliot,

is not a substitute for philosophy or theology or religion; it has its own function. But as this function is not intellectual but emotional, it cannot be defined adequately in intellectual terms. We can say that it provides 'consolation', strange consolation, which is provided equally by writers so different as Dante and Shakespeare.[16]

T. S. Eliot's words take us back to our starting-point – the difficulties of defining poetry. But they are also an attempt to bring poetry into a true and proportionate relationship with those activities with which it is linked but from which it differs by virtue of its emotional and intellectual *immediacy*. Eliot's view may represent a scaling-down of poetry's historic claims, but it is also a confident affirmation of poetry's distinctive function – directly to compel the mind through an appeal to feeling.

Another way of affirming that function in the modern world is by showing how poetry's most fundamental process – metaphorical connection – is an intensive form of the imaginative reflex which operates in most ways of engaging with reality – religious, philosophical, political, or even scientific. This is how the American poet Robert Frost in a lecture entitled 'Education by Poetry' (given in 1930) presents his twentieth-century 'defence of poesie'. Frost proclaims as the highest function of poetry that attempt to reconcile those ultimate binary opposites, the material and the spiritual. But he insists that the way in which poetry brings together seemingly disparate or contrary things – by metaphor – is basic to all human ways of trying to understand the world:

> it is the height of poetry, the height of all thinking, the height of all poetic thinking, that attempt to say matter in terms of spirit, spirit in terms of matter . . . It is wrong to call anybody a materialist simply because he tries to say spirit in terms of matter, as if that were a sin. Materialism is not the attempt to say all in terms of matter. The only materialist – be he poet, teacher, politician, or statesman – is the man who gets lost in his material without a gathering metaphor to throw it into shape and order.[17]

This is what poetry's power to bring together things ordinarily apart or opposed depends upon – the 'gathering metaphor'. For a metaphor is a means of being in two places at once – metaphorically speaking.

What is a poem?

Take heart, a boy
Could do worse than be a spotter of metaphors.[18]

Having looked briefly at the question of how poetry has been thought of as a cultural phenomenon, we shall now consider what a poem is before moving on to see how it works. Earlier I pointed out that while it is possible to define a poem, any definition is likely to be a rather qualified one. Defining a poem is rather like throwing a stone into a still pool of water and watching the ripples it creates. The first few ripples are sharply outlined against the surface but the last lose their distinctness as the water absorbs the energy of disturbance. In the case of our attempts at definition, the watery element in which the effort is absorbed is the fluid question of what poetry is generally. (Alert readers will note my recourse to a figure of speech in an attempt to deal with this question.) The entry in *The New Shorter Oxford Dictionary* (1993) under 'poem' makes the point for me. It gives three variants: '(i) A metrical composition of words expressing facts, thoughts, or feelings in poetical form; a self-contained piece of poetry. (ii) A non-metrical composition of words having some quality or qualities in common with poetry. (iii) A thing (other than a composition of words) having poetic qualities.' The definition given here starts with the identification of a poem as a verbal construct which has *particular technical characteristics* but moves onwards and outwards to define a poem by association with certain *general qualities of language* which may be considered 'poetic'. This is a recognition of the fact that while, in English culture at least, a poem has traditionally been marked by certain formal and structural features, the conventions of poetry have loosened to the point at which, in a technical compositional sense, only the poet's willed act of writing in shortened lines necessarily differentiates poetry from prose.

Once we have decided, on the basis of this fundamental criterion, that a piece of writing is a poem, we can go on to consider whether or not it has those formal features which enable us to describe it as *verse*. In order to be so described, it must have that regularly recurring pattern of rhythm to which we give the name *metre*. It may, in addition, be characterised by *rhyme* and it may also be organised into structurally equivalent groups of lines called *stanzas*. But an organised rhythm is the only necessary condition for designating lines of poetry as verse. To summarise: while poetry need not be verse, verse *must* be poetry but *may* be so only in the most basic, technical sense described above. *Paradise Lost* and *The Ballad of Eskimo Nell* are both verse and, therefore, both poetry, but, even in these postmodern times, are not to be counted as poems of the same order. To say why not takes us, of course, into the area of the different themes and scope that poetry may have, but most fundamentally leads us into the question of how syntax (the order of words in relation to the rules of grammar) and diction (the choice of words in a text) are manipulated in order to influence our emotional receptivity. These two categories bridge over the distinction which I made earlier between the particular technical characteristics of a poem and its general qualities of language.

Of the main recurrent technical features which a poem may have – metre, rhyme and stanzaic form – the last two are relatively unproblematical. *Rhyme* is the effect produced by the repetition of the same sound or group of sounds, usually at the ends of lines of verse, in different words or groups of words. Numerous rhyme schemes are possible, including some traditional ones which accompany stanzas of a particular length and pattern. Poets sometimes also make lines of verse rhyme internally and may use half-rhymes – sounds which are near, not full, phonetic equivalents. But whatever form rhyme takes, it invariably has two functions. The first is *mnemonic*, that is to make the lines easy to memorise. Poetry is written to preserve and memorialise, so making poems memorable is important. But of course they also need to stimulate immediate attention and, since one way in which human attention is caught is by linguistic contrivance, the effect of arranging a pattern of different words with equivalent sounds is inherently arresting.

Any discussion of rhyme takes us to the heart of the essential function of a poem which is to intensify our apprehension of the sense of things. Notice that I do not say to intensify the sense of things, but rather our *apprehension* of it. All good poetry should leave us with a heightened awareness of the significance of some aspect or other of experience, but without distorting or exaggerating that significance. Rhyme is one of the basic heightening devices available to poets. Available but, of course, not always used. Much of the finest English poetry is written in what we call *blank verse*. Blank verse is not just any poetry which is unrhymed, but poetry without rhyme written in the commonest of all English metrical forms, the iambic pentameter (see below). It became a feature of English dramatic writing in the sixteenth century and was first used in non-dramatic poetry as early as the 1530s. But the establishment of blank verse as an acceptable vehicle for poetic expression really dates from the middle of the seventeenth century and its adoption by John Milton for his great epic poem *Paradise Lost*. Milton prefaced his epic with a note on the verse used, arguing that rhyme was 'no necessary adjunct or true ornament of poem or good verse' but merely the 'jingling sound of like endings'.[19] Although rhyme, particularly in the form of the *heroic couplet* (a pair of rhyming iambic pentameter lines) predominated in poetic composition throughout most of the eighteenth century, the advent of blank verse begins that general process of the loosening of poetic conventions which I described earlier. At the same time, it must be stressed that rhyme remains a commonly used and extremely powerful device.

The *stanza* represents another level at which a poem may be organised. Stanzas are groups of lines, usually no less than four in number, demarcated by spaces on the printed page. In a given poem, the stanzas usually all have the same number of lines, line-lengths and rhyme scheme. The stanza is not to be confused with the irregular groupings of lines which may occur, particularly in long blank verse poems, and which are sometimes called *verse paragraphs*. The forms that stanzas take vary enormously. Some, with a strictly set pattern, have their own names, such as *rhyme royal* and *ottava rima*. A good glossary of literary terms will provide you with a list of the less common traditional stanza forms. The form that you are most likely to encounter is the *quatrain*, a stanza of four lines.

How may stanzas affect the way in which a poem functions? First, a stanza may quite simply be used as a means of marking off one stage from another in the sequence of ideas, the argument or the dialogue which make up the poem. But there are also more subtle ways of using stanzaic form. The poet may choose to continue the grammatical unit of a sentence across the gap separating two poetic units, the stanzas. This has the calculated effect of making the reader aware of the tension between the artifice of poetic form and the natural structures of grammar and/or conventional, non-poetic syntax. This is just one of the means, rhyme and metre being others, whereby poetry declares itself as performance – a willed departure from the merely functional norms of spoken and written language, which creates, productively, a sense of tension between two orders of communication. And poetry works by generating tension in order to compel attention.

Of all the technical attributes which poetry may have, *metre* is the one about which it is most difficult to be categorical. This is partly because, as we shall see, the theory of metrical composition according to which much English verse has been written and most analysed since the Renaissance is a borrowed suit of clothes which does not fit very well. This connects with a second problem – that of getting the presence and function of metre into proportion in the analysis we make of a poem. A student's commentary on a poem can be marred by her fixation upon metre and the consequent neglect of other less classifiable aspects of language use. On the other hand, where metre is at work in a poem, its function is a fundamental one and, precisely because it is basic to the sound and sense generated, it can easily be overlooked. So when metre is present – and it may not be – we need to treat it as an integral rather than a superimposed element of composition.

What is metre? In simple terms, metre – in English at least – is the creation of equal units out of the patterns of stressed and unstressed syllables which occur naturally in the language. When we speak, we emphasise some syllables more than others by uttering them more loudly, in a higher tone and by lengthening their pronunciation relative to the syllables which surround them. Composing poetry in metre means adapting this phenomenon by making a certain pattern of stressed and unstressed syllables recur and by fixing the number of these recurring units which appear in a line of the poem. In traditional metrical analysis, each of these units is called a *foot*. There are many different types of metrical foot recognisable in English verse, but of these the four set out below are much the commonest. Note that the convention for denoting the pattern of stress in metrical anaylsis is to mark unstressed syllables with a cross (x) and stressed ones with an oblique stroke (/) , immediately above the line of verse. The names and stress patterns of the most common types of metrical foot with their stress pattern are:

iamb x /	anapaest x x /
trochee / x	dactyl / x x

(Thus: *arrive* is an iamb, *quickly* is a trochee, *understand* is an anapaest, and *imitate* is a dactyl.)

We also have names for different lines of verse, according to how many metrical feet there are in them. These are:

monometer:	one foot
dimeter:	two feet
trimeter:	three feet
tetrameter:	four feet
pentameter:	five feet
hexameter:	six feet
heptameter:	seven feet
octameter:	eight feet

The most frequently used of all combinations of foot and line in English verse written in the last five hundred years is that of iambs in a line of five feet – the iambic pentameter (as in the line, 'My father and my mother died of want').

These are the essential forms and terms used in metrical analysis. More detailed accounts can be found in M. H. Abrams's *A Glossary of Literary Terms* and Geoffrey Leech's standard work on poetic language, *A Linguistic Guide to English Poetry*. Remember, though, that I spoke earlier about the system of metrical analysis as a poor fit for the patterns of stress which occur in normal spoken English. This is because the principles of absolute regularity and equivalence of sound value which have determined the system outlined above have been borrowed from classical Greek and Latin and do not accord with the way in which word-forms and grammatical structures combine in English to locate stress powerfully but variably across phrases and sentences. As Leech states, in the naturally occurring rhythms of English ' [a] number of unstressed syllables, varying from nil to four, can occur between one stressed syllable and the next'.[20] This leads him to argue, as many other commentators have done, that the concept of the metrical foot is ill-adapted to English:

> The importance of the foot lies mainly in its historical position in the body of theory which poets through the centuries have learnt, and have more or less consciously applied in their poetry. This theoretical apparatus originated in a misapplication of classical metrics to the rhythm of English, and there is reason to feel that despite its longstanding hold over English versification, it has never become fully assimilated.[21]

It is possible to see this mismatch between the rhythms of English and classical metrical principles in two ways. On the one hand, it may be seen as restrictive, a hindrance, the result of which has been to reduce too much English verse to what Keats, referring to the highly regulated metre of neo-classical poetry, called 'rocking horse' rhymes. On the other hand, the very same act of imposing an artificial order upon naturally determined stresses can enable the poet to play off the emotional and intellectual energies of direct utterance against the restraint of poetic convention. The tension which this can generate is like that created by setting the discontinuities of stanza form against the continuities of grammatical and syntactic structure. And the effect can be, as Coleridge said, writing of metre, to suggest 'the interpenetration of passion and of will, of spontaneous impulse and voluntary purpose' – in other words, the reconciliation of binary oppositions.[22]

All of the devices which I have just outlined – rhyme, stanza, metre – represent the basic formal means (over and above the typographical convention of shortened lines) by which a poetic structure marks itself off from prose. But of course, in order to be intelligible, it must utilise essentially the same rules of grammar and syntax as prose; hence, the two orders of communication which I spoke of earlier. This dual nature of

poetic utterance has been termed by some linguists 'the double pattern'.
Richard Bradford, in his recent study, *A Linguistic History of English
Poetry*, writes that

> [a]ll poems consist of two linguistic patterns, one which corresponds with
> and organises the structure of the poetic line, and one which poetry shares
> with other linguistic discourses, the structural keystone of which is the
> sentence, and the broader signifying functions of which (the generation of
> metaphor, the use of irony, the employment of grammatical deviation, etc.)
> are unlimited.[23]

Let us turn now to those broader signifying functions which poetry
shares with prose – the general qualities of language to which I referred
earlier – in order to see whether anything remains to differentiate the
language of prose from that of poetry once all the technical conventions
of versification have been allowed for.

The language of the poem

The question of how the language of the poem differs from that of other
non-poetic modes of expression is an old and vexed one. If we look at the
history of English literature since the Middle Ages, we can see that there
have been long periods in which the language of poetry has been regarded
as necessarily special, distinct from that of prose and certainly distinct
from that of common speech. In the middle of the eighteenth century,
just such a phase, the poet Thomas Gray could flatly assert that '[t]he
language of the age is never the language of poetry'.[24] But there have
been important moments when poets have made a deliberate attempt to
pull poetry back towards everyday usage in the belief that *poetic diction*,
that is the range of words and phrases chosen for use in poetry, had
become too rigidly conventionalised, too elitist, and therefore exhausted.
By far the most significant such moment occurred at the start of the
nineteenth century, when Wordsworth turned Gray's assertion on its
head, insisting in his poetic manifesto, the Preface to the *Lyrical Ballads*,
that poets should follow his example and use 'the language really spoken
by men'.[25] Of course, between these two particular polarised views lies a
zone of complexity and controversy; the assertions of both Gray and
Wordsworth beg questions. The positions they adopt have much to do
with power relations in society, a fundamental issue with which the

history of poetic language and form is inextricably bound up. There is not the space here to open up this important area of discussion, but as you widen your reading of poetry, it will become clear to you that the conflicting impulses of elitism and egalitarianism have had a powerful bearing on the nature of poetic language.

Setting that issue aside – important though it is – I want now to examine more closely the precise nature of poetic language. Let us start by reminding ouselves of the distinction I made earlier between the performative and the functional uses of language. When I use the word 'performative', I mean it in its specific sense of a speech act which is both formal and emotive, calculated yet impassioned. But it is arguable that prose, just as well as poetry, can be the vehicle of such utterances. In prose, just as in poetry, you can heighten the effect of your words by deviating from the everyday functional or referential norms of language. This is possible because words may have a power of *connotation* as well as one of *denotation*, a distinction which broadly correlates with their performative and functional roles. Whereas denotation implies a strict, referential indication of meaning, connotation refers to the associations and overtones which a word or phrase may have acquired over and above its literal sense, and which may be drawn on by choosing to use the word in a recognised cultural context. A simple example of this would be the word 'flesh'. To the essential meaning of the word there have been added powerful connotations to do with human nature and behaviour. Use the word in the context of a literary form – a poem, a novel, or a play – and you can signify much more than its root meaning.

Largely because of the power of connotation, coupled with the customary force of convention, there are various ways in which language can be used *rhetorically*, that is to say used in order to persuade or compel the reader emotionally and intellectually. Some of these ways in which literary language differs from language used pragmatically may be common to both poetry and prose. That is partly why those poets who have felt most urgently the need to revitalise poetic form and diction have, paradoxically, also been the ones who have challenged the distinction between prose and poetry. Two of the most innovative poets of the last two hundred years, William Wordsworth and T. S. Eliot, came at particular stages of their careers to regard the division between the language of poetry and that of prose as artificial. As a young man, inspired by a democratic urge to correct the over-refinement of taste, Wordsworth went so far as to affirm 'that there neither is, nor can be, any essential difference between the language of prose and metrical composition'.[26]

More circumspectly, T. S. Eliot, after a lifetime of writing poetry, contended that 'the moment the intermediate term *verse* is suppressed, I do not believe that any distinction between prose and poetry is meaningful'.[27]

The most basic level of language at which poetry and prose can be said to operate in the same spectrum, rather than as distinct categories, is that of *vocabulary*. By using words with particular connotations, you can make prose poetic and poetry prosaic. Despite the best efforts of Wordsworth, Byron, Browning, Clough and a handful of other reforming spirits, poetry, until the early twentieth century, was characterised by a restricted vocabulary, a stock of words and phrases clustered at one end of the spectrum. As I indicated earlier in this chapter, the inability of poetry to free itself from a self-perpetuating sense of its elite status and the self-perpetuating vocabulary that went with it was one reason for its eclipse by prose fiction. Archaic words such as 'darkling' and 'perchance' and forms such as 'thou' and 'hath' survived into the early twentieth century. By contrast, in most poetry of the mid- to late twentieth century, there has been a marked tendency to move to the prosaic end of the spectrum which, given the accompanying shift away from metre and rhyme, has meant that the risk of stylistic inflation has been replaced by that of uninspired flatness.

Once we move beyond the level of vocabulary to that of grammar and syntax, we find a sharp difference in the degree to which poetry on the one hand and rhetorical prose on the other can depart from the norms of spoken and written communication. A very important feature of poetry's historically privileged status has been the assumption of *poetic licence*, the special dispensation granted to poets which permits them to deviate from the normal rules of grammar, syntax and (sometimes) pronunciation for the sake of rhyme and metre and in the more general interests of impact and immediacy. And the convention that allows poets to miss out words, rearrange their order, invent compound phrases and juxtapose seemingly unrelated ones, or even uncouple one unit of grammar from that to which it is normally attached is a long-established tradition. Notwithstanding the positions taken by Wordsworth and Eliot, then, we can say that the frequency and extent of grammatical and syntactical deviation is one notable way in which the language of poetry may distinguish it from that of prose.

Before we look at examples of poetry in order to illustrate some of the characteristics which I have described, it is important to mention the most vital of all the constituents of poetic language – *metaphor*. John Williams provides one definition of metaphor in Chapter 4. Chris

Baldick's definition differs slightly; he defines metaphor as the 'most important and widespread figure of speech, in which one thing, idea, or action is referred to by a word or expression normally denoting another thing, idea or action, so as to suggest some common quality shared by the two'.[28] As Baldick points out, metaphor is simply the most important of a range of figures of speech, few of them peculiar to poetry. Some of this range are common, such as *metonymy* (the figure of speech which substitutes something closely associated with the thing for the thing itself), *simile* (the explicit likening of one thing to another) and *oxymoron* (the combination of words normally taken to be contradictory). Others such as *zeugma* (connecting words which occur in different phrases by one part of speech) are more narrowly literary in application. As with types of metre and poetic line, a good glossary of literary terms will provide you with explanations and illustrations of these and other figures of speech.

What I am concerned to do here is not just to emphasise the centrality of metaphor to poetic language but also to suggest that the metaphorical impulse is fundamental to the way we interpret and enhance reality. The drive behind all art is not simply to represent the world by imitation, but to invest in reality through imaginative addition. This is why metaphor is so important, for it enables us to present one thing in terms of another, to take painful truths and appease them by displacement, and to take pleasant truths and increase them by elaboration. Thus, when Shakespeare's Macbeth calls life a tale

> Told by an idiot, full of sound and fury,
> Signifying nothing

he confronts us with the starkest of all truths, the essential meaninglessness, the absurdity, of existence. Yet by metaphoric transference, that which signifies nothing has been signified by something; if imagination cannot overturn the fact of absurdity, it can mitigate it by pulling it closer to the field of human comprehension and acceptance.

Metaphor is always present in our daily speech; sometimes we have conscious recourse to it, but often we use it without thinking in phrases such as 'he ploughed on without stopping' and 'she stuck to her guns'. Frank Kermode in his essay, 'The Plain Sense of Things', holds that imaginative addition is so basic to human apprehension that we can scarcely think without the metaphoric reflex cutting in. ' Metaphor', he writes, 'begins to remodel the plain sense as soon as we begin to think or to speak about it.'[29] And I want to argue that if metaphor, as Kermode puts it, 'runs in the world's blood', its prevalence in poetry makes poetry important to our sense of what we are. Metaphor has certainly always run in the blood of poetry; Old Norse and Old English verse were characterised by a rudimentary form of metaphorical usage known as *kennings*, a convention by which familiar phenomena were figuratively enlarged, so, for example, a battle might be termed a 'metal storm'. In the poem from which I quoted at the start of the previous section, 'The Metaphor Now Standing At Platform 8', Simon Armitage inverts the well-worn idea of the train as metaphor by wittily converting metaphor into train – and the train has a rather brusque conductor:

> Feet off the seats, please. Lady, for the last time,
> extinguish that cigarillo. This is a metaphor
>   I'm running here,
> not a jamboree, and as soon as we get that straight
> we're rolling. Till then, no one goes nowhere.[30]

Just so. And without poetry to keep the metaphors rolling, no one goes nowhere.

How poetry works

We still expect the poetic imagination to be sympathetic rather than analytic. 'Intellect' still tends to summon its rhyme from Wordsworth's pejorative 'dissect'.[31]

The truth is that poetry is both sympathetic and analytic. Poems never really succeed unless the impulse of sympathy is guided by a controlling and inquiring intelligence. And this holds true of reading as well as writing them. I began this chapter by saying that pleasure is increased, not diminished, by the effort involved in understanding how a poem works. And I want to conclude by demonstrating that this is so.

In Chapter 5, Chris Walsh took you carefully through a reading of a single short poem, Tennyson's 'Break, break, break'. My own examples will be extracts from two longer poems, William Wordsworth's 'The Old Cumberland Beggar' (1800) and Tony Harrison's *v.* (1990). These poems, separated by nearly two hundred years, have several things in common. First, they originate in the emotional ground of deeply felt individual experience but develop from this source into diagnoses of the

general condition of society. Both Wordsworth and Harrison are poets
who see human identity in personal *and* social terms. Consequently, their
work affirms the social function of poetry itself. Secondly, they both seek
to combine formal and traditional elements of poetic composition – metre
and, in Harrison's case, rhyme and stanza form – with diction and expression that communicate lived experience with as much immediacy as
possible. In each case, the poetry is carefully composed so as to concentrate rather than attenuate the originating force of feeling and insight.
Finally, both the poems from which these extracts come are about the
need for social and moral cohesion. Poetry may make nothing happen,
but its ability to stabilise the sense and significance of things within a
constructive order has a powerful exemplary force in a disordered world.

Wordsworth, 'The Old Cumberland Beggar', lines 22–51

Him from my childhood have I known, and then
He was so old, he seems not older now;
He travels on, a solitary man,
So helpless in appearance, that for him   25
The sauntering horseman-traveller does not throw
With careless hands his alms upon the ground,
But stops, that he may safely lodge the coin
Within the old Man's hat; nor quits him so,
But still when he has given his horse the rein   30
Towards the aged Beggar turns a look,
Sidelong and half-reverted. She who tends
The toll-gate, when in summer at her door
She turns her wheel, if on the road she sees
The aged Beggar coming, quits her work,   35
And lifts the latch for him that he may pass.
The Post-boy when his rattling wheels o'ertake
The aged beggar, in the woody lane,
Shouts to him from behind, and if, perchance
The old Man does not change his course, the Boy   40
Turns with less noisy wheels to the road-side,
And passes gently by, without a curse
Upon his lips, or anger at his heart.
He travels on, a solitary Man,
His age has no companion. On the ground   45
His eyes are turned, and as he moves along,

They move along the ground; and evermore
Instead of common and habitual sight
Of fields with rural works, of hill and dale,
And the blue sky, one little span of earth   50
Is all his prospect . . .[32]

This is a poem about seeing connections and connection through seeing. Wordsworth has a *didactic* purpose; he aims to teach the importance of those everyday acts of charity which keep alive not only the beggar who receives them, but also the humanity within those who perform them. Those who bestow kindness and consideration on the old man are connected to each other through him. He acts as a cynosure, a focus of attention, for those with whom he comes in contact. Later in the poem, Wordsworth attacks those politicians who would confine the begging poor to institutions, so removing them beyond the reach of alms-giving. The poet, one might say, has his own version of that modern political slogan 'care in the community'.

How does Wordsworth communicate these ideas? When we analyse poetry, there are two basic questions we need to ask: how does the poem cohere, and how does it progress? Poems tend to work by balancing two organising principles, one stabilising and the other dynamic. Here, the two meet and are balanced in the figure of the Old Cumberland Beggar. He picks up *meaning*, as well as alms, in his progress along the country road. At the beginning of the extract, we see him solely through the eyes of the poet, for whom he represents the continuity against which change in his own life may be measured. As the passage proceeds, we see the beggar being seen by horseman, toll-gate keeper and post-boy and, in the process, acquiring the cumulative significance of ever wider association. This connection through sight culminates in what the beggar himself sees as his eyes 'move along the ground' – 'one little span of earth', the earth to which, for Wordsworth, the great poet of nature and humanity, we are all indissolubly bound. In other words, the community is connected by line of sight through the beggar to the world itself. Here the public road is realised with a naturalistic exactness – note the carefully detailed nature of each encounter – yet at the same time it acquires metaphorical overtones as the totality of these encounters comes to suggest the moral choice – to ignore or to recognise – we are faced with on 'the road of life'.

At the same time, the beggar is a point of fixity around which the variegated movement of life circulates and the sense of the poem coheres.

Notice how Wordsworth frames the beggar's wanderings and his encounters with the line 'He travels on, a solitary Man' as if to affirm the beggar as a moral if not a physical constant in a moving, changing world. A few lines beyond where this extract ends, Wordsworth describes the beggar as 'so still/In look and motion'. The idea of stillness and motion paradoxically reconciled is one which held great appeal for Wordsworth. So automatic, so slow, so unswerving is the beggar's progress, so fixed upon the earth is his gaze, that we are made to think of him as if he were unmoving yet in motion – a resolution of binary opposites if ever there were one.

This relationship between fixity and progression is mirrored and reinforced at the level of the poem's verbal structure. The basic metrical form of 'The Old Cumberland Beggar' is that of the blank verse (iambic pentameter) line:

$$x \quad / \quad | \; x \quad / | \; x \quad / \quad | \; x \quad / | x \quad /$$
He was so old, he seems not older now;
$$x \quad / \quad | x \quad / | \; x \quad / | x / | x \quad /$$
He travels on, a solitary man . . .

The recurrence of this metre represents a constant. But pulling forward against the metrically identical lines are features of grammar, syntax, punctuation and natural stress which transform the artifice of regular metre into a subliminal – though still important – element in the way the poem is read. For example, the poet's judgement of how long to dwell on each of the beggar's various encounters so as to achieve optimal emotional effect is what determines where one episode ends and another begins, not the contrivance of line length. Consequently, relatively few of the lines are *end-stopped* (i.e. end where a unit of grammar such as a clause, phrase or sentence also ends) while most lines are characterised by *enjambement* (i.e. the running on of sense and syntax from one line to another). Clearly, one of the principal advantages of blank verse is that, without rhyme to draw attention to the line end, the poet can easily play off the momentum of varying grammatical and syntactical units against the fixed entity of the metrical line. Wordsworth valued spontaneity and immediacy, and blank verse lent itself to his purpose by making possible the unobtrusive regulation of powerful thoughts and feelings.

Finally, let us consider the diction and syntax of the poem. Everyone knows the saying, 'Actions speak louder than words'. It is very precisely *actions* that Wordsworth here commends, so his aim must be not to let the words he uses speak louder than the gestures he describes. By that I mean that he must not over-articulate his sense of what these actions signify or else they will not speak for themselves. So the poet must ensure that the force of the verbs is relatively undiluted by adjectival or adverbial qualification. This he does: if you look carefully at the extract, you will see that the verbs have a positional prominence within it. If Wordsworth needs to qualify them, he makes sure that qualification is a carefully judged extension of verbal meaning. A good example of this occurs in the following lines:

> The sauntering horseman-traveller does not *throw*
> With careless hands his alms upon the ground,
> But *stops*, that he may safely *lodge* the coin
> Within the old Man's hat . . . [my emphasis]

By locating the verbs 'throw' and 'stop' at the end of the first and near the beginning of the third line and separating them by a second line which has no verb in it, Wordsworth accentuates their structural and emotional importance. Arranging the words in this way enables him to achieve the force of contrast between thoughtless and thoughtful acts. What the horseman might have done (throw the money to the ground) is eclipsed by what he does do, and what eclipses the less thoughtful act is the shadow cast over it by that qualificatory second line ('with careless hands his alms upon the ground'). The third line, with two verbs in it denoting right action, of which only one is adverbially qualified, thus acquires force through the contrast between itself and the line which precedes it.

In general, the vocabulary of this poem is plain and the phrasing simple. But its syntax, the order in which words and phrases occur, is quietly sophisticated. I have said that Wordsworth is at pains not to over-elaborate his meaning by adverbial or adjectival extension. When he does qualify a verb or noun, the effect is calculated to animate to just the right degree. So, for example, when Wordsworth wants to suggest how the sauntering horseman's attention lingers on the beggar, he gives grammatical extension to the noun 'look' by placing the adjectives 'Sidelong and half-reverted' after, rather than before, the noun. That is to say, he makes the sentence linger as the horseman's look does. By such careful attention to words and their order an action performed and perceived two hundred years ago is brought instantly alive – and allowed to speak for itself.

Tony Harrison (1937–) v., stanzas 11–21

The language of this graveyard ranges from
a bit of Latin for a former mayor
or those who laid their lives down at the Somme
the hymnal fragments and the gilded prayer,

how people fell 'asleep in the Good Lord';
brief chisellable bits from the good book
and rhymes whatever length they could afford,
to CUNT, PISS, SHIT and (mostly) FUCK!

Or, more expansively, there's LEEDS v.
the opponent of last week, this week, or next,
and a repertoire of blunt four-letter curses
on the team or race that makes the sprayer vexed.

Then, pushed for time, or fleeing some observer;
dodging between tall family vaults and trees
like his team's best ever winger, dribbler swerver,
fills every space he finds with versus Vs.

Vs sprayed on the run at such a lick,
the sprayer master of his flourished tool,
get short-armed on the left like that red tick
they never marked his work much with at school.

Half this skinhead's age but with approval
I helped whitewash a V on a brick wall.
No one clamoured in the press for its removal
or thought the sign, in wartime, rude at all.

These Vs are all the versuses of life
From LEEDS v. DERBY, Black/White
And (as I've known to my cost) man v. wife,
Communist v. Fascist, Left v. Right,

class v. class as bitter as before,
the unending violence of US and THEM,
personified in 1984
by Coal Board MacGregor and the NUM,

Hindu/Sikh, soul/body, heart v. mind,
East/West, male/female, and the ground
these fixtures are fought out on 's Man, resigned
to hope from his future what his past never found.

The prospects for the present aren't too grand
when a swastika with NF (National Front) 's
sprayed on a grave, to which another hand
has added, in a reddish colour, CUNTS.

Which is, I grant, the word that springs to mind,
When going to clear the weeds and rubbish thrown
on the family plot by football fans, I find
UNITED graffitied on my parents' stone.[33]

Actions speak louder than words. But there are times when the power of words must be affirmed in the face of actions – particularly when language itself is the instrument of abuse. The extract above comes from the long poem *v.* by the contemporary poet Tony Harrison. It is occasioned by a visit to his parents' grave and the discovery that their gravestone has been vandalised. This prompts the poet to reflect upon a series of interrelated contrasts – unity and opposition, culture and barbarism, the sacred and the profane, the past and the present. Later in the poem, the poet enagages in imaginary argument with the foul-mouthed skinhead who has defiled his parents' headstone. This battle of words is also a battle over words. Can words make reason prevail over hatred and violence? Harrison thinks he has his imaginary skinhead cornered when he challenges him to sign his name under the word UNITED, sprayed on the grave, to take responsibility for his words. The skinhead contemptuously does so – writing the name Harrison under his handiwork. The vandal is the poet's – and our – *alter ego*.

v. is a fine poem, intensely personal and yet reaching to the heart of our most urgent public concerns. Harrison is both a poet and a classical scholar. From this comes in part his sense of the formal and social function of poetry. His own is almost always rhymed and frequently, as here, takes traditional stanza forms. Yet he is also strikingly successful at introducing dialect and a pungent colloquial idiom alongside literary language. He can often make his poems work by exploiting the tension between the careful, studied reflectiveness of the educated mind and the customary, emotional responses of common life.

v. is about signification, about making signs and assigning meanings. The title of the poem plays upon the multiple sense of the letter 'v'. To make the sign of a 'v' with two fingers may be either a gesture of obscenity or a victory salute. This second use has powerful emotional connotations in Britain, since it is associated with Winston Churchill and victory over Fascism in the Second World War. But as an obscene gesture it is also associated with the brutality and racism of skinhead subculture. While the letter itself may carry two meanings, one suggesting victory and unity, the other anger and hostility, the word for which it may stand – versus – means opposite or against. But 'versus' rhymes with 'verses', meaning made by combining sound and sense. By giving his poem this punning title, Harrison is signalling to readers not only the ironies embedded in language, but also the key to how we may read the poem – as a challenge to us to reconcile the conflicting marks of our civilisation and our barbarism.

The extract I have chosen begins with a powerful image of that conflict – the graveyard headstones bearing prayers for the dead and curses for the living. By focusing on the two kinds of inscription side by side, he turns these stones into a powerful metaphor for all that we are in life and in death. Working at both literal and metaphorical levels, the image of the vandalised grave becomes the controlling point of reference for the poem. With this image as its constant, the extract moves through the following stages – the marks, the making of the marks, their meaning and then back to the marks themselves in the form of the word 'UNITED' sprayed on his parents' grave. The predominant tone of the poem is one of ironical reflection. Here the ironies of signification stand for the disparities of social history – the disapproved of 'v' sign resembles the tick of approval denied the skinhead at school and is identical to the (approved of) victory sign which the poet helped whitewash on a wall during the Second World War. From the changes and failures of British history, the passage widens in scope and deepens in the gravity of its sense that opposition and conflict lie ineradicably at the heart of all human life. That sense is secured by the metaphor of Man as the (football) ground on which all fixtures are fought out. The culminating point of the passage – the discovery of the word 'UNITED' – resolves the interplay between the ideas of division and unity which has moved the poem forward. Such has been the implicating reach of the passage that by the time we get to the word 'UNITED', it is clear that neither the poet nor ourselves as readers are any less involved in the desecration than the skinhead perpetrator. We are 'UNITED' in our responsibility for the signs we make because the language is common property.

Language is common property. Earlier in this chapter, I indicated how poetry has periodically had to check its own drift away from everyday speech. And yet it is self-evident that poetry must also find ways of marking itself off from common usage. Tony Harrison's *v.*

resolves this dilemma in a distinctive way. It squeezes new life out of unexceptional words and phrases by exerting upon them the constant pressure of tight formal control – through rhyme, through stanza and through the use of images (whether metaphorical or not) to regulate and monitor meaning. His technique is to adopt a strict poetic framework and then maximise the emotional and intellectual energies to be gained by compression. In this his work calls to mind the method and spirit of the neo-classical period, when poets last saw their function as unambiguously social.

When the form is so regular and definitive as it is in *v.*, the poet can gain much from the slightest pauses, reversals and irregularities of sound, sense and rhythm that occur within it. Take, for example, the way in which the poem uses metre. The guiding metrical line is that of the iambic pentameter, but it is by no means continuously adhered to. When Harrison departs from it, introducing a stress pattern which syntax dictates must work against the metre, or a line which is longer or shorter by the odd syllable, the resulting calculated awkwardness works as a reminder that it is a struggle with intractable problems with which we are dealing. So too with the relationship between rhyme and punctuation in the poem. The rhyme is unvarying, absolute, but there is a great deal of mobility in the punctuation (and variety in the playful use of typographical convention). The contribution which this makes is to suggest the weaving and linking activity of associative thought (imagination working through punctuation and parenthesis) as it tries to make sense of a fixed predicament or condition (life represented by rhyme) which is ultimately not negotiable. The relationship of formal and grammatical elements in the poem mirrors its concern with 'Man, resigned/To hope from his future what his past never found'.

This line from *v.* takes us back to our original concern with binary opposites and poetry's effort to mediate between them. That effort is condensed into Harrison's suggestive phrase 'resigned to hope', which registers as a paradox rather than a contradiction. It reminds us that poetry has to confront realities, however unpalatable, but keep open possibilities, however improbable. This even the bleakest poetic statement does. For by existing without having to exist, a poem exercises the freedom of signification. It represents, if you like, a 'v' sign (however you care to take it) made in the face of 'all the versuses of life'.

Notes

1. *Boswell's Life of Johnson*, ed. G. B. Hill and L. F. Powell (Oxford: Oxford U.P., 1964), pp. iv, 218.
2. Philip Larkin, *Required Writing* (London: Faber and Faber, 1983), pp. 81–2.
3. Frank Kermode, *An Appetite for Poetry* (London: Collins, 1989), pp. 50–1.
4. *William Wordsworth: The Oxford authors*, ed. Stephen Gill (Oxford: Oxford U.P., 1984), p. 608.
5. W. H. Auden, 'In Memory of W. B. Yeats', *Collected Shorter Poems 1927–1957* (London: Faber and Faber, 1990), p. 142.
6. Samuel Johnson, *The History of Rasselas, Prince of Abissinia*, ed. D. J. Enright (Harmondsworth: Penguin, 1976), p. 61.
7. Plato, *The Republic*, quoted in *Classical Literary Criticism*, ed. D. A. Russell and M. Winterbottom (Oxford: Oxford U.P., 1989), p. 47.
8. Seamus Heaney, *The Government of the Tongue* (London: Faber and Faber, 1989), p. 108.
9. Aristotle, *Poetics*, quoted in *Classical Literary Criticism*, p. 84.
10. Ibid., p. 62.
11. *Sir Philip Sidney: The Oxford authors*, ed. Katherine Duncan-Jones (Oxford: Oxford U.P., 1989), p. 232.
12. John Dryden, *Essays*, ed. W. P. Ker (Oxford: Clarendon Press, 1900), vol. I, pp. 100–1.
13. *Rasselas*, p. 62.
14. *The Portable Matthew Arnold*, ed. Lionel Trilling (Harmondsworth: Penguin, 1980), p. 299.
15. *The Poems and Prose Remains of Arthur Hugh Clough*, ed. Mrs Clough, 2 vols (London: Macmillan, 1869), vol. I, p. 360.
16. T. S. Eliot, *Selected Prose* (Harmondsworth: Penguin, 1955), pp. 55–6.
17. Robert Frost, 'Education by Poetry: A Meditative Monologue', in *Writers on Writing*, ed. Robert Neale (Oxford: Oxford U.P., 1992), p. 129.
18. Simon Armitage, 'The Metaphor Now Standing at Platform 8', *Kid* (London: Faber and Faber, 1992), p. 52.
19. *John Milton: The Oxford authors* (Oxford: Oxford U.P., 1990), p. 355.
20. Geoffrey Leech, *A Linguistic Guide to English Poetry* (London: Longman, 1990), p. 106.
21. Ibid., p. 113.
22. *Samuel Taylor Coleridge: The Oxford authors* (Oxford: Oxford U.P., 1985), p. 350.
23. Richard Bradford, *A Linguistic History of English Poetry* (London: Routledge, 1993), p. 7.
24. *Letters of Thomas Gray*, ed. John Beresford (Oxford: Oxford U.P., 1951), p. 83.
25. *William Wordsworth: The Oxford authors*, p. 602.

26. Ibid., p. 602.
27. Quoted in Christopher Ricks, *The Force of Poetry* (Oxford: Clarendon Press, 1984), p. 89.
28. Chris Baldick, *The Concise Oxford Dictionary of Literary Terms* (Oxford: Oxford U.P., 1992), p. 13.
29. *An Appetite for Poetry*, p. 188.
30. *Kid*, p. 53.
31. *The Government of the Tongue*, p. 45.
32. *William Wordsworth: The Oxford authors*, pp. 50–5.
33. Tony Harrison, *Selected Poems* (Harmondsworth: Penguin, 1987), pp. 237–8.

Further reading

Bradford, R., *A Linguistic History of English Poetry* (London: Routledge, 1993). (An alert and informative book which interprets the history of English poetry in the light of recent theoretical developments. Challenging yet accessible.)

Leech, G., *A Linguistic Guide to English Poetry* (London: Longman, 1990). (The standard work on poetic form. A comprehensive and well-written guide to the reading of poetry. Packed with clear illustrations of the points made.)

Lucas, J., *Modern English Poetry from Hardy to Hughes* (London: Batsford, 1986). (A study of most of the major figures and significant trends in modern English poetry. Lucas does what many writers fail to do – he locates poetry firmly in the sphere of social, political and moral values while remaining sensitive to the structures of poems and the texture of poetic language.)

Miller, R., and Greenberg, R.A., *Poetry, An Introduction* (Basingstoke and London: Macmillan, 1985). (Both an anthology and an introduction to the elements of poetry. One of the best of many such books, clear and sensible in approach without in any way patronising the reader.)

Quinn, K., *How Literature Works* (Basingstoke and London: Macmillan, 1992). (A general discussion which contains some helpful advice about reading poems, delivered in a readable and reassuring form.)

7
Reading prose fiction

Susan Watkins

Introduction: What is prose fiction?

How can we define prose fiction? To help us understand what distinguishes this category of literature from other categories, it makes sense to separate its two terms. 'Prose' is anything that is not poetry and fiction is anything that is not true; but what about prose poems and what about that odd mixture of fact and fiction known as 'faction'? Drama can be in prose and be fictional so why is it not appropriate to label drama 'prose fiction'?

Criticism divides literature into different categories, or genres, which consist of similar characteristics. Obviously there will be grey areas, and it may seem that prose fiction is an all-embracing term, but there are identifiable features which can be used to discriminate between poetry, drama and prose fiction. In asking the above questions some of the main differences have been identified. First, everyone understands that fiction is invented, and is not literally 'true', despite the apparent efforts of many early novelists to pass off their novels as edited manuscripts or auto-biographies. Secondly, prose language is not divided up according to poetic principles of rhyme, rhythm, metre or word patterning. Thirdly, prose fiction is written to be read rather than acted or performed, and the events described are told to us by a narrator, not enacted or dramatised for us.

A very important feature of prose fiction is its use of *narrative*. Narrative can be defined as the linking together of events, the way in which we put things into some kind of order so that we can understand, or explain them.

Although narrative is also important in both drama and poetry, it is particularly crucial to prose fiction, which makes use of it in specific ways.

As readers and students of literature, you will most commonly encounter prose fiction in the form of novels and short stories. You may initially feel more confident about reading and studying these forms than poetry. After all, everyone reads novels, and they have traditionally been perceived as a 'popular' form of literature. Indeed, their literary reputation has not always been particularly high. As Jane Austen wrote in *Northanger Abbey* (1818):

> Although our productions have afforded more extensive and unaffected pleasure than those of any other literary corporation in the world, no species of composition has been so much decried. From pride, ignorance, or fashion, our foes are almost as many as our readers . . . There seems almost a general wish of undervaluing the labour of the novelist, and of slighting the performances which have only genius, wit, and taste to recommend them.[1]

You may very well feel, then, that you already know how to read novels and short stories. It is certainly true that readers of prose fiction use well-developed skills. Without these, it would not be possible to reach the end of the book. In some sense then, the purpose of this chapter is to make you more aware of the skills that you already use in reading. It will also encourage you to consider how various different writers have used particular features of prose fiction to create certain effects. The experience of reading a novel or short story is a transaction between writer and reader, and in this chapter you will be encouraged to develop your critical ability to understand what happens when you read prose fictions. After all, reading a novel or short story is uniquely under your control. It is a private experience, unlike being a member of a theatre audience. Even supposing you sat down with a friend and both began to read two copies of the same book, no one can simultaneously read the text at the same pace as you. You can decide whether to stop for a while, skip bits, sneak a look at the end, or go back and re-read something.

A short story

What follows is a short story, 'The Snow Child' (1979) by Angela Carter.[2] Although extremely brief, it is a complete story in its own right.

While it would be a mistake to claim that this story is representative or typical of prose fiction, nevertheless it is a good example, in compressed form, of many of the features that are important when we read prose fictions – of whatever length.

The Snow Child

Midwinter – invincible, immaculate. The Count and his wife go riding, he on a grey mare and she on a black one, she wrapped in the glittering pelts of black foxes; and she wore high, black, shining boots with scarlet heels, and spurs. Fresh snow fell on snow already fallen; when it ceased, the whole world was white. 'I wish I had a girl as white as snow,' says the Count. They ride on. They come to a hole in the snow; this hole is filled with blood. He says: 'I wish I had a girl as red as blood.' So they ride on again; here is a raven, perched on a bare bough. 'I wish I had a girl as black as that bird's feather.'

As soon as he completed her description, there she stood, beside the road, white skin, red mouth, black hair and stark naked; she was the child of his desire and the Countess hated her. The Count lifted her up and sat her in front of him on his saddle but the Countess had only one thought: how shall I be rid of her?

The Countess dropped her glove in the snow and told the girl to get down to look for it; she meant to gallop off and leave her there but the Count said: 'I'll buy you new gloves.' At that, the furs sprang off the Countess's shoulders and twined round the naked girl. Then the Countess threw her diamond brooch through the ice of a frozen pond: 'Dive in and fetch it for me,' she said; she thought the girl would drown. But the Count said: 'Is she a fish, to swim in such cold weather?' Then her boots leapt off the Countess's feet and on to the girl's legs. Now the Countess was bare as a bone and the girl furred and booted; the Count felt sorry for his wife. They came to a bunch of roses, all in flower. 'Pick me one,' said the Countess to the girl. 'I can't deny you that,' said the Count.

So the girl picks a rose; pricks her finger on the thorn; bleeds; screams; falls.

Weeping, the Count got off his horse, unfastened his breeches and thrust his virile member into the dead girl. The Countess reined in her stamping mare and watched him narrowly; he was soon finished.

Then the girl began to melt. Soon there was nothing left of her but a feather a bird might have dropped; a bloodstain, like the trace of a fox's kill on the snow; and the rose she had pulled off the bush. Now the Countess had all her clothes on again. With her long hand, she stroked her furs. The

Count picked up the rose, bowed and handed it to his wife; when she touched it she dropped it.

'It bites!' she said.

The following analysis will elaborate some of this story's main features and discuss its possible effects on readers, before extrapolating from this analysis some important features of prose fiction which will then be discussed in more detail.

The opening sentence of the story sets the scene in a particular context in which the action that we expect to follow will presumably take place. This 'scene setting' is not particularly elaborated or detailed – we are briefly told the season in which the story is set, which is (also briefly) described for us.

We are then introduced to two of the story's main characters (although at this stage we do not know how important they will turn out to be). There is a strong emphasis on the Countess's clothing, although no description of her features, and there is no description of the Count. We are not given their names, or any other information about them. Despite this, as we read the story we do develop a mental picture of both characters. You may like to ask yourself what colour you think the Countess's hair is. Usually you will have an answer, because you have filled in the gaps the text leaves to form a more complete mental picture. This is one reason why film adaptations of texts can be so unsatisfactory: the actor playing a particular role may not correspond to your imagined version of a character.

The Count's first wish may remind us of the Snow White fairy tale, and this suggestion will be reinforced by the title of the story. In this way, any other reading we may have done will affect our response to a new text. The Count's wish also suggests to us what kind of story this is. It is obviously not a *realist* text (a text which conveys the sense of 'reflecting' actual life) – this is a story where magic and sudden and surprising events seem appropriate. The similarity with fairy tale also creates expectations about the plot. In fairy tales characters are granted three wishes, or their wishes may be suddenly and surprisingly granted, and this is also what happens here.

The event of the snow child's creation provokes reactions in the characters. The line 'she was the child of his desire and the Countess hated her' creates a mixed sense of anticipation and foreboding. We begin to wonder what is going to happen, and perhaps speculate about the Countess's possible reaction. The behaviour of the characters encourages us to develop our response to them: the Countess's cruelty may reduce our sympathy for her, unless we identify with her jealousy. We may feel sorry for the snow child as the victim of both the Count's desire and the Countess's jealousy.

When the Countess begins her attempts to destroy the snow child we may guess that she will make three attempts, only the third of which will be successful. In this way, the child's destruction will mirror her creation after three wishes, and we may feel that this would be a balanced movement in the story, especially given its fairy-tale quality. The text also signals this change of direction with the return of the Count's sympathy to his wife rather than the child.

The Count's actions in having sex with the dead girl are shocking, and will significantly alter our perceptions of his character. Once we know that he does this, any re-reading of the story will be affected by our knowledge of his actions here. One phrase which is bound to evoke some kind of reaction, whether surprise, laughter or disgust is the phrase 'virile member'. This is because the choice of words seems so inappropriate in this kind of story. This makes us aware of the voice telling the story, which has up until this point appeared to be quite neutral, calm and distant. Our feelings about the sudden intrusion of a different kind of vocabulary may well make us reassess the tone of voice elsewhere. Is there not a suggestive, perhaps even sadistic quality in the description of the Countess's clothes: 'high, black, shining boots with scarlet heels, and spurs'? This is perhaps especially significant on a second reading, given that we know she will temporarily lose her garments to the snow child. It is also apparent in the sensuous stress on colour, and in phrases like 'she was the child of his desire'. Perhaps this story is not merely the innocent tale it first appeared to be.

At the end of the story the disruption is over and the girl has been destroyed, returning (almost) to what she was. The Countess has her clothes back again. In this sense the story follows a fairly typical narrative pattern of stasis, disruption, resolution and return to stasis. The small kickback or surprise at the end lies in the rose biting the Countess. Things are not quite the same as they were before.

What is this story really about? How can we set about understanding it? Taking account of some of the points made earlier allows us to begin to interpret the text. Although the story uses many fairy-tale motifs and references (the three wishes suddenly granted; the similarity with Snow White), it differs in its suggestive and highly sexualised tone. The tone encourages us to read more into the text than appears to be on its surface, and we see that what lies under the surface is sexual desire. We also see the structural and symbolic importance of the clothing and nakedness of women in the story. It is on the transference of clothing from one woman to another that the narrative focuses. And clothing (or its absence) is consistently associated with desire. It is also associated with power. The Countess drops her glove in order to exercise power over the girl by forcing her to pick it up, hoping to destroy her in the process. Once the Countess is naked the Count's sympathy returns to her. We could therefore interpret this short story as an examination of the role of desire, power and possessions (clothing, jewellery) in relationships between men and women. It would obviously help to support these comments to know that this text forms part of a collection of stories entirely devoted to rewritings of fairy tales, that Angela Carter has been associated with *magic realist* writing (writing that blends myth, fairy tale and sudden and surprising events with realistic representations of life), that in others of her works she also addresses the question of female desire and sexuality. This kind of contextual explanation aids interpretations based on a close reading of a text.

Reading prose fiction: Significant features

From this analysis of Carter's short story it is possible to extrapolate some important features of reading prose fiction. We could isolate them as follows:

- Characterisation.
- Narration.
- Language.
- Reader response.

We see the importance of characterisation in the story in the development of our response to the child, the Count and the Countess. The brief, but distinctive descriptions of them, focusing particularly on colour and clothing, mean that we have some sort of mental picture of the characters and we inevitably take up a perspective on their behaviour as the story progresses. Narrative technique, or the way in which the story is told, is crucial in conditioning this response. The calm, distant, yet suggestive perspective and tone of the narrator, the order in which events are told, are all relevant, as is language. The sudden intrusion of a very different type of language develops the suggestive quality we may not previously have noticed. The response of the reader is certainly important in many ways. We want to know, and speculate about, what may happen; we apply knowledge we have already gained from the story to the rest of it as we continue reading; we apply what we know will happen to what is happening on a second reading, and we make connections and contribute to the story ourselves, filling in any gaps and bringing certain types of relevant prior reading to bear on the text. All these features are important when reading prose fiction, and being aware of them helps in interpreting or understanding the text.

Characterisation

It is undoubtedly true that novels have provided us with some of the most interesting and memorable characters in literature, and this fact is one of the reasons why we read prose fiction. *Characterisation* has a large impact on our engagement with, and response to, a text, and therefore, it is important to investigate how this can work.

Authors often describe the experience of writing a novel as crucially linked with characterisation. Many feel taken over by their characters as if they were real people outside their control, who begin to direct the course of the narrative through the way in which they respond to events. George Eliot quotes one of Novalis's 'questionable aphorisms – "character is destiny" ' in *The Mill on the Floss* (1860),[3] going on to qualify this assertion somewhat by suggesting that the shape of Hamlet's life would have been different if circumstances had been other than they were. It has been debated, however, whether or not Eliot's novels suggest that character is the most important influence on life. In his preface to *The Portrait of a Lady* (1880), Henry James writes that character was the mainspring of his own creative process in writing the novel:

> My dim first move toward *The Portrait*, which was exactly my grasp of a single character . . . I had my vivid individual – vivid, so strangely, in spite of being still at large, not confined by the conditions, not engaged in the tangle, to which we look for much of the impress that constitutes an identity.[4]

Charlotte Brontë felt compelled to give the heroine of *Villette* (1853), her last novel, a cold name, and after considering Lucy Frost settled for Lucy Snowe.[5] Jane Austen remarked that in her novel, *Emma* (1816), she was writing about 'a heroine whom no one but myself will much like'.[6] Both instances suggest that writers frequently treat characters as real figures outside their own writing process who must be 'truthfully' described and named, regardless of their subsequent impact on the reading public.

How do writers set about creating their characters and making them memorable to us? Frequently, certain characters may become associated with particular characteristics or traits, whether visual or verbal. Charles Dickens is a master at this. In *Bleak House* (1852–3) Mr Chadband, the unsympathetic preacher, is described as having 'a good deal of train oil in his system'[7] and constantly mops his perspiring, oily forehead. His specific style of speech is also important in distinguishing him for the reader:

> 'I say, my friends,' pursues Mr Chadband . . . 'why can we not fly? Is it because we are calculated to walk? It is. Could we walk, my friends, without strength? We could not. What should we do without strength, my friends? Our legs would refuse to bear us, our knees would double up, our ankles would turn over, and we should come to the ground.' (p. 318)

The narrator subsequently comments on 'Mr Chadband's piling verbose flights of stairs upon one another after this fashion' (pp. 318–19), a memorable metaphor. Dickens can also make more complex metaphorical or metonymical connections between his characters and something with which he wishes to identify them. In *Bleak House*, Miss Flyte, the woman whose mental health has been ruined by her concern with her seemingly interminable lawsuit, is linked metaphorically with the caged birds she keeps. This comparison is made more obvious by her name. Naming is also important in prose fiction. Nineteenth-century novels made great use of names that indicated something to the reader about the character. Trollope's Mr Slope, in his novel *Barchester Towers* (1857), is rumoured to have changed his name from Slop, and although the alteration is intended as an improvement, it accurately suggests this particular character's furtive, deceptive qualities.[8] These ways of identifying characters may seem somewhat crude to us, but in a period when novels were first published in serial form with intervals between the appearance of each 'episode', such visual, verbal and metaphorical 'tags' were important.

A *modernist* novel like Virginia Woolf's *To the Lighthouse* (1927), which is told in a way which concentrates on the internal thoughts and reflections of its characters, still makes some use of these features: when Lily Briscoe first appears in the text she is described as follows: 'With her little Chinese eyes and her puckered-up face she would never marry'.[9] The use of visual characteristics is still important, but the description is extended to form part of a character (Mrs Ramsay's) thoughts about Lily's marriage prospects. *To the Lighthouse* also uses verbal characteristics to describe its characters: 'They were walking on and Mrs Ramsay did not quite catch the meaning, only the words, here and there . . . dissertation . . . fellowship . . . readership . . . lectureship. She could not follow the ugly academic jargon, that rattled itself off so glibly' (p. 16). This is Mrs Ramsay's response to Charles Tansley's distinctive way of speaking.

Some novelists make the reader party to the kinds of decisions that they make about naming, or otherwise identifying, their characters. In David Lodge's novel, *How Far Can You Go?* (1980), the narrator vacillates over what to name a particular character: 'Let her be called Violet, no, Veronica, no Violet, improbable a name as that is for Catholic girls of Irish extraction, customarily named after saints and figures of Celtic legend, for I like the connotations of Violet – shrinking, penitential, melancholy.'[10]

As we continue reading a text we learn about characters in different ways: through their interactions with each other and their responses to particular situations; or from things we are told by the narrator, or other characters. Who introduces us to the characters and tells us about them is obviously very important in a text, and this question will be addressed later in the section on narration.

Critics have written about character in different ways. E. M. Forster, in his book *Aspects of the Novel*, distinguishes between 'flat' and 'round' characters; or, to use a different metaphor, between those who are merely two-dimensional, and those who are three-dimensional or have depths.[11] We may initially see the usefulness of this distinction in a novel like Jane Austen's *Emma*, where the subtleties of the heroine's personality, thoughts and feelings are elaborated, unlike those of less significant characters like Miss Bates, who, it could be argued, are merely caricatures or stereotypes. However, although we may initially think that Jane Fairfax is a 'flat' character, standing for the stereotype of the poor female relation, destined to be a governess, she eventually emerges as the secret fiancée of Frank Churchill, and has therefore had 'hidden depths' all through the novel. Indeed, it could be suggested that the trick on Emma is that she assumed Jane to be a flat character when she was actually a round one.

Our response to characters will implicitly involve liking or disliking them and approving or disapproving of what they do, and to some extent the two things are linked. If we read the opening letter of Alice Walker's novel *The Color Purple* (1983), which details the sexual abuse of a young black southern American girl by her father, with the covert consent of her mother, we will inevitably identify with Celie's incomprehension at what is happening to her and dislike her father because of what he is doing.

However, Vladimir Nabokov's novel *Lolita* (1959) treats a similar subject very differently. This novel tells the story of a middle-aged man's passion for a 12-year-old girl, but from the man's perspective. The account of their first sexual encounter is from his point of view, and is narrated by him:

> 'You mean,' she persisted, now kneeling above me, 'you never did it when you were a kid?'
> 'Never,' I said quite truthfully.
> 'Okay,' said Lolita, 'here is where we start.'
> However, I shall not bore my learned readers with a detailed account of Lolita's presumption. Suffice it to say not a trace of modesty did I perceive in this beautiful hardly formed young girl whom modern co-education, juvenile mores, the campfire racket and so forth had utterly and hopelessly depraved. She saw the stark act merely as part of a youngster's furtive world, unknown to adults.[12]

Again we read about a character who abuses a young girl, but in this extract he appears to be the innocent, seduced by the sexually depraved Lolita. Although we may know rationally that this character is an exploitative victimiser, prolonged exposure to his witty, urbane, amusing narrative voice (to which this brief extract does not do justice) may result in our understanding his fascination and almost liking him. This leads us on to the next important feature of prose writing: narration.

Narration

Narration could be described as 'the way the story is told', and encompasses several important decisions that writers can make about how to tell their story. One important issue that we should address at the outset is the distinction between the author and the narrator. This is not usually a problem when we have a first-person narrative (where the narrator participates as a character in the story and speaks as 'I' like Jane in *Jane Eyre* (1847), for example), but is it fair to assume that the opinions expressed by the narrator of a novel like E. M. Forster's *Howards End* (1910) or George Eliot's *Middlemarch* (1871–2) are exactly identical with the opinions of that novel's author? Novels such as *Howards End* and *Middlemarch* make use of the convention of the omniscient (all-knowing), third-person narrator (the narrator is outside the story and speaks of the characters as 'he', 'she', 'they'). An omniscient narrator seems able to enter the minds of all the characters at will, has the freedom to wander in time and space, may comment on characters' behaviour and actions, and knows the outcome of the novel's plot. We may well be justified in assuming that there is a fairly close correspondence between the views of the author and the views expressed by this type of narrator, but we should recognise that there are limits to this correspondence that arise from the fact that omniscient narration is a convention, just like any other way of telling a story. To give an example, E. M. Forster had frequent doubts about *Howards End* as he wrote it, remarking in a letter to a friend: 'written some of the new novel. A deal too cultured, and from hand to mouth.' After another year's progress he comments:

> Thought my novel very bad, but . . . It's not quite as bad as I thought, for the characters are conceived sincerely. Will it ever be done? A fortnight ago I should have said not, but am hopeful now . . . But take it all round, I've lost inspiration, and not adequately replaced it by solidity.[13]

None of Forster's fluctuating feelings about his novel, moving from despair to hope and back to despair again, are reflected in the tone of the narrator of the novel, who tells the story confidently and ironically, managing his material with ease and control. If the author and the narrator were identical, we might well expect some of Forster's doubts to rub off in the narrator's tone, but it is not part of the convention of omniscient narration to openly express doubts about the text under construction.

There has been much controversial critical debate about the best way of *further* distinguishing the series of relationships or transactions that develop when reading a piece of prose fiction. Any reader who picks up a novel or short story and starts reading enters into a number of relationships with the different voices of the text. In a conventional reading situation the reader is unable to access the real author of the text: that author may be dead, or if alive, not available. But we do develop a sense of the authorial voice that we are listening to, and in some situations we may want to distinguish between that voice and the voice of the narrator, for example, when we have a first-person narrator whose behaviour is grossly at odds with the assumptions we can make *from reading the novel* about the novelist's beliefs. Two terms are important here. The first is the *implied author*. This term, first used by Wayne C. Booth,[14] identifies the particular characteristic features of the authorial voice of the novel we are reading. It encompasses the assumptions, beliefs and moral horizons of a particular novelist, *as we derive them from reading the text itself*, not from any relationship with the real flesh and blood author. The second term is the *unreliable narrator*, whom Booth describes as follows:

> I have called a narrator *reliable* when he speaks for or acts in accordance with the norms of the work (which is to say, the implied author's norms), *unreliable* when he does not . . . the narrator is mistaken, or he believes himself to have qualities which the author denies him. (*The Rhetoric of Fiction*, pp. 158–9)

A good example of this kind of reading relationship arises in Henry James's 'The Turn of the Screw' (1898), about which Booth says, 'the governess is only one of the indeterminately unreliable narrators who have led readers into public controversy' (*The Rhetoric of Fiction*, p. 315). The problem here is how we determine whether a narrator is reliable or not, which depends on what we assume the implied author's values are as contrasted with those of the narrator. These judgements will vary from reader to reader (and 'The Turn of the Screw' is a good example here as some readers will find the governess to be entirely reliable).

These terms are much less useful in a situation where there is no first-person narrator, although, as Booth remarks: ' "Narrator" is usually taken to mean the "I" of a work, but the "I" is seldom if ever identical with the implied image of the artist' (*The Rhetoric of Fiction*, p. 73). However, to return to the examples of *Howards End* and *Middlemarch*, it is arguably less appropriate to distinguish between narrator and implied author in these novels.

It is also appropriate to consider the other 'side' of the relationship: the author in writing a novel or short story inevitably imagines a reader's response to that text, thereby creating an *implied reader*. (This term is first used by the critic Wolfgang Iser.[15]) When George Eliot pauses in *Adam Bede* (1859) to defend herself against an imaginary reader's response she is creating two sorts of implied readers: the reader who would prefer her to put 'truly spiritual advice' into the mouth of the Rector of Broxton, rather than the limited and unhelpful remarks he does make to Arthur; and the reader who would appreciate her decision to give 'a faithful account of men and things'.[16] It is clear she prefers the latter response. However, the actual reader's response may differ in various ways from the response of the 'implied reader' of the text. Does, for example, an author mentally create an 'ideal reader' who is able to grasp all the intended nuances and subtleties of the text?

Some texts may also contain what critics term a 'narratee': a character to whom the story is told, whose role as listener to the events recounted by the narrator may be presumed to have an impact on the way they are told by that narrator. In epistolary novels, for example, the letter form can make great play of the fact that letters written with a particular recipient (or narratee) in mind can be read by the wrong person. In Samuel Richardson's *Pamela* (1740), the heroine's letters to her parents complaining of her treatment by her master, Mr B., are misappropriated by him, with the result that Mr B. becomes convinced of Pamela's virtue and is persuaded to marry her. All these different ways of describing the intricacies of the reader's relationship with the voices of the novel or short story are useful to describe appropriate situations in particular texts, although it is unlikely that hard and fast rules using these terms could be made to apply in every situation.

Another important distinction that should be made when considering narrative method is that between the person who speaks and the person who sees. If we compare the moments in Jane Austen's *Emma* and Charlotte Brontë's *Jane Eyre* where each heroine realises that the hero loves her this point is clarified. From *Emma* we get the following:

> While he spoke, Emma's mind was most busy, and, with all the wonderful velocity of thought, had been able – and yet without losing a word – to catch and comprehend the exact truth of the whole; to see that Harriet's hopes had been entirely groundless, a mistake, a delusion, as complete a delusion as any of her own – that Harriet was nothing; that she was everything herself.[17]

From *Jane Eyre* the following:

> And if I loved him less I should have thought his accent and look of exultation savage; but, sitting by him, roused from the nightmare of parting – called to the paradise of union – I thought only of the bliss given me to drink in so abundant a flow.[18]

The extract from *Emma* is from Emma's perspective: it is she who *sees* but it is not she who *speaks*. If she were speaking the passage would begin 'While he spoke, *my* mind was most busy . . .' This is what happens in *Jane Eyre*, where the heroine, Jane, both sees *and* speaks.

Writers can make a number of decisions about who is going to speak, or actually tell the story, and about who is going to see (whose perspective to give on the story). They can have one person telling the story or more than one, and these narrators may be characters within the story or not. They can privilege one character's viewpoint throughout the text, or can have several viewpoints in any proportion.

Some complex effects are possible from the more inventive use of these combinations. Charles Dickens's *Bleak House* is made up of two narratives, Esther's first-person narrative and the omniscient narrator's, which are interspersed throughout the novel, providing two perspectives on many events, for example both describe the Court of Chancery. One critic, Hillis Miller, has argued that the end result of the double narrative is to leave the novel permanently unresolved.[19] However, it could be argued that readers will inevitably fill in the gaps between the two narratives.

The effect of embedding multiple narratives within each other is used to singular effect in two nineteenth-century novels by women writers, Mary Shelley's *Frankenstein* (1818) and Emily Brontë's *Wuthering Heights* (1847). In *Frankenstein* the central part of the narration consists of the monster's experiences since his creation, which are contained within Victor Frankenstein's account of his making of the monster. This in turn is contained within Robert Walton's account of meeting Victor Frankenstein, recorded in journal form and sent to his sister in the form of letters. The embedded structure is even more complex in *Wuthering Heights*, where different characters' accounts of the strange relationship between Cathy and Heathcliff are filtered through the consciousness of the servant, Nelly Dean, and ultimately presented by the tenant of Thrushcross Grange, Lockwood. This device of using multiple embedded narrators offers the opportunity to play with the reader's sympathy and offer various different (and sometimes contradictory) ways of interpreting the novel.

A third-person narrative can also make clever use of changes of perspective to great ironic effect. Both Jane Austen, in *Emma*, and Henry James, in *The Portrait of a Lady*, confine themselves for large amounts of time to the point of view of their central characters, Emma and Isabel. However, important scenes that provide the reader with more knowledge than the central character are seen from the perspective of other characters. In *Emma*, Mr Knightley's growing suspicions about the exact nature of the relationship between Jane Fairfax and Frank Churchill are provided for the reader in an account of an evening party which is seen from his point of view. In *The Portrait of a Lady* some scenes between Osmond, Madame Merle and Ned Rosier are not presented from Isabel's perspective. Such scenes alert the reader to possible interpretations of events which the central character in each case has not considered (sometimes because the character is unaware of the events themselves). However, neither novelist provides the reader with a complete understanding of events in advance of the heroine's recognition, and the moment when both reader and heroine come to fully understand things is seen from the heroine's point of view.

As well as considering the question of who sees and who speaks, it is also important to remember that novelists have choices about how to plot their particular story. This distinction between *story* and *plot* is a useful way of describing the difference between the story as we may assume it 'actually' happened, and the way in which the writer chooses to order the events for the reader. A good example is provided by the detective story, which begins with the discovery of a body and ends with the discovery of the murderer's identity and the explanation of the murderer's motives. In this case, the 'actual' story as we may presume it to have happened is reversed, in order to provide the maximum of suspense for the reader.[20] We could subdivide the different ways in which plot can differ from story into three categories: *order*, *frequency* and *duration*, terms first used by the critic, Gérard Genette.[21]

Order describes the way in which the writer chooses to order the telling of events for the reader. Writers can make use of retrospective narrative and of anticipation. Retrospective narrative means recounting events that are in the past, that have already happened, when compared with the current time scheme of the text. For example, many first-person narratives in the autobiographical style entail narrators recounting the whole of their lives as a retrospective: an account of their past lives leading up to the point at which they are actually writing the narrative. Lucy Snowe, the narrator of Charlotte Brontë's novel, *Villette*, frequently reminds readers that the events they are reading about are in her past, commenting on her now white hair as she sits and writes of her early life.[22] 'Autobiographical' retrospective narratives can make subtle use of the play between the voice of the experienced, knowledgeable narrator, looking back on her inexperienced earlier self, and the remembered ignorance and naivety of the younger self. In Daphne du Maurier's novel, *Rebecca* (1938), the narrator compares her youthful, sensitive former self with the hardened middle-aged woman she has become:

> I am glad it cannot happen twice, the fever of first love. For it is a fever, and
> a burden too, whatever the poets may say. They are not brave, the days when

we are twenty-one. They are full of little cowardices, little fears without foundation, and one is so easily bruised, so swiftly wounded, one falls to the first barbed word. Today, wrapped in the complacent armour of approaching middle age, the infinitesimal pricks of day by day brush one lightly and are soon forgotten, but then – how a careless word would linger, becoming a fiery stigma, and how a look, a glance over a shoulder, branded themselves as things eternal. A denial heralded the thrice crowing of a cock, and an insincerity was like the kiss of Judas. The adult mind can lie with untroubled conscience and a gay composure, but in those days even a small deception scoured the tongue, lashing one against the stake itself.[23]

It is also possible for novelists to anticipate events: to provide a hint (or more than a hint) of what is going to happen later in the story. In *Howards End* the narrator remarks: 'Leonard – he would figure at length in a newspaper report, but that evening he did not count for much' (p. 303). We may well speculate on why Leonard Bast would merit mention in a newspaper report. He is not famous, and the most likely reason for someone appearing in a newspaper is because of their birth or death (especially if it occurs in unusual or tragic circumstances). The narrator here anticipates (admittedly in a veiled way) Leonard's death at the end of the novel.

The term *frequency* is useful to describe the number of times a writer tells events. An event that happened once can be told once or several times, an event that happened several times can be told several times or only once. This is a way for a writer to be selective, and to assign importance to events. A crucially important event can be told repeatedly, perhaps from different perspectives, to emphasise its impact, or an event that happens several times can be told only once, the reader assuming that that account stands true for the other occasions. The self-conscious narrator of David Lodge's novel, *How Far Can You Go?* discusses this issue in relation to the representation of marital sex:

It is difficult to do justice to ordinary married sex in a novel. There are too many acts for them all to be described, and usually no particular reason to describe one act rather than another; so the novelist falls back on summary, which sounds dismissive. As a contemporary French critic has pointed out in a treatise on narrative, a novelist can (*a*) narrate once what happened once or (*b*) narrate *n* times what happened once or (*c*) narrate *n* times what happened *n* times or (*d*) narrate once what happened *n* times. Seductions, rapes, the taking of new lovers or the breaking of old taboos, are usually narrated according to (*a*), (*b*) or (*c*). Married love in fiction tends to be narrated according to mode (*d*). *Once or twice a week, perhaps, if they happened to go to bed together at the same time, and Angela was not feeling too tired, they would make love.* (p. 150)[24]

Duration (or how much time is spent in a text in recounting a particular event or events) is also relevant in signifying to readers the importance accorded to particular events or occurrences. The narrator of *Howards End* skims over two years of the characters' lives as follows: 'Over two years passed, and the Schlegel household continued to lead its life of ignoble ease, still swimming gracefully on the gray tides of London' (p. 115). The two years mentioned are obviously unimportant for the novel's plot, and readers must accept the narrator's extremely brief account of what filled them. It is also possible for writers to spend a good deal of time in a text on a very brief, but perhaps very significant moment, in a particular character's story: for example the account of Helen and Paul's kiss at the beginning of *Howards End* (pp. 38–9).

Language

It is important to recognise that narration is closely connected with the different ways of using language in fiction to record voice. To serve as an example of various ways in which this can work, the following extract from Virginia Woolf's *To the Lighthouse* is useful:

> There wasn't the slightest possible chance that they could go to the Lighthouse to-morrow, Mr. Ramsay snapped out irascibly.
> How did he know? she asked. The wind often changed.
> The extraordinary irrationality of her remark, the folly of women's minds enraged him. He had ridden through the valley of death, been shattered and shivered; and now she flew in the face of facts, made his children hope what was utterly out of the question, in effect, told lies. He stamped his foot on the stone step. 'Damn you,' he said. But what had she said? Simply that it might be fine to-morrow. So it might.
> Not with the barometer falling and the wind due west.
> To pursue truth with such astonishing lack of consideration for other people's feelings, to rend the thin veils of civilisation so wantonly, so brutally, was to her so horrible an outrage of human decency that, without replying, dazed and blinded, she bent her head as if to let the pelt of jagged hail, the drench of dirty water, bespatter her unrebuked. There was nothing to be said.

He stood by her in silence. Very humbly, at length, he said that he would step over and ask the Coastguards if she liked.
There was nobody whom she reverenced as she reverenced him.
She was quite ready to take his word for it, she said. (p. 37)

Perhaps the most useful initial distinction is between *direct* and *indirect speech*. What difference does it make to represent a character's words in direct rather than indirect speech? In the above extract, although Woolf often dispenses with inverted commas as formal indications of direct speech (as in Mr Ramsay's opening remark) there is a marked difference between ' "Damn you," he said', and 'Very humbly, at length, he said that he would step over and ask the Coastguards if she liked'. In the first instance, direct speech gives the illusion that the reader is close to the character speaking, and hears Mr Ramsay's words 'as he spoke them', without, apparently, a mediating narrative presence. Indirect speech reminds us that a narrator is accounting for the words of the character, which may give the reader a sense of being 'once removed' from the dialogue. Mr Ramsay may have used slightly different words from those with which the narrator summarises what he said in the second instance.

Much prose fiction makes use of what is known as the *free indirect style*, a way of representing thought or speech which fluctuates, or is on the borderline between, direct and indirect speech, where it is unclear whether we are listening to the voice of the character or the voice of the narrator. For example, in the passage from *To the Lighthouse*, large parts of the narrative are in free indirect mode. Whose voice thinks 'There was nobody whom she reverenced as she reverenced him'? It is unclear whether it is the narrator or Mrs Ramsay's voice here.

Another important way of representing voice in fiction is through *stream of consciousness* and *interior monologue*. Stream of consciousness can be defined as a way of recording the complete mental process of a particular character, without any narrative commentary. The term 'interior monologue', although often seen to be synonymous with 'stream of consciousness', is a more precise term for the all-inclusive, linguistically fragmented depiction of a character's thought process, including conscious and unconscious thoughts, feelings and desires, and random associative mental connections. James Joyce's *Ulysses* (1922) makes particularly effective use of interior monologue. One excellent example is the following extract from the beginning of Molly Bloom's soliloquy at the end of the novel:

Yes because he never did a thing like that before as ask to get his breakfast
in bed with a couple of eggs since the *City Arms* hotel when he used to be
pretending to be laid up with a sick voice doing his highness to make
himself interesting to that old faggot Mrs Riordan that he thought he had a
great leg of and she never left us a farthing all for masses for herself and
her soul greatest miser ever was actually afraid to lay out 4d for her
methylated spirit telling me all her ailments she had too much chat in her
about politics and earthquakes and the end of the world let us have a bit of
fun first God help the world if all the women were her sort[25]

Different ways of using language to record voice allows for different
effects. The Russian critic Mikhail Bakhtin argues that the many voices
in a text are in conversation or dialogue with each other and with the
reader.[26] In some texts there may be a well-defined 'hierarchy' of voices,
which privileges, for example, the voice of the narrator as the focus for
interpreting the text. In other texts there may be no single voice which
dominates. A distinction that is relevant when discussing this issue in
third-person narration is that between *showing* and *telling*. Are events,
characters and conversations shown or told to us? Although all stories are
told to us by a narrator, in some texts narrated in the third person the
commentary, or 'voice' of the narrator telling us about, or interpreting
events and conversations is at least as important as the showing or enactment of events and conversations themselves. In the following childhood
scene from *The Mill on the Floss*, Tom Tulliver has just cut off his sister
Maggie's hair:

'O Maggie,' said Tom, jumping round her and slapping his knees as he
laughed. 'O, my buttons, what a queer thing you look! Look at yourself in
the glass – you look like the idiot we throw our nutshells to at school.'
Maggie felt an unexpected pang. She had thought beforehand chiefly of
her own deliverance from her teasing hair and teasing remarks about it,
and something also of the triumph she should have over her mother and
her aunts by this very decided course of action: she didn't want her hair to
look pretty – that was out of the question – she only wanted people to
think her a clever little girl and not find fault with her. But now when Tom
began to laugh at her and say she was like the idiot, the affair had quite a
new aspect. (pp. 120–1)

This extract shows a high proportion of telling by the narrator of Maggie's thoughts and feelings. The proportion of telling, or intrusion by the
narrative voice in a text has particular effects. It could be argued that the

reader is left at liberty to interpret events that are shown rather than told; however, it is also possible that the very obviousness of an intrusive narrative voice could provoke or encourage an individual reader's different interpretation.

Reader response

To conclude with a discussion of the reader's response is strategic, in that it is arguably only with a particular reading of a novel or short story that questions of interpretation and evaluation can be addressed. The reader is of primary importance as the focus not merely for *responding* to some of the devices of characterisation, narration and language discussed above, but also for creating in her mind a particular reading of a text. After all, each reader's reading experience is to some extent unique.

In order to read a text a certain amount of investment and desire is necessary in the reader. One of the most obvious examples of this process is the reader's experience of responding to particular characters in fiction and identifying with them. Thackeray wrote the following of his experience of reading *Jane Eyre*:

> I wish you had not sent me *Jane Eyre*. It interested me so much that I have lost (or won if you like) a whole day in reading it at the busiest period with the printers I know waiting for copy . . . Some of the love passages made me cry, to the astonishment of John, who came in with the coals.[27]

Thackeray's experience here is a common one, but how and why is it possible for him to feel so deeply involved with the characters and the story that he is reduced to tears? Georges Poulet comments that while reading the reader takes on and actually thinks the thought processes and experiences narrated in the text: 'Whenever I read, I mentally pronounce an *I*, and yet the *I* which I pronounce is not myself.'[28] It is this odd experience of becoming the 'I' of a novel or short story which encourages a reader's investment in a text, and this experience can transcend expected boundaries of empathy. We might not predict that Thackeray, a successful male novelist, would become so involved with the story of Jane Eyre, a poor orphaned governess, but the reading process itself makes this identification possible.

Once we begin to read we experience the desire to know what happens: we invest in the story and its potential outcome. E. M. Forster's famous remark, 'Yes – oh dear yes – the novel tells a story' (*Aspects of the Novel*, p. 40), implies that the novel should also do something more, as if successful plotting is an easy, and rather inferior part of the novelist's repertoire. However, the creation of suspense, and sustaining the reader's interest are no mean feats. The endings of novels and short stories crucially affect and concern readers, critics and authors. The ending of Charlotte Brontë's *Villette*, in which the heroine waits for the return of her lover, Monsieur Paul, from overseas by ship was particularly controversial. The narrator, Lucy, describes the onset of a storm at sea. Charlotte Brontë leaves the decision about the fate of the hero up to each individual reader, suggesting that optimistic readers with 'sunny imaginations' may create a happy ending. The last paragraph of the novel, however, catalogues the long lives of all the heroine's worst enemies, as if to leave the story on an ominous note. Charlotte Brontë was convinced that the hero should die at sea, but her father disliked that ending so much that she was persuaded to compromise with an ambiguous conclusion to the novel. She was plagued with letters from readers wanting to know the 'truth'.[29]

Similarly, Charles Dickens changed the ending of his novel, *Great Expectations* (1860–1), to hint strongly at the union of the hero, Pip, with Estella, the woman he has fruitlessly and mistakenly loved throughout the novel. He commented: 'I have no doubt the story will be more acceptable through the alteration.'[30] This comment on readers' preferences for definite (and happy) endings is interesting in that it reveals what Dickens assumed readers wanted from endings, and from novels generally. A contemporary novel like *The French Lieutenant's Woman* (1969), which contains parodies of many Victorian fictional conventions, has three endings, from which the reader must choose. The desire to know what happens and to reach a satisfying conclusion has been compared by some critics to the sexual act. Robert Scholes writes:

> In the sophisticated forms of fiction, as in the sophisticated practice of sex, much of the art consists of delaying climax within the framework of desire in order to prolong the pleasurable act itself. When we look at fiction with respect to its form alone, we see a pattern of events designed to move toward climax and resolution, balanced by a counter-pattern of events designed to delay this very climax and resolution.[31]

It is certainly true that the narrative process relies on desire to a great extent. Do ambiguous endings mean that it is more difficult for readers to close off and conclude their engagement with a text? The ending of a short story like James Joyce's 'The Dead', in *Dubliners* (1914), has provoked extensive critical commentary in an attempt finally to close what is ultimately an open ending.

Comparisons of first and second readings are particularly interesting when discussing reader response. On a second reading of a novel or short story entirely different effects, and in many ways, an entirely different reading, may be produced. This is because on a second reading our knowledge of events and characters is fuller, and we are able to anticipate. Our understanding of what will happen can be applied to what is happening at the point at which we read. On a first reading we can only refer backwards to what we have already read; on a second reading we can refer forwards as well. A second reading may appreciate effects of dramatic irony which were not apparent or were only implied on a first reading. A second reading of any Jane Austen novel would perceive more subtle ironic effects of plot and characterisation than a first reading. Think, for example, of the scene in *Emma* where Mr Elton admires Emma's portrait of Harriet. It would be much clearer on a second reading (when we know that it is Emma Mr Elton is interested in, and not Harriet) that it is the skill of the painter rather than the beauty of the sitter which has attracted him.

Second readings could be said to be synchronic as well as diachronic, meaning that whereas a first reading is more concerned with the forward-moving, linear development of the plot, a second reading pays more attention to other ways in which the text can be interpreted, linking events, characters and images in different combinations. A second reading may often pay more attention to imagery and symbolism; for example, a second reading of E. M. Forster's novel *Howards End* might well notice the recurrence of the image of goblin footfalls, which begins when the Schlegels are at the concert and meet Leonard Bast, and continues throughout the rest of the novel to be associated with the Basts and the threat they pose to the ordered world of the Schlegels and the Wilcoxes. Some novels encourage us to read them in a way which stresses the importance of plot and narrative progression, others encourage a reading which takes account of imagery, symbolism and language. A novel like Jeanette Winterson's *Sexing the Cherry* (1989) has a very disrupted time scheme, more than one narrator, and makes great use of magic, myth and fairy tale. As such it frustrates the reader's search for a consistently developing plot, and encourages a reading which makes connections in other ways: for example through considering questions of imagery and symbolism (such as the visual symbols of the banana and the pineapple which are associated with the dog-woman and Jordan respectively).

Sexing the Cherry is also a particularly good example of a novel that makes reference to other literature. Among some of the texts it refers to are the Grimms' fairy tale 'The Shoes that were Danced to Pieces', Browning's poem 'My Last Duchess' and Byron's poem 'She Walks in Beauty like the Night'. Although not all prose fictions contain such explicit *allusions* to specific texts, it is certainly the case that anyone reading a novel or short story brings their prior reading experience to bear on the text they are currently reading. From when we first begin to read we learn the conventions of story-telling, and as we become more experienced readers we are able to see the influence of certain texts on others. Some novelists exploit this fact: Margaret Atwood's novel *Lady Oracle* (1977) parodies the conventions of romance fiction, David Lodge's *Nice Work* (1988) refers to nineteenth-century industrial novels like *North and South* (1854–5). But whether or not such references are made explicit to the reader, it helps to think of prose fictions as *intertextually* related to one another, as using the common features of prose fictions, either implicitly or explicitly, whether in order to challenge or to modify or to endorse them.

Conclusion

It is certainly crucial, then, for any reader to be aware both of the *skills* needed to read prose fictions, and the *devices* writers can use to tell their stories. All readers invest in the reading process, perhaps through the specific process of identification with a particular character. Everyone wants to know what happens 'in the end', and we can all be aware of how the text we are reading refers to other texts we may have read. We should consider our own reading response: how it changes and develops as we read, how it may alter drastically on a second reading. Being aware of the devices writers use to tell their stories means considering issues of characterisation, narration and language. It means asking ourselves questions about who sees and who speaks, and about the ways in which writers distinguish between story and plot.

An understanding of both our own response as readers, and the devices used by the writer to tell a story, creates a sense of how they intertwine, creating a particular reading of a text. With this knowledge, readers can begin the process of interpreting and evaluating the novel or short story they are reading with greater confidence.

Notes

1. Jane Austen, *Northanger Abbey*, ed. Anne Henry Ehrenpreis (Harmondsworth: Penguin, 1972), p. 58.

2. Angela Carter, 'The Snow Child' in *The Bloody Chamber and Other Stories* (Harmondsworth: Penguin, 1981), p. 91.

3. George Eliot, *The Mill on the Floss*, ed. A. S. Byatt (Harmondsworth: Penguin, 1979), p. 514.

4. Henry James, *The Portrait of a Lady*, ed. Geoffrey Moore (Harmondsworth: Penguin, 1984), p. 46.

5. See Charlotte Brontë's letter to W. S. Williams, 6 November 1852, quoted in Elizabeth Gaskell, *The Life of Charlotte Brontë*, ed. Alan Shelston (Harmondsworth: Penguin, 1975), p. 485.

6. Quoted in J. E. Austen-Leigh, 'A Memoir of Jane Austen', in Jane Austen, *Persuasion, with A Memoir of Jane Austen*, ed. D. W. Harding (Harmondsworth: Penguin, 1985), p. 376.

7. Charles Dickens, *Bleak House*, ed. Norman Page (Harmondsworth: Penguin, 1971), p. 316.

8. Anthony Trollope, *Barchester Towers*, ed. Robin Gilmour (Harmondsworth: Penguin, 1983), p. 22.

9. Virginia Woolf, *To the Lighthouse*, ed. Stella McNichol (Harmondsworth: Penguin, 1992), p. 21.

10. David Lodge, *How Far Can You Go?* (Harmondsworth: Penguin, 1981), p. 15.

11. E. M. Forster, *Aspects of the Novel* (Harmondsworth: Penguin, 1990).

12. Vladimir Nabokov, *Lolita* (Harmondsworth: Penguin, 1980), p. 133.

13. See the introduction to the Penguin edition of E. M. Forster's *Howards End*, ed. Oliver Stallybrass (Harmondsworth: Penguin, 1975), pp. 11–12.

14. Wayne C. Booth, *The Rhetoric of Fiction*, 2nd edn (Harmondsworth: Penguin, 1991).

15. Wolfgang Iser, *The Implied Reader: Patterns of communication in prose fiction from Bunyan to Beckett* (Baltimore: The Johns Hopkins U.P., 1974).

16. George Eliot, *Adam Bede*, ed. Stephen Gill (Harmondsworth: Penguin, 1980), p. 221.

17. Jane Austen, *Emma*, ed. Ronald Blythe (Harmondsworth: Penguin, 1966), pp. 417–18.

18. Charlotte Brontë, *Jane Eyre*, ed. Q. D. Leavis (Harmondsworth: Penguin, 1966), p. 284.

19. See the introduction to the Penguin edition, p. 33.

20. See Tzvetan Todorov, 'The Typology of Detective Fiction', in *Modern Criticism and Theory: A reader*, ed. David Lodge (London: Longman, 1985), pp. 158–65.

21. Gérard Genette, *Narrative Discourse*, trans. Jane E. Lewin (Oxford: Basil Blackwell, 1980).
22. Charlotte Brontë, *Villette*, ed. Mark Lilly (Harmondsworth: Penguin, 1979), p. 105.
23. Daphne du Maurier, *Rebecca* (London: Arrow, 1992), p. 38.
24. Lodge is here referring to Genette's *Narrative Discourse*.
25. James Joyce, *Ulysses* (Harmondsworth: Penguin, 1992), p. 871.
26. Mikhail Bakhtin, *The Dialogic Imagination: Four essays*, ed. Michael Holquist (London and Austin: Texas U.P., 1981).
27. Letter to W. S. Williams, 23 October 1847, quoted in Winifred Gérin, *Charlotte Brontë: The evolution of genius* (Oxford: Oxford U.P., 1977), p. 342.
28. Georges Poulet, 'Criticism and the Experience of Interiority', in *Reader-Response Criticism: From formalism to post-structuralism*, ed. Jane P. Tompkins (Baltimore: The Johns Hopkins U.P., 1988), pp. 41–9 (pp. 44–5).
29. See her undated letter to W. S. Williams quoted in Elizabeth Gaskell's *Life of Charlotte Brontë*, p. 500.
30. Quoted in Appendix A in the Penguin edition of Charles Dickens's *Great Expectations*, ed. Angus Calder (Harmondsworth: Penguin, 1965), p. 494.
31. Robert Scholes, *Fabulation and Metafiction* (Urbana: Illinois U.P., 1979), p. 26.

Further reading

Allen, W., *The Short Story in English* (Oxford: Clarendon Press, 1981). (An introductory section discusses the rise of the short story form in England in the late nineteenth century, considers its roots in journalism and French literature and makes comparisons with its American counterpart. There is then extensive coverage of many different individual exponents of the genre.)

Allott, M., *Novelists on the Novel* (London: Routledge, 1965). (A fascinating collection of novelists' writings about their own and others' fictional processes.)

Bakhtin, M., *The Dialogic Imagination: Four essays*, ed. Michael Holquist (London and Austin: Texas U.P., 1981). (Wide-ranging, complex but fascinating book which develops the notion of the 'dialogic' text as an appropriate way of understanding and analysing how prose fictions have developed and function as a genre.)

Booth, W., *The Rhetoric of Fiction*, 2nd edn (Harmondsworth: Penguin, 1991). (Examines the strategies authors of prose fiction use to communicate with their readers. Introduces the valuable concepts of the implied author and the unreliable narrator. However, Booth's preference for a clear authorial stance and reliable narration implies a belief in the coherent unified text which has been questioned.)

Forster, E. M., *Aspects of the Novel* (Harmondsworth. Penguin, 1990). (Originally a series of lectures, this is engaging to read, though a very personal view. Not explicitly critical, in fact the opposite. His distinction between 'flat' and 'round' characters and his comments on story have been widely referred to.)

Genette, G., *Narrative Discourse* (Oxford: Basil Blackwell, 1980). (Although this book focuses on Proust, and is extremely complex, it provides a detailed and thorough system with which to analyse narrative discourse. A structuralist masterpiece.)

Hanson, C., *Short Stories and Short Fictions 1880–1980* (London and Basingstoke: Macmillan, 1985). (A rather more theoretical discussion than Allen's, though not as comprehensive. Considers the type of short story that focuses on plot versus the 'plotless', 'proto-modernist' variation. Organised thematically rather than by author.)

Hawthorn, J., *Studying the Novel: An introduction* (London: Edward Arnold, 1985). (Introductory level. Usefully structured around ways of analysing, studying and critically approaching fiction.)

Kettle, A., *An Introduction to the English Novel*, 2 vols, 2nd edn (London: Hutchinson, 1967). (For the reader looking for an historical survey, this covers the novel from its beginnings to the mid-twentieth century. Consistently sets the novel in its social and historical context, and contains analyses of specific texts.)

Rimmon-Kenan, S., *Narrative Fiction: Contemporary poetics* (London: Methuen, 1983). (Organised in sections around Genette's distinctions between story, text and narration, this book has a rather structuralist feel to it, moving on to consider reader response at the end.)

Scholes, R. and Kellog, R., *The Nature of Narrative* (Oxford: Oxford U.P., 1966). (Considers many diverse narrative forms as well as the novel, which sets it in an illuminating context.)

8
Reading plays
Graham Atkin

The theatrical medium

Plays have unique features which make them differ from poems and prose fiction. To be aware of what these unique features are, and of what possibilities they open up for both author and reader is essential for a thorough appreciation of how plays work. To begin to appreciate drama more fully we must try to understand more about the theatre as a medium, a medium through which the dormant play-text can come to life.

Of course there is a tension here, which is what makes dramatic texts so fascinating. The tension exists between the play as a text (some print on a page), and the play as an enacted, colourful, noisy, 'real' spectacle. From the author on *one* end of this rope of meaning to the audience in the theatre on the first night on the *other* end there stretches a complex of threads involving writing, reading, interpretation, rehearsal, production and reception.

The reader of a play-text might be an actor looking for a part, a director searching for a subject, or a student studying drama. A particular reader will always have an advantage over any theatre in the world no matter what the resources of that theatre. This advantage exists due to the potency of the human imagination. Shakespeare's *Henry V* opens with the figure of the Chorus appealing to the audience to exercise their imagination in order to flesh out the action that is to be presented before them:

Piece out our imperfections with your thoughts,
Into a thousand parts divide one man,
And make imaginary puissance;
Think, when we talk of horses, that you see them
Printing their proud hoofs i' the receiving earth;
For 'tis your thoughts that now must deck our kings.[1]

This appeal, and the later request in the prologue to act three, to 'eke out
our performance with your mind' is just as if not more applicable to the
reader of plays as it is to the audience in the theatre. However, to 'make
imaginary puissance', to bring the power of imagination to the words on
the page, is not sufficient in itself. The imagination needs to be informed,
directed and disciplined if a play-text is to be fruitfully realised in the
mind of the reader.

Knowledge is an aid to the imagination; it gives it more resources.
Knowledge of the history of the theatre, of its evolution and continuing
changeability, can strengthen and deepen our enjoyment of reading plays.
Dramatic literature and the theatre have a rich and immense history. What
we read and see today has evolved over the centuries, and playwrights,
directors, actors and audiences bring a knowledge of this history to bear
every time they write, interpret, enact or envision the dramatic. The history
of the theatre comes down to us not only in those texts, those plays which
have been set in print, but also in architecture where theatre has been staged,
in criticism and theory, in set and costume design and in music and song.

The word *drama* derives from the ancient Greek word meaning 'to do'.
Drama is always concerned with action and performance, with representation through the use of body and voice. Due to its special combination
of artistic forms dramatic representation can include painting, sculpture,
dance, music, poetry and prose. It is this multiplicity of media which
makes the play an attractive option for writers and readers. Plays have an
openness, a flexibility of modes of expression which, when realised either
by a company of committed artists in the theatre, or through the concentrated sensitive imagination of the reader, can come closer than any other
artistic form to a representation or imitation of life.

Unlike poetry and prose fiction a play-text can be thought of as a set of
instructions. These instructions are to be followed by actors and directors
according to their understanding and interpretation of the script. The
point about plays is that they are not only literary *texts*, but also the bases
for potential *performances*: as many possible performances, it would seem,
as there are companies of actors, directors, set designers and technicians

to perform them. The trouble is, putting on a play requires a lot of time
and effort and people. The reading of a play-text is not particularly time-
consuming and requires only one person – the reader. The level of effort
is of course another matter. The more plays you read, the smaller the
effort required – the effort, that is, to stage the play in the theatre of the
mind. 'The theatre of the mind.' What a grand phrase. But what exactly
is the theatre of the mind? It is an imaginary place where the reader of the
play-text attempts to stage the play she is reading. The aim of this
chapter is to convince you that the more you know about the whole
process of writing, reading, interpreting and performing plays, the easier
and more rewarding the study of plays will become.

Theatre of the mind

When we *read* a play we are doing something very different from when
we *watch* a play. When we sit in the audience at the theatre and the
curtain is raised, or the lights are dimmed, we are presented with an
interpretation of a particular text. Many, many factors have combined
and resulted in the action put before us. But when we read a play we are
alone with the words. We must build the entire production up from those
words. To this end stage directions, titles, character names and additional
information provided by the author are vital components of the text and
must be carefully attended to.

All this is making use of what is often referred to as the *side-text* or
secondary text. Included under this title are stage directions. To ignore
stage directions, or to pay scant attention to them, will lead to a partial or
incorrect conception of the play. David Birch has convincingly argued
that Roman Ingarden's distinction between the main and the side-text is
'not a particularly useful one' and he goes on to claim:

> The stage directions, amongst other things like character naming, textual
> and production histories, critical reception, mise-en-scene, and so on, are
> as much a part of the main text as the words assigned to characters to speak
> and should not, therefore, be marginalised as 'side-texts'.[2]

While it might be arguable whether 'critical reception' is 'as much part of
the main text as the words assigned to characters to speak', nevertheless
Birch alerts the reader of plays to the necessity of working on the script
and of digging deeper than the dialogue alone.

Look Back in Anger is a play in three acts which was first performed in London on 8 May 1956. Many critics and commentators consider John Osborne's play the most influential and ground-breaking work of drama in post-war Britain. The reader of this play today, whether in Britain or elsewhere, faced with the task of staging the play in the theatre of her mind, must attend closely to Osborne's lengthy *stage directions*. Even before reading these opening directions the reader may have read or heard some details of the history of the play's production and reception. Certainly the *title* of the play will already be known, and that is not an insignificant matter. Osborne wrestled with a number of possible titles for the play before opting for the impressive and highly successful *Look Back in Anger*. One wonders whether the play would have achieved its fame had Osborne opted for one of the following possibilities, which he scribbled in his writing pad: *Man in a Rage, Farewell to Anger, Angry Man, Bargain from Strength, Close the Cage Behind You, My Blood is a Mile High*. So never underestimate the importance of the title of a play. Who comes home in Harold Pinter's *The Homecoming* (1965)? Who or what is saved in Edward Bond's *Saved* (1966)? What is the meaning of the title of Edward Albee's play *Who's Afraid of Virginia Woolf?* (1962)?

Osborne's opening stage directions in *Look Back in Anger* run to almost two pages and contain details about the set and the properties on stage. In addition Osborne also provides us with insights into the psychology of his characters. Before we read Jimmy Porter's first line we have already read that 'he may seem sensitive to the point of vulgarity'. Arguably Osborne's comment that Jimmy is a 'disconcerting mixture of sincerity and cheerful malice, of tenderness and freebooting cruelty; restless, importunate, full of pride' does as much to create in our minds the sense of his character as anything he himself says.

Do these detailed stage directions show a distrust of actors and directors, or are they genuinely helpful to all? They make for a readable play which works at times like a novel with an omniscient narrator. These directions are written for the reader rather than the audience. But there are clear differences between reading thorough and unequivocal stage directions as an actor or director, and reading them as a student. Workers in the theatre may find that overly prescriptive directions limit and constrain their freedom to interpret the text; on the other hand, such directions might be seen by some as invaluable production notes. Certainly, these details must be considered carefully by the student of drama for they enable and assist the enactment of the play in the theatre of the mind.

In some extreme cases the secondary text of a play seems to drown and obliterate the primary text. George Bernard Shaw's *Androcles and the Lion* (1916) opens with a preface twice as long as the play itself. Some have seen such authorial strategies as a weakness. Hugo von Hofmannsthal has starkly claimed: 'The more powerful the dramatic dialogue, the more it will convey of the suspense, tension and atmosphere, and the less it will entrust to the stage directions.'[3] Though stage directions may sometimes be sparing they are an integral part of the playtext. The reader who does not bring a powerful mind to bear on such brief but crucial stage directions as 'they fight', or 'exit pursued by bear', or 'she hits him with the teapot', will be inadequately realising the text in her mind.

For a number of reasons Shakespeare used few stage directions. He was writing his plays at a time when drama was not really considered 'serious' literature and few plays were published with a wide readership in mind. Plays were written for performance not for reading. In 1616, the year of Shakespeare's death, Ben Jonson published his own plays as *Works* in a volume containing dedications, prologues and stage directions. Though Jonson, against a background of some ridicule, thus sought to enhance the reputation of drama as literature, it was not until 1623 that Shakespeare's plays were published in the earliest collected edition of his works. Partly due to Shakespeare's beneficial influence on the literary reputation of drama, and partly as a consequence of the development of printing technology, plays became more widely available in published form from the seventeenth century on, and editions of play-texts are now readily accessible to today's students.

The difference between Shaw and Shakespeare is the difference between realism and rhetoric. In rhetorical plays the details of action and appearance are generally integrated within the primary text, that is, within the dialogue. In *Henry IV, Part One* Shakespeare's greatest comic creation, the larger than life Sir John Falstaff, relays a tall tale of his bravery in combat to Prince Hal and company:

Prince Hal: Pray God you have not murdered some of them.
Falstaff: Nay, that's past praying for, I have peppered two of them. Two I am
    sure I have paid, two rogues in buckram suits. I tell thee what, Hal, if I tell thee
    a lie, spit in my face, call me horse. Thou knowest my old ward – here I lay,
    and *thus* I bore my point. Four rogues in buckram let drive at me –
Prince Hal: What, four? Thou saidst but two even now.
Falstaff: Four, Hal, I told thee four.

Poins: Ay, ay, he said four.
Falstaff: These four came all afront, and mainly thrust at me. I made me no more
   ado, but took all their seven points in my target, *thus*!

(II.iv.184–97; my italics)

Here there is no need for even the simplest stage direction. Falstaff's
exclamations of 'thus' suffice to indicate to any interpreter of the script
that the actor playing the part needs to enact the skirmish. Taking other
cues from Falstaff's lively language the actor's movements would doubt-
less be outlandish and exaggerated, adding to the humour of the scene.

Dialogue and character

At the other end of the scale from Osborne and Shaw exist many plays
with a minimum of stage directions. Such plays have little secondary text
and consist almost wholly of primary text: speech assigned to character.
Consider the opening of *Hamlet*:

Enter Barnardo and Francisco, two Sentinels.
Barnardo: Who's there?
Francisco: Nay, answer me. Stand and unfold yourself.
Barnardo: Long live the King!
Francisco: You come most carefully upon your hour.
Barnardo: 'Tis now struck twelve. Get thee to bed, Francisco.
Francisco: For this relief much thanks. 'Tis bitter cold,
         And I am sick at heart.
Barnardo: Have you had quiet guard?
Francisco: Not a mouse stirring.
Barnardo: Well, good night.

(I.i.1–12)

Thus begins probably the most celebrated play in the history of literature. The scene is set immediately. There is uncertainty, even fear (as
well as cold) in the air. The mood is despondent and sickly. The guard
coming on duty questions the guard already on duty. It is the witching
hour and we sense the supernatural. Sure enough we are soon to witness
the ghost of Denmark's dead King Hamlet.
   What is it that is so riveting about dialogue? When you read a novel it
is the speech of characters, especially when they are involved in quick,
tense exchanges, which catches the eye and rivets the attention. In drama
we get dialogue, dialogue, and more dialogue.

Dialogue is at the heart of drama. The playwright has the freedom to create a polyphony of voices, a battle of character in which each of the players in the *dramatis personae* fight for dominance. This dimension of drama has been very evident in some forms of modern drama, where the action seems little more than an adjunct to linguistic skirmishes that dwarf mere physical violence. In Harold Pinter's *The Homecoming* brothers Lenny and Teddy fight it out not with fists but through a dispute over a cheese roll.

Lenny: You took my cheese roll?
Teddy: Yes.
Lenny: I made that roll myself. I cut it up and put the butter on. I sliced a piece of
    cheese and put it in between. I put it on a plate and I put it in the sideboard. I
    did all that before I went out. Now I come back and you've eaten it.
Teddy: Well, what are you going to do about it?
Lenny: I'm waiting for you to apologize.
Teddy: But I took it deliberately, Lenny.
Lenny: You mean you didn't stumble on it by mistake?
Teddy: No, I saw you put it there. I was hungry, so I ate it.
Pause.
Lenny: Barefaced audacity.[4]

When we think about *character* in a play we inevitably think about character in real life. How do we judge the character of others? By observing what they do and listening to what they say. Yes, but also by hearing what is reported of them and assessing such comments as to their truthfulness. Similarly, when we watch a play we judge of characters based on these things: *speech, action* and *report*. When we read a play we must imagine the presence of a character in all the scenes in which they appear. They may not have any words, but their actions and reactions, even their inactions, are vital to any talk of character. In Edward Bond's *Saved* the 'hero' Len watches silently from the trees as a group of his friends stone to death a baby in an English park. Len's quiet voyeuristic fascination and his incapacity to intervene are as important in a consideration of his character and place in the play as his usual curious questioning.

The reader of plays needs to engage with characters by imagining the words of dialogue on the page being spoken by bodies in motion on the stage. The meat of most plays, the essence of the drama, lies in the impact of speeches and actions. These words and movements are indicated in the play-text with the intention that they be spoken and enacted in actual space and real time, though set in a theatrical 'frame'. At times words and actions ascribed to characters can be seemingly contradictory, producing meaningful and memorable moments of dramatic irony. Samuel Beckett's *Waiting for Godot* (1956) ends with just such a moment:

Vladimir: Well? Shall we go?
Estragon: Yes, let's go.
   They do not move.[5]

Caryl Churchill's innovative use of an oblique stroke to indicate an interruption of one speaker by another is a good example of the flexibility of the play-text. This simple invention allows Churchill to write dialogue in which characters speak simultaneously, with speakers occasionally speaking right through each others' lines. In *Top Girls* (1982) the device creates a strong sense of the confusion of argumentative conversation:

Joyce: Don't talk to me.
Marlene: Why shouldn't I talk? Why shouldn't I talk to you? / Isn't she my
   mother too?
Joyce: Look, you've left, you've gone away, / we can do without you.
Marlene: I left home, so what, I left home. People do leave home / it is normal.
Joyce: We understand that, we can do without you.[6]

For the audience the clash of lines and characters is all too obvious, but the reader has to produce the effect for herself. The words on the page may all seem to carry equal weight, but Churchill's intent is that certain phrases will be contending with others. The reader must, to the best of her ability, realise the intended effect of such colliding words.

Speeches assigned to characters need not be part of a dialogue. The use of *soliloquy* enables the playwright to reveal the inner thoughts of a character directly to the audience through the conventional device of talking aloud to oneself. Soliloquy functions rhetorically to lay bare what would otherwise remain hidden and unknown, and can add greatly to the level at which we engage with the character. Shakespeare discloses Hamlet's melancholic, suicidal temperament through soliloquy before the prince is aware that his father has been murdered by his uncle:

O that this too too sullied flesh would melt,
Thaw and resolve itself into a dew,
Or that the Everlasting had not fix'd
His canon 'gainst self-slaughter. O God! God!

How weary, stale, flat and unprofitable
Seem to me all the uses of this world!
(I.ii.129–34)

When we read or hear soliloquy we are being drawn into the private consciousness of character.

The theatre allows the playwright to represent the inner workings of the human mind through methods other than soliloquy. Willy Loman, Arthur Miller's confused and pathetic protagonist in *Death of a Salesman* (1949), blurs past and present in a series of exchanges (with his dead brother Ben, with his ex-lover, with his sons Biff and Happy as young children) which portray the turmoil within. It is through these dialogues that Miller's play explores the psychology of a man whose mind and life are in crisis:

[Howard exits, pushing the table off left. Willy stares into space, exhausted. Now the music is heard – Ben's music – first distantly, then closer, closer. As Willy speaks, Ben enters from the right. He carries valise and umbrella.]
Willy: Oh, Ben, how did you do it? What is the answer? Did you wind up the Alaska deal already?
Ben: Doesn't take much time if you know what you're doing. Just a short business trip. Boarding ship in an hour. Wanted to say good-bye.
Willy: Ben, I've got to talk to you.
Ben [glancing at his watch]: Haven't the time, William.
Willy [crossing the apron to Ben]: Ben, nothing's working out. I don't know what to do.[7]

Ben does not exist in the play as a character in his own right but as the product of Willy's troubled and tired brain. Indeed Miller originally envisaged the stage-design as a huge head inside of which all the action would take place. By enmeshing the past and the present in his play Miller is able to show not just the final moments of Willy's life but the process which has brought about his decline.

Semiotics of drama

Semiotics is the study of signs, communication and meaning. The reader of plays is unlikely to neglect the words, or verbal signs, which will be spoken by actors portraying characters as these are all too apparent when faced with a text. However there is one potential pitfall, which must be strenuously avoided, and that is the danger of neglecting the multimedial aspect of actual theatrical performance. When we read a play we must, if we can even start to claim to understand and appreciate it as an aesthetic object, a work of art, contemplate the *non-verbal* dimensions of that play. What is meant by non-verbal? Quite simply all those signs, codes and channels of communication which are not words. These non-verbal signifiers include, but are not limited to: noise, lighting, costume, mask, make-up, gesture, music, properties and set-design.

To illustrate the importance of maintaining an awareness of non-verbal aspects of drama we may turn to the comments Thomas De Quincey makes in his compelling essay 'On the Knocking at the Gate in *Macbeth*' (1823):

> Hence it is, that when the deed is done, when the work of darkness is perfect, then the world of darkness passes away like a pageantry in the clouds: the knocking at the gate is heard; and it makes known audibly that the reaction has commenced: the human has made its reflux on the fiendish; the pulses of life are beginning to beat again; and the reestablishment of the goings-on of the world in which we live, first makes us profoundly sensible of the awful parenthesis that had suspended them.[8]

Here De Quincey has taken a sound-effect and convincingly argued for a possible interpretation of its meaning and effect in relation to the whole play. The knocking is interpreted as a pivotal moment of reversal, or peripeteia, in the play. It is the non-verbal sign that Macbeth's murder of Duncan will be countered by forces of life. The knocking further unnerves the murderous Macbeths. There is a sense of divine judgement. Who is it that is knocking? Macduff: Macbeth's eventual executioner. When the reader of *Macbeth* sees the innocent-looking stage direction 'Knock within' she must employ an imagination unassisted by further detail. The knock is not a tap on the neighbour's door, it is a loud, echoing pounding which might wake the dead:

> Wake Duncan with thy knocking! I would thou couldst!
> (II.ii.73)

The strength and importance of these non-verbal modes of signification is by no means restricted to Shakespeare's craft. Modern plays similarly contain powerful non-verbal signs. In *Look Back in Anger* Jimmy's trumpet-playing gives him a presence and a voice even when he is off-stage. Both Helena and Alison wear Jimmy's shirts in symbolic deference to his ego. In the theatre these non-verbal signifiers are imposs-ible to ignore, but the reader of plays must remain vigilant and attentive if she is to fully appreciate the theatrical effects intended. In scene four of *Saved* Bond includes the following stage direction: 'Slowly a baby starts to cry. It goes on crying without a break until the end of the scene.'[9] The reader determined to stage a performance of the play in the mind will hear in the mind's ear the crying baby as the concluding pages of the scene are read.

Just as the reader must be sensitive to sound effects so too must she be sensitive to lighting effects. In *The Homecoming* the academic Teddy makes a speech which ends with this address to his family: 'You're just objects. You just . . . move about. I can observe it. I can see what you do. It's the same as I do. But you're lost in it. You won't get me being . . . I won't be lost in it' (p. 62). Teddy's futile hope is that he somehow stands outside the process of historical inevitabilities which he feels everyone else is subject to. By operating '*on* things and not *in* things' (p. 61) he hopes to free himself from the past and the social necessities of the present which arise because of the past (or present interpretations of the past). His belief that he thereby gains a sort of freedom and independence is implicitly ridiculed, perhaps even directly contradicted, by the stage direction which immediately follows: 'BLACKOUT.'

Teddy is already faltering at this point, seemingly unsure about the validity of what he is saying. In spite of his brave intellectual claim that he is the one who can see, he is lost with the others as the light goes. The attentive and imaginative reader of Pinter's play would be aware that the audience in the theatre experiences the blackout along with the actors on stage. It is not only Teddy and his family, but all the members of the audience, who are plunged into the uncomfortable gloom.

Sound and light are only two of the many non-verbal modes of theatrical communication. There is insufficient space here to consider all the other non-verbal signs which are potentially at work on the stage, but the reader of plays must remain aware of the potential use of properties, costume, make-up, set-design, gesture and facial expression as important contributing factors to the meaning of plays. The leafy boughs of Birnam Wood carried across the stage by Macduff's and Malcolm's army in *Macbeth* function as powerful visual signs of the resurgent forces of life. Martha's change into a voluptuous, enticing costume in *Who's Afraid of Virginia Woolf?* signals a readiness for combat with her husband George. Harold Pinter's indication in

Moonlight (1993) of three main playing areas, one of which serves as a location for dream-like scenes, is an example of the specific use of stage space to produce meaning.

Structure and time

Aristotle makes a series of suggestions as to the qualities of tragic drama in his immensely influential *Poetics*. His observations form the basis of much of the literary criticism of dramatic texts which was to follow. Knowledge of some of Aristotle's formulations can only serve to enhance the play-reading experience. Aristotle claimed that the dramatic elements which have been used by nearly all playwrights and possessed by all plays are: spectacle, character, plot, diction, song and thought.

Of these characteristics of drama Aristotle argued that the *plot*, or the ordering of the action, was the most important. It is the plot to which all the other elements are subjugated. Furthermore it is qualities of the plot, particularly 'reversals' (*peripeteia*) and 'recognitions' (*anagnorisis*), which create the most profound effects on the audience. Reversals are crucial points in the drama where the situation changes, often due to a discovery or recognition. Aristotle cites the example of Oedipus who, in *Oedipus Rex*, discovers that he has married his mother and killed his father. The moment of discovery or recognition is also the moment of reversal. The fortunes of Oedipus change in an awful dawning of awareness. The effect of the action of Sophocles' play is, according to Aristotle, that it awakens fear and pity in the audience, which in turn produces a purging or *catharsis* of these emotions. While fear and pity can be evoked by spectacle the superior dramatist works to excite these emotions in the audience through the very structure of the play's plot.

Drama consists of action, but the audience or reader often needs to know a certain amount of 'background' information in order to understand the action. This information is known as *exposition*. Exposition can be dull and uninteresting if it is not treated skilfully. In the hands of a great playwright the exposition is finely bound into the structure of the drama. To appreciate *Hamlet* we need to know that Claudius has murdered his brother in order to seize the throne. How does Shakespeare reveal this necessary information? Through the apparition of the dead king's ghost. There is suspense in that the ghost will not speak to Horatio. While Shakespeare makes us wait to hear what the ghost has to say, King Claudius and his new queen, Gertrude, are shown at court.

Suspense builds as the brooding Hamlet is told of the apparition of his
father's ghost by Horatio. After setting in motion the stories of Laertes,
Ophelia and Polonius, Shakespeare brings together Prince Hamlet and
his father's ghost, and we finally hear the chilling account of the murder
of Hamlet's father:

> Sleeping within my orchard,
> My custom always of the afternoon,
> Upon my secure hour thy uncle stole
> With juice of cursed hebenon in a vial,
> And in the porches of my ears did pour
> The leprous distilment, whose effect
> Holds such an enmity with blood of man
> That swift as quicksilver it courses through
> The natural gates and alleys of the body,
> And with a sudden vigour doth it posset
> And curd, like eager droppings into milk,
> The thin and wholesome blood. So did it mine,
> And a most instant tetter bark'd about,
> Most lazar-like, with vile and loathsome crust
> All my smooth body.
> Thus was I, sleeping, by a brother's hand
> Of life, of crown, of queen at once dispatch'd.
>
> (I.v.59–75)

The traditional plot consisting of exposition, action leading to *climax*, and finally *denouement* or resolution has not been so evident in
contemporary drama. Dramatic representation has become more unpredictable, flouting conventions and not tying up all the loose ends. Many
consider Georg Büchner's *Woyzeck* (1836) to be the first truly modern
play. With its fragmented structure, in which each scene functions as
another piece in the jigsaw, Büchner's play shows a dissatisfaction with
traditional play structure which can truly be said to be an anticipation
of the modern. Writers such as Beckett and Ionesco have developed the
sense of absurdity, uncertainty, even nihilism to which Woyzeck gives
expression when he says: 'Everyone's an abyss. You get dizzy if you
look down.'[10]

Scene changes are immensely important. They can offer chances for
shifts in the action or focus of the play. Often scene changes work to
build suspense. They offer the opportunity for the playwright and the
play to slide through time. The reader is not witness to the gap, only to

what things are like at the other side of the gap. Our powers to compare the new situation with the old will in large part determine our view of the play. Sometimes vital transitions will have taken place during the gap. In David Mamet's *Oleanna* (1992) Carol, perhaps surprisingly, transforms from an inarticulate student to a person who has gained power and control over language and its interpretation, in between acts one and two. Shakespeare would often use scene changes to set up oppositions and contrasts as he does in *Henry IV, Part One,* with the action moving between a court of verse-speaking political intrigue and a tavern of prose-speaking drunken indolence, Falstaffian wit and revelry. In *Look Back in Anger* the action at the opening of act three, with Helena standing at the ironing board, presents an obvious echo of Alison at the ironing board in act one.

One of the most important tasks for the reader of plays is to pace the reading of the text. In this respect plays can be more demanding than other types of reading. The play-text is written with timing very much in mind. Silences and pauses (the latter are shorter) must be imagined by the reader, not hurried over to get to the next line of speech. A pause can create a real sense of expectation or unease, often enhancing the effect of words spoken either side of the gap. This is certainly the case in Beckett's *Waiting for Godot*:

Vladimir: We'll hang ourselves tomorrow. (Pause.) Unless Godot comes.
Estragon: And if he comes?
Vladimir: We'll be saved.

(p. 94)

Just as a play's pace will often be slowed by hesitations, pauses and silences so at times the action will be fast and furious. The reader of *Macbeth* should be alert to the quickening of the pace immediately following the murder of Duncan:

Macbeth: I have done the deed. Didst thou not hear a noise?
Lady Macbeth: I heard the owl scream and the crickets cry. Did you not speak?
Macbeth: When?
Lady Macbeth: Now.
Macbeth: As I descended?
Lady Macbeth: Ay.
Macbeth: Hark! Who lies i' th' second chamber?

(II.ii.14–18)

Such short sharp exchanges of speech, or *stichomythia*, produce a powerful dramatic effect, heightening the sense of nervous tension and speed-
ing along the action.

Some playwrights deliberately disrupt any sense of 'real' time. In *The
Winter's Tale* Shakespeare presents the figure of Time as Chorus to
explain that the action slides forward over sixteen years. This is just time
enough for a new generation to grow and heal the tragic wounds of the
first part of this bitter-sweet play. In Harold Pinter's *Betrayal* (1978) each
scene shows us a previous component of the action. Time is flowing
backwards. Caryll Churchill uses a similar device in *Top Girls* in which
act three takes place a year earlier than act two. Such experimentation
with time can produce intense dramatic moments. The climactic class-
war exchange between sisters Joyce and Marlene is thus placed at the
very end of Churchill's play, though chronologically it occurs before
other less heated words:

Marlene: I hate the working class / which is what you're going
Joyce: Yes you do.
Marlene: to go on about now, it doesn't exist any more, it means lazy and stupid.
    / I don't like the way they talk. I don't
Joyce: Come on, now we're getting it.
Marlene: like beer guts and football vomit and saucy tits / and brothers and
    sisters –
Joyce: I spit when I see a Rolls Royce, scratch it with my ring / Mercedes it was.
Marlene: Oh very mature –

(p. 85)

Performance

When reading a play the reader must do the work of the performers, at
least in the mind's eye and ear, if not in part with actual body and voice.
While paying close attention to the text of a play the reader should ideally
be continually aware of the requirements and possibilities of actual
performance. With the exception of deliberately written *closet drama*, intended purely for private reading, plays are written so that they can be
performed. Once a play-text is completed by an author it travels a variable
and unpredictable road to performance. It is read, analysed and interpreted. It is cast, rehearsed and performed. These few words do little to
demonstrate the elaborate interaction of persons and ideas involved in
dramatic performances.

During the process leading to performance a play passes out of the domain of the isolated reader and becomes the focus for a group of people, consisting of a variety of directors and actors, set-designers and makers, lighting and sound technicians, costume designers and makers, make-up artists and others. The interpretation of the play evident in performance is the product of the interplay of all the theatrical workers involved. The meanings and significances which the rehearsal procedure, culminating in performance, can make manifest are multiple. Just as performances of plays involve facets of interpretations from all those involved in the production, so the reception of theatrical performance involves another group of people – the audience. The audience is an always unique combination of individual subjectivities who form the crowd which views, listens to and responds to each individual performance, through laughter, applause, silence, groans or yawns.

How does an awareness of the complexity of theatrical performance and reception assist the reader of plays? In order to perform a play the text has to be translated from words into light, sound, objects and bodies in action in a definite space. It is the actuality of performance which the reader needs constantly to bear in mind. Performance necessitates decision. The reader may feel she has fully comprehended a particular scene, but it is not until words are spoken aloud, and actors playing characters move in relation to each other in space, that comprehension of the requirements and possibilities of stage performance can begin. The reader of plays should be prepared to create a performance not just in the mind, but partly physically by use of voice and body. The reader of *Macbeth* might be content silently to scrutinise Lady Macbeth's famous soliloquy, but reading the passage aloud necessitates the making of certain choices:

> The raven himself is hoarse
> That croaks the fatal entrance of Duncan
> Under my battlements. Come, you spirits
> That tend on mortal thoughts, unsex me here,
> And fill me, from the crown to the toe, top-full
> Of direst cruelty! Make thick my blood,
> Stop up th' access and passage to remorse,
> That no compunctious visitings of nature
> Shake my fell purpose, nor keep peace between
> Th' effect and it! Come to my woman's breasts,
> And take my milk for gall, you murd'ring ministers,
> Wherever in your sightless substances
> You wait on nature's mischief! Come, thick night,

And pall thee in the dunnest smoke of hell,
That my keen knife see not the wound it makes,
Nor heaven peep through the blanket of the dark,
To cry 'Hold, hold!'

(I.v.39–55)

The danger when reading a play is that it remains a silent script. When the speeches of a play are spoken rather than silently read the words unavoidably acquire tone and emphasis. Any speaker of the above speech will lend the words certain qualities they simply do not possess while they sit dead on the page. J. L. Styan has usefully described these 'elements in the voice' as the five Ps or the five Ss. The five Ps are *Pressure, Pace, Power, Pitch, Pause*. The five Ss are *Stress, Speed, Strength, Song, Silence*.[11] If you read the above soliloquy aloud you will deliver the words with a distinct pressure or stress, a particular pace or speed, a definite power or strength, a certain pitch or song, and a specific use of pause and silence. Which words do you stress? How do you pace the speech? At what points do you increase or reduce the strength of your voice? What alterations of pitch do you make? Where do you pause and for how long? These are the questions that an actor in performance must answer.

Performing plays involves answering many more questions about the text than those solely concerned with the speaking of words. Other questions concerning movement, gesture and facial expression, not only when delivering lines, but also when reacting to the lines of others, must be addressed by the actor. Questions concerning stage space, set-design, properties, costume, make-up, lighting and sound effects must also be addressed. If a chair is called for in the play-text then those involved in the production of the play must decide on a specific chair to use. The workers in the theatre cannot vaguely think of a chair as a reader might, they must decide on one particular chair.

As a reader of plays you should not be content to leave unanswered questions that those working in the theatre must decide upon. If you were playing Lady Macbeth how would your face and body move when performing the above soliloquy? What would you be wearing? How would you be made-up? Would you still be holding the letter from your husband Macbeth which has sparked off these dark thoughts? What sort of lighting should be used? A consideration of these sorts of questions can only serve to deepen our involvement and understanding of the way plays work. Jonathan Miller has written of plays:

The text is in fact an extremely impoverished promisory note with a view to performance. We don't know what it means until we tether it into a world, our world, and it doesn't become lucid or interesting or *drama* until it's in a world.[12]

The essential aspect of drama, that which distinguishes drama from all other types of literature, is the aspect of enactment or performance. The play-text is a blueprint for action but until enacted it does not live as theatre. When a play is performed the text itself recedes temporarily, the focus moves from page to stage, and the extraordinary and magical relationship between theatre and the world is evident. Yet while theatrical performance offers a living interpretation of a play it is, by its nature, an ephemeral art form. When studying plays you may be unable to see them performed on stage. But it is always worth making an effort to see as many theatrical performances as possible (whether of set texts or not). Moreover, many plays are widely available in audio or video form, and you may find it helpful to make use of them. In the final analysis, your interpretation of a play must be based on the words of the play-text, and you must try to enact a performance of that play-text in your imagination.

Notes

1. William Shakespeare, *Henry V* (Prologue: lines 23–8). Subsequent references to and quotations from Shakespeare's plays will be given in the main body of the chapter. The Arden edition of the plays has been used throughout.
2. David Birch, *The Language of Drama* (London: Macmillan, 1991), p. 11.
3. Manfred Pfister, *The Theory and Analysis of Drama* (Cambridge: Cambridge U.P., 1988), p. 16.
4. Harold Pinter, *The Homecoming* (London: Methuen, 1965), pp. 63–4.
5. Samuel Beckett, *Waiting for Godot* (London: Faber and Faber, 1956), p. 94.
6. Caryl Churchill, *Top Girls* (London: Methuen, 1982), p. 78.
7. Arthur Miller, *Death of a Salesman* (London: Penguin, 1949), p. 66.
8. Thomas De Quincey, quoted from Pfister, *The Theory and Analysis of Drama*, p. 217.
9. Edward Bond, *Saved* (London: Methuen, 1966), p. 36.
10. Georg Büchner, *Woyzeck* (London: Methuen, 1979), p. 22.
11. J. L. Styan, *The Dramatic Experience* (Cambridge: Cambridge U.P., 1965), pp. 38–9.

12. Jonathan Miller, 'From Page to Stage: Text, Interpretation, Performance', *Strawberry Fare* (Autumn, 1988), p. 10.

Further reading

Birch, D., *The Language of Drama* (London: Macmillan, 1991). (Deals with issues of literary theory, social semiotics, discourse and performance analysis in order to delineate a 'drama praxis'.)

Dawson, S. W., *Drama and the Dramatic* (London: Methuen, 1970). (One of the *Critical Idiom* series. Raises many important points of contention. Especially clear on dramatic irony, character and idea, and the differences between drama and the novel.)

Elam, K., *The Semiotics of Theatre and Drama* (London: Methuen, 1980). (As the blurb says, this 'leads us to an area of inquiry whose complexity may be daunting but whose very openness makes it particularly inviting and challenging'.)

Esslin, M., *An Anatomy of Drama* (London: Temple Smith, 1976). (A practical introduction to theatrecraft.)

Esslin, M., *The Field of Drama* (London: Methuen, 1987). (A thought-provoking consideration of the boundaries of drama with attention paid to cinema and television.)

Griffiths, S., *How Plays Are Made* (London: Heinemann, 1982). ('A guide to the technique of play construction and the basic principles of drama.' A useful introduction to the most important elements of dramatic writing with a wide variety of references to plays throughout history.)

Hayman, R., *How to Read a Play* (London: Methuen, 1977). (A book designed to encourage a self-conscious and critical approach to the reading of plays.)

Kelsall, M., *Studying Drama* (London: Edward Arnold, 1985). (Another good general introduction to reading plays. Questioning, with an extensive array of examples.)

Mamet, D., *Writing in Restaurants* (London: Faber and Faber, 1988). (Rumination on life in the theatre from one of America's greatest contemporary playwrights.)

Pfister, M., *The Theory and Analysis of Drama* (Cambridge: Cambridge U.P., 1988). (Extremely thorough analysis which makes for heavy going at times, but is full of valuable insights and some splendid diagrams.)

Scolnicov, H. and Holland, P. (eds), *Reading Plays: Interpretation and reception* (Cambridge: Cambridge U.P., 1991). (A challenging collection of essays dealing with a fascinating variety of issues of concern to contemporary critics of drama.)

Styan, J. L., *The Dramatic Experience* (Cambridge: Cambridge U.P., 1965). (Full of plainly expressed wisdom and a vast array of visual aids. An influential writer of dramatic criticism.)

Wright, N., *Ninety-nine Plays* (London: Methuen, 1992). (A highly personal but stimulating introduction to a selection of key plays from *The Oresteia* on.)

9

Practising criticism and theory

Katherine A. Armstrong

Introduction: Criticism and theory

When you begin to study for your degree you will find that all literature
courses will make some reference to works of criticism and theory, and
most course bibliographies will strongly recommend or even prescribe
the reading of critical and theoretical texts alongside the primary reading
which forms the core of the study programme. Even where criticism and
theory are not highlighted by a course, as students you will often find
yourselves turning to critical and theoretical works for enlightenment of a
difficult author or from curiosity about her or his context, critical reception and significance for other readers, whether specialist or general. And
all literature courses involve students in practising their own critical and
theoretical skills, both through informal class discussions and through the
writing of essays or dissertations.

It is, therefore, important to understand what is meant by criticism
and theory, how they differ from one another and how they interact. This
chapter seeks, first, to define the related functions of criticism and theory;
secondly, to explain why as students of literature you will benefit from
studying critical and theoretical works in addition to primary literary
texts; thirdly, to offer some practical suggestions about how to use criticism and theory to help with your own readings and analyses of literature; and fourthly, to suggest some of the techniques which will help you
to become insightful and interesting practitioners of criticism and theory
in your own right.

What are criticism and theory?

Criticism and theory are closely related, and a theoretical work may often be indistinguishable from a critical one, but we might tentatively say that 'Theory' *defines* various methods of reading and interpreting, whilst 'Criticism' *applies* those methods to particular texts. Another way of putting this is to say that all literary critics work from a theoretical base, whether explicitly acknowledged or not, whereas theorists foreground their methodology in their discussions of authors and texts. Thus Tzvetan Todorov's *Genres in Discourse*[1] is for the most part an exposition of structuralist theory which has general applications for the study of literature, whereas Roland Barthes's essay, 'Textual Analysis of Poe's "Valdemar"'[2] is a structuralist critique of a particular literary work. Of course, the distinction is a gross oversimplification, for theorists refer to individual works and critics will frequently outline their theoretical standpoints. But so long as we bear in mind that the boundaries between Theory (which we might term 'pure') and Criticism ('applied') are in practice almost always blurred, an awareness of the basic difference in emphasis between criticism and theory is helpful when beginning to read secondary materials. As students of literature you will also be both critics and theorists yourselves, on the one hand examining and questioning your own methods and assumptions and on the other attempting to broaden and strengthen your critical skills.

Criticism and theory have gone hand-in-hand with art since classical times: the first great work of theory, Aristotle's *Poetics*, was written in the fourth century BC in response to contemporary Greek tragedy; and from the Roman poet Horace to the medieval Italian poet Dante and the poets of the English Renaissance, Sir Philip Sidney and Ben Jonson, writers have produced works of criticism and theory alongside their 'creative' works of art. It is ironic, then, that people sometimes object to criticism and theory on the grounds that they are parasitic on art, and derivative rather than original; or alternatively because criticism and theory are seen to dissect texts and destroy them in the process. We only have to think about the number of poets, dramatists and novelists who have written criticism or formally addressed questions of theory to see that literature, criticism and theory are not opposed but closely connected. Samuel Johnson, S. T. Coleridge, George Eliot, Virginia Woolf, T. S. Eliot, George Orwell, A. S. Byatt, Margaret Atwood, Angela Carter and Salman Rushdie have all written criticism, explored the theoretical implications of their stances, and are well known both as artists and as critics.

It is worth forestalling this and other objections to criticism and theory before we begin to consider them in depth. Criticism and theory are often attacked for their obscurity and dependence on what we might call jargon. It is true that some critical and theoretical writings may be unintentionally opaque in style; but this is very often a consequence of their authors' grappling with subjects which are themselves opaque and difficult: writers are unlikely to make themselves deliberately unreadable. It is equally true that a minority of critics use an unnecessary amount of technical language to express their ideas, but most critical language serves the same purpose as the terminology of any other specialist sphere: it is a convenient shorthand for the discussion of recurring problems and ideas.

The word 'text', for example, is, strictly speaking, a 'jargon' word in literary studies, borrowed from theological and religious discourse. Initially 'text' was used to denote the body of a literary work which was subject to the scrutiny of editors and bibliographers, on an analogy with the texts studied by biblical scholars. Nowadays it is a word which readers and critics use to signify any piece of written or spoken discourse when they want to avoid weighted or value-laden terms (including 'literary'). If we describe Mary Shelley's *Frankenstein* (1818) as a 'text' we are acknowledging that this is a work which is amenable to the same kinds of serious critical analysis as a play by Christopher Marlowe or a poem by Sylvia Plath. If, however, we choose to refer to *Frankenstein* as a romance, a horror story, a thriller or a Gothic tale, we would be prejudging the work before we so much as began to make any explicit analyses or evaluations of it. To someone unused to common critical terms the word 'text' might seem to have pretentious or exclusive overtones. In fact it has been adopted by critics for fundamentally egalitarian reasons, in the hope that it is a reasonably neutral term (in so far as any critical term can be neutral).

Criticism and theory are, of course, rarely neutral. They have at times been perceived as irrelevant, the intellectual posturings of an ivory-tower elite. While some critics and theorists may wish to ignore the social and political dimensions of their own works and the works they study, many are overtly committed to some kind of ideological standpoint. It is worth noting that various critics and theorists have promulgated radical, even revolutionary analyses of society. Some have been persecuted or imprisoned by totalitarian regimes, so subversive was their work considered: Viktor Shklovsky; Georg Lukacs; Antonio Gramsci, for example. The Russian Formalists worked and wrote underground in Stalinist Russia, and one of their leading exponents, Roman Jakobson, was forced to leave

Czechoslovakia when the Nazis invaded in 1939. The Communist critic Gramsci was victimised by the Fascist government of Italy in the 1920s; Mikhail Bakhtin was persecuted under Stalinism in the Soviet Union; and Marxist critics are still regarded with outspoken hostility by many academics and public figures in the United States. Within the 'academy' – the many thousands of educational and research institutions across the world engaged in literary studies – theoretical debates and individual critical interpretations of texts have been and remain sources of fierce controversy. Criticism and theory increase our understanding of the relationships between literary texts and their societies: their ideological functions as well as their formal properties. Far from rendering primary works academic or remote, criticism and theory ultimately root them in the material world in which we live, showing us, whether explicitly or implicitly, that literature operates in relation to social, political and economic systems. Thus the practice of criticism and theory should not be thought of as the prerogative of specialists or a cultural elite: quite the opposite.

Why do we read criticism and theory?

In this section these fundamental reasons for reading criticism and theory will be discussed in some depth. First, however, it should be acknowledged that both criticism and theory have a number of what might be termed 'pragmatic' uses for the student of literature, not least of which is an exemplary one. By familiarising yourself with the work of a range of eloquent and perceptive critics and theorists, you provide yourself with models for your own analytical practice. Coleridge's lectures on Shakespeare, for example, delivered in the early nineteenth century, remain provocative and inspiring for late-twentieth-century readers and critics. You may or may not wish to place the same emphasis as Coleridge does on the psychological authenticity and complexity of Shakespeare's characters, but all critics, even the most inflexibly formalist, will make some reference to characters when interpreting a text, in which case Coleridge's tenacity and sensitivity serve to demonstrate the benefits of close reading and strenuously logical deduction. The brilliant and unpredictable twentieth-century critic, William Empson, insists in his *The Structure of Complex Words*[3] on an inquisitive, challenging approach to key words in texts and historical periods; and any student who has followed Empson's vigorous pursuit of an apparently straightforward word such as 'honest' through all its transformations and mutations in post-medieval English is likely to develop a more acute ear for subtle semantic shifts as a result.

In addition, reading critical and theoretical works will gradually furnish you with an enlarged vocabulary, technical and non-technical, for the discussion of literature, and thus will help you to write with authority and precision. Some students, however, undoubtedly find that reading other critics and theorists actually impedes them in their own writing about texts, perhaps because they are inhibited by the spectacle of acknowledged experts displaying their skills or perhaps because they sense themselves losing the directness and freshness which characterised their written work hitherto. This directness is largely a matter of confidence; and it is one of the purposes of academic study to instil confidence or rather, perhaps, to restore it along with a new self-awareness and breadth of knowledge. A huge compensation for suddenly feeling yourself to be a relative novice in the field of literature is the discovery and acquisition of facts and interpretations from the reading of established theorists and critics. Our understanding of the nineteenth-century novel, for example, may be greatly enhanced by a complementary reading of Raymond Williams's *Culture and Society 1780–1950*,[4] in which the novels are related to their socio-economic context. Our appreciation of recurrent ideas in nineteenth-century novels may also deepen as we learn from critics and theorists about the intellectual preoccupations of the period. For example, the intensity with which certain nineteenth-century novelists deal with questions of growth, transformation, determinism and sexual selection is lucidly explained by the critic Gillian Beer in relation to the impact of contemporary evolutionary theories such as Darwin's.[5]

Narrowly biographical criticism can raise problems for students and professional critics alike, since it is never possible to determine with certainty how far a writer's life has influenced her or his work or, more importantly, how we can justify interpreting the meaning of a text with reference to external sources. The fact that Charlotte Brontë spent some years at a school resembling the fictional Lowood in *Jane Eyre* (1847) does nothing to help us in deciding about the significance or importance of this experience for Brontë's portrayal of Lowood in the novel though Lowood might be very useful to us if we were writing a biography of Brontë and attempting to estimate the psychological effects on her of her school days.

Some kinds of biographical information which can be obtained from critics are, however, very useful. If we feel perplexed by John Donne's

Songs and Sonets (1633), and find them bewildering in their catholicity of references to such diverse and sometimes difficult subjects as theology, astronomy, medicine, geography, geometry, alchemy and philosophy, we will want to know that the poems were originally written for individual manuscript circulation within a coterie of aristocratic and learned friends and patrons. Their witty intricacies and recondite allusions are intimately bound up with their conditions of production.[6] A similar clarification takes place when we learn that Richardson's voluminous novels *Clarissa* (1747–8) and *Sir Charles Grandison* (1754) were published over a protracted length of time and were designed for a leisured readership and to be read collectively: typically, as with Richardson's own immediate circle of friends, to be read and discussed aloud.

These two functions of criticism and theory – the demonstration of the skills which we wish to develop ourselves in writing about texts, and the contextualisation of works (in the broadest sense) – are relatively straightforward to identify and define. That criticism and theory also help us to understand the relationships between texts and society on an ideological level is a more complex issue to expound since we are not always accustomed either to questioning our reasons for focusing on certain texts (or aspects of texts) in preference to others, or to justifying our particular methods and value-judgements. In what follows, therefore, various examples are given to illustrate the consequences of learning about certain critical or theoretical approaches. My underlying concern is to show that criticism and theory are chiefly valuable for the ways in which they oblige us to scrutinise our assumptions as readers; it is this, rather than any particular methodological approach, which I wish to stress. This is not the place for an extended account of individual critical theories; instead I hope to offer some instances of the value of critical and theoretical reading in contesting and refining our own analysis of literature and society.

The uses of criticism and theory

My first example is taken from Virginia Woolf's immensely influential and stimulating critical work, *A Room of One's Own*.[7] This is a polemical defence of the woman writer and intellectual in which Woolf is ultimately concerned to assert the vitality of contemporary women's writing. In order to do so she also surveys various epochs in which women have been excluded from dominant literary culture, either during their lifetimes or shortly after their deaths. Woolf's essay is a key text in the twentieth-century feminist tradition which has sought to restore women writers to the canon and to analyse the reasons for their previous exclusion from anthologies, bibliographies, college syllabi and so on.

One of the most welcome effects of this branch of feminist inquiry which Woolf helped to inspire and which has been consolidated by the work of later critics such as Ellen Moers, Elaine Showalter, Sandra Gilbert, Susan Gubar and many others, is the steady rediscovery and republication of a host of women writers from earlier periods. To take a random example, the work of the early-seventeenth-century poet Aemilia Lanyer, *Salve Deus Rex Judaeorum* (Hail God, King of the Jews) has recently been re-issued in a scholarly edition;[8] and individual poems from it are included in two important new anthologies: *The New Oxford Book of Seventeenth-Century Verse* (1991)[9] and *The Penguin Book of Renaissance Verse* (1992).[10] As well as contributing to the original impetus behind such revisionist republishing ventures, Woolf's analysis of women's writing from the time of Shakespeare to her own is of use to us when we begin to read writers such as Lanyer. Woolf draws attention to the problematic theme of female friendship in women's writing; to the anger and resentment of male dominance which is either expressed or carefully repressed in many pre-twentieth-century texts by women; and to the vernacular language and absence of learned allusions in women's literature: this, Woolf points out, is a reflection not of any supposed intellectual inadequacy on the part of women but a consequence of society's refusal to educate them. Lanyer, we notice, addresses most of her poems to women, challenging the reader to reconsider certain conventional views of women's failings, and, by the by, proving that, contrary to Woolf's assumption, some seventeenth-century women were indeed extremely well-read.

Woolf's essay is, therefore, a highly suggestive one for feminist critics and theorists, and it is this aspect of criticism and theory – their suggestiveness – which is more important than any other. Criticism and theory offer us new – sometimes radical – ways of reading, and we are able to select and adapt from them as our own critical theories evolve, ensuring that our work remains reflective, rigorous and self-conscious.

My second example of a work which invites literature students to revise substantively their assumptions was published much more recently: *Political Shakespeare*,[11] edited by Jonathan Dollimore and Alan Sinfield. This book is a good example of the fusion of criticism and theory since most of its contributors are concerned both to challenge traditional methods of reading and teaching Shakespeare and also to demonstrate the consequences of their radical theory for individual readings of Shakespeare's plays. In addition, *Political Shakespeare* explicitly defines its political agenda – 'the transformation of a social order which exploits people on grounds of race, gender and class' (p. viii) – an agenda which we might choose to label as 'cultural materialist'. Cultural materialist critics and theorists have as one of their stated aims the foregrounding of the political and ideological assumptions underlying not only literature itself but also their own work and those of other critical and theoretical practices. In the foreword to *Political Shakespeare* Dollimore and Sinfield explain why:

> cultural materialism does not pretend to political neutrality. It knows that no cultural practice is ever without political significance – not the production of *King Lear* at the Globe, or at the Barbican, or as a text in a school, popular or learned edition, or in literary criticism, or in the present volume. Cultural materialism does not, like much established literary criticism, attempt to mystify its perspective as the natural, obvious or right interpretation of an allegedly given textual fact. (p. viii)

This assertion of the fundamentally partisan nature of what has been thought of by many as a branch of objective and disinterested scholarship is a perfect illustration of the value of reading criticism and theory alongside 'primary' works of literature (I insert the quotation marks here to signal what is becoming increasingly clear as we investigate the more innovative critics and theorists: that the distinction we erect between primary and secondary texts is often artificial). Whether or not we share Dollimore and Sinfield's specific ideological commitments, and whether or not we decide to accept the individual interpretations of Shakespeare offered in their collection of essays, none of us is able to ignore the point that criticism too often involves an evasion of its underlying implications. If we are to meet the challenge offered by Dollimore and Sinfield we must begin to critique our own interpretative methods and outline their ideological assumptions and political significance unequivocally: to do otherwise is to vindicate the charge in *Political Shakespeare* that literary criticism all too often cries out for demystification.

My third example is the essay 'The Intentional Fallacy' by the American New Critics W. K. Wimsatt and Monroe C. Beardsley.[12] New Criticism has been largely overtaken in literary studies by more recent and more self-conscious critical and theoretical movements, but Wimsatt's work demonstrates that issues raised long ago may still provoke debate and still require us to articulate our guiding critical principles with care and exactitude. Wimsatt argues persuasively for the irrelevance of authorial intention for those attempting to evaluate literary texts. This intention is, he points out, impossible to understand conclusively, but even if we could be certain about an author's intention we would be no closer to evaluating the actual effects she or he achieves, both because there may be a 'shortfall' between the artist's conception and her or his execution and because we are unlikely to understand the historical context of the work in sufficient detail to respond to it exactly as the author originally intended. For example, we do not know for certain whether Shakespeare wrote *Richard II*, a play about the deposing of a monarch, as an oblique comment on the latter end of Elizabeth's reign and the possibility of her deposition, but many late-twentieth-century readers and theatregoers will be unaware of this aspect of Richard's possible significance and would prefer in any case to respond to the play in terms of its transcendent, timeless themes and qualities. Certainly we have no way of telling with any accuracy how Elizabethans might have viewed *Richard II*, or to what extent contemporary reactions may have varied from one individual to another: the range of possibilities includes an interpretation of the play as an attack on Elizabeth; as a defence of her; or as a treatment of kingship in the abstract.

It could be argued that Wimsatt's refutation of the 'intentional fallacy' looks increasingly shaky in the light of newly rehistoricised critical trends, including feminism and cultural materialism, both of which emphasise the need to understand the contexts of literary works and our responses to them. Yet Wimsatt reminds us that even if we do not subscribe to many of the tenets of New Criticism, our reply to them must be rational and responsible. At the very least 'The Intentional Fallacy' underlines for us the immense difficulty in establishing an author's motives or a text's original implications, and guards us against making oversimplistic assumptions about them.

This role of criticism and theory – to prompt you to ongoing self-examination about your procedures and preoccupations as students of literature – is especially true in the case of one of the most controversial critical and theoretical developments of the twentieth century, structuralism. The premise on which all structuralist studies, whether anthropological, linguistic or literary, are based – that meaning is always derived from the place of an utterance or act within a system – transforms cultural studies because it reveals that our beliefs and value-systems are constructed and maintained through convention. Language governs our perceptions of what we term 'reality'; it could be argued that, strictly speaking, there is no reality prior or external to language. Equally, a literary text does not depict a world which exists *outside* language. Since the only world we know is the one mediated through language and other systems of meaning, the meaning of a literary text is not inherent but exists only as part of a system or 'langue' (as the Swiss linguist Ferdinand de Saussure termed it). Since the author was thus seen as unable to operate outside existing literary and linguistic conventions, Roland Barthes could, in 1977, proclaim the 'Death of the Author', explaining that 'The text is a tissue of quotations drawn from the innumerable centres of culture'.[13] Charles Dickens's *Great Expectations* (1860–1), for example, exploits certain narrative techniques which we may choose to denote as 'realist' but the novel is in fact as stylised and dependent on convention as the most avant-garde of fictional texts. Certain narrative techniques are by consensus understood in certain ways, so that, for example, Dickens has no need to give plausible psychological reasons for his hero's detailed and lengthy autobiography: Pip's account is just what we expect to encounter when we open a novel, and hence we need no one to tell us who the narrating 'I' is at the beginning of the story. Structuralist theory, then, recognises that characters in literature are not to be regarded as 'real' people: they are fictional constructs which we simply choose to view as more or less 'rounded' personalities. We can see that structuralism is particularly useful when we try to make sense of, say, the narrator of Jonathan Swift's *Gulliver's Travels* (1726), who is not a very credible creation in terms of human motive and feeling but who makes perfect sense if we view him as the mouthpiece for a satirical exploration of certain moral and social issues.

More radical and perhaps disturbing is the challenge posed by structuralism to the very notion of individual people – let alone fictional characters – as stable and independent entities. Since the Renaissance, Western culture has promoted individualism, which the critic Ian Watt has defined as 'the idea of every individual's intrinsic independence both from other individuals and from the multifarious allegiance to past modes of thought and action denoted by the word "tradition" '.[14] Watt's implication is that individualism ignores or denies the fact that individuals are the product of tradition, and he goes on to identify the ideology which profits from this denial and from the privileging of the 'economic individual':

> Capitalism brought a great increase of economic specialization; and this, combined with a less rigid and homogeneous social structure, and a less absolutist and more democratic political system, enormously increased the individual's freedom of choice. For those fully exposed to the new economic order, the effective entity on which social arrangements were now based was no longer the family, nor the church, nor the guild, nor the township, nor any other collective unit, but the individual: he alone was primarily responsible for determining his own economic, social, political, and religious roles. (p. 67)

Watt has already identified a political and economic function for individualism, then, but it was to be the task of structuralists and post-structuralists to attack explicitly the humanist belief in the individual. These critics and theorists went on to argue that the individual is an unconscious product of various cultural and ideological practices, and that consciousness is neither coherent nor autonomous. An example of this 'decentring of the subject' is in the area of gender studies where gender and sexuality are seen to be constructed socially rather than to be 'essential'.

Clearly structuralism is at odds with common sense, and it is precisely this which constitutes its usefulness. Structuralism and post-structuralism require us to scrutinise many of the assumptions we take for granted, and incidentally to begin to unravel some of the coercive functions of humanism. With structuralism, as Terry Eagleton puts it:

> The confident bourgeois belief that the isolated individual subject was the fount and origin of all meaning took a sharp knock: language pre-dated the individual, and was much less his or her product than he or she was the product of it. Meaning was not 'natural', a question of just looking and seeing, or something eternally settled; the way you interpreted your world was a function of the languages you had at your disposal, and there was evidently nothing immutable about these.[15]

Eagleton welcomes the resistance structuralism offers to intellectual complacency, but he goes on to question the political commitment of a theory which privileges form over content so absolutely that the meaning of a text is discarded in favour of tracing and classifying the structural relationships of its narrative components. His objection highlights one of the reasons why we read theory and criticism: to enable us to follow and engage with current intellectual controversies. We may turn either by design or chance from Eagleton to Paul De Man's equally persuasive essay, 'The Resistance to Theory' and note that De Man's response to critics such as Eagleton is to defend post-structuralism's fundamental opposition to (repressive) ideology. De Man argues that it is precisely because post-structuralism unmasks the deceptions practised by ideology and shows reality to be constructed rather than transcendent that we need to retain it at the centre of literature studies: 'In a genuine semiology as well as in other linguistically oriented theories, the referential function of language is not being denied – far from it; what is in question is its authority as a model for natural or phenomenal recognition.'[16]

And from De Man we might move in turn to A. D. Nuttall's provocatively titled *A New Mimesis: Shakespeare and the representation of reality* which insists on the mimetic function of literature and which finds that Jacques Derrida's decentring of the subject had been anticipated – and partially but crucially refuted – by the philosopher David Hume in the eighteenth century. Hume knew that there is no 'single being which we can recognize as a self' but also that 'if the Self is not forthcoming, there is still experience'.[17] For Nuttall the scepticism of post-structuralists such as Derrida and De Man is arid and destructive, but also disingenuous in the charge of conservatism which it levels at its opponents. Socialism, Nuttall points out, requires a 'conservative' (p. 38) belief in 'meaning and reason' (p. 192): *logical* conservatism, a belief in the referentiality of literature, is not, as the post-structuralists would have it, the same as *political* conservatism.

I have followed some of the arguments and counter-arguments which structuralism and post-structuralism have prompted in order to suggest that practising criticism and theory is a process which is without intellectual or chronological end. There are certainly some critics and theorists who maintain their adherence to a position which for others has been effectively superseded – there are still some classical structuralists who are exclusively devoted to questions of narratology, for example – but most critics and theorists envisage their work as part of a continual project of cultural and theoretical investigation. The prefaces of some works of criticism and theory illustrate this provisionality very well. In 1975 Jonathan Culler began his *Structuralist Poetics* with the hope that he would 'show how such a poetics emerges from structuralism . . . indicate what it has already achieved, and . . . sketch *what it might become*' (my emphasis).[18] David Lodge makes a broader claim for theory in general, but places a similar emphasis to Culler's on the currency and immediate relevance of theoretical debate: 'The aim of the collective enterprise would appear to be nothing less than a totalizing account of human consciousness and human culture (or else a tireless demonstration of the impossibility of such a project).'[19] We have already seen that a sense of political urgency prompts Jonathan Dollimore and Alan Sinfield to offer their criticism in the service of an explicit agenda; and feminist criticism is likewise conscious of its participation in contemporary re-envisionings of history and society. Clare Brant and Diane Purkiss's *Women, Texts and Histories* explains that 'this collection and all its contributors are part of a general feminist project to reshape perceptions of the early modern period by replacing women in it.'[20] For the Black critic and theorist Henry Louis Gates part of the value of contemporary theory is its refusal of a monolithic approach: '*Black Literature and Literary Theory* is not a programmatic manifesto announcing a unified set of responses to these questions. Indeed, I have edited it carefully to reveal the *diversity* of the criticism practised by these citizens of literature.'[21]

Gates's rationale serves to introduce my fifth and final example of the uses of criticism and theory, postcolonialism. Postcolonialism illustrates rather differently the way in which the insights of critics and theorists may oblige us to revise our views of what we had assumed was reality. The most influential postcolonialist writer is Edward Said, whose *Orientalism*[22] confronted European and North American readers with the realisation that their time-hallowed 'world picture' was profoundly and unselfconsciously racist, ignoring or distorting the experience of non-'Western' peoples. In the years since the publication of *Orientalism* there have been new and radical reformations of the literary canon in order to make it more inclusive; re-readings of the traditional canon in order to analyse its representation of people of colour; and the transference of Said's conclusions about Western perpetuations of 'Orientalism' to other relationships between the Western and non-Western worlds. The Orientalist critique has become paradigmatic for all studies of culture and literature which seek to avoid the errors and occlusions of Eurocentric criticism.

Said and successive postcolonialists have led European readers to question more thoroughly the portrayal of, say, Black characters in Renaissance English drama, or Indian figures in eighteenth-century English fiction, and to turn their attention increasingly to the work of writers of other literatures in English. Within a few years it has become an embarrassment to talk of 'Commonwealth literature' or to overlook the implications of imperialist rhetoric in Elizabethan plays, eighteenth-century poetry and nineteenth-century novels. Postcolonialism has changed for ever the study of literature in the West since, like all the critical and theoretical movements I have discussed here, it has raised questions which cannot be dismissed about how and what we read.

Perhaps because criticism and theory are potentially so explosive, threatening to shatter our cherished notions about why we study literature, students may remain wary of them and prefer to work around them rather than with them. Such hesitancy is understandable, for although I have here touched on some of the more accessible and populist ideas we can derive from reading criticism and theory, actually tackling some critical and theoretical works in their original form may produce at best only dim and flickering illumination of a writer's thought. In the third section of this chapter, therefore, I shall suggest some practical solutions to the difficulties of reading criticism and theory, the rewards of which, I would argue, compensate for any initial experience we might have of indigestibility.

How do we read criticism and theory?

In the first section of this chapter I discussed the 'jargon' which arguably obtrudes between text and reader in some works of criticism and theory, and suggested that this language usually functions as a shorthand which is convenient for the specialist though it may exasperate the non-specialist. As mentioned in Chapter 1, the obvious first task, therefore, for those wishing to extend their critical and theoretical reading is to acquire a vocabulary of literary and theoretical terms, since like all authors, critics and theorists will be unintelligible to us unless we familiarise ourselves with their language.

To a certain extent reading criticism and enlarging our critical vocabularies go hand-in-hand, but there is no shortage of dictionaries, glossaries and guides available to the student. These range from very basic reference books with brief, unproblematic entries for such terms as 'irony', 'metaphor' and 'heroic couplet', to more ambitious readers which give potted accounts of theoretical trends alongside definitions of standard critical terms, and from these to substantial works containing original essays on aspects of literary theory which assume a knowledge of critical terms on the part of the reader. All three kinds are useful, and a selection of them is given in the section on further reading below, but it is clearly unwise to rely exclusively on a textbook which oversimplifies complex ideas or on one which does not define the terms which are puzzling us. Only by attempting to work with such reference books will you discover their uses and limitations, and begin to determine at what level you need to approach critical and theoretical concepts.

Your technical vocabulary will expand automatically as you widen your reading of criticism and theory, and finding works of criticism and theory beyond those listed in course bibliographies also happens automatically to a certain extent. Independent study involves following up leads: one book will contain references which point you to others; or will be found on the library shelf next to others which deal with related topics; or may be located in an online catalogue search by subject or author. You may be directed to critical and theoretical books when you find them reviewed in newspapers or specialist journals, and finding past reviews of such books is straightforward if you have access to newspaper indices on CD-ROM. Serendipity, however, plays an important part in forming an individual's reading, and we all need to spend time browsing in libraries so that we can discover where to look for material: in essay collections and periodicals as well as in monographs; in books relating to disciplines other than literature (such as history, art and media studies); and in non-printed media such as audio cassettes and videos. You should also use criticism and theory selectively, taking down accurate references for quotations and seeking to understand and paraphrase an author's arguments but also suppressing the urge to read a work in its entirety if time is short. By consulting a book's contents pages and index it should be possible to identify those sections which will be of most use, and the other sections can either be ignored, skimmed or set aside for further study at a later time.

Although it is evident that some critical works are principally useful as sources of empirical data about an author, a text or a historical period, most secondary reading provides a mixture of fact, criticism and theory in varying proportions. I have already stressed that criticism and theory are inextricably linked, and it is as reductive to skip theoretical prefaces and introductions as it is to dismiss critical writing out of hand from a sense that it is somehow less rigorous than theoretical material. The most successful students will engage with a variety of critical and theoretical texts, thereby learning both how to produce perceptive analysis and simultaneously how to critique their analytical methods.

My emphasis throughout this chapter has been on criticism and theory as sources for stimulating ideas about the nature and function of reading literature, and this is especially pertinent in the light of strictures from examiners and assessors on the perils of plagiarising published critics in examination scripts and coursework essays. As is made clear in Chapter 3, raiding secondary works for material to pad out an essay is neither intellectually rewarding nor likely to find favour with those marking essays. For a number of reasons, then, criticism and theory should not be used to substitute for your own ideas, and not only because you need to produce original work for the purposes of passing courses, but also because intellectual satisfaction comes from your own interpretations, and because works of criticism and theory are intended not to elicit your blanket approval but to make you question and reflect. Practising criticism and theory should not mean learning to apply a single methodology whilst ruthlessly excluding all others from our terms of reference; it is about learning to modify, revise and continually refine our opinions about what constitutes the study of literature.

Practising criticism and theory

Scrutinising our assumptions as critics and theorists means we must ask questions about our preoccupations, preferences and implicit value-judgements. These are embedded in personal reading choices, both as regards formal course requirements and beyond them, including 'popular' texts, non-fiction, newspapers and magazines. As a student of literature you also need to question the critical and theoretical attitudes of your fellow-students, and your teachers and lecturers. You need to try to understand the reasons for the selections involved in the creation of your course by an institution or an individual: why, for example, 'Literature in English' (not 'English Literature' or 'European Literature'); or why 'The Victorian Novel' (and not 'Nineteenth-Century Prose Narratives'); or 'Renaissance Drama from 1580 to 1700' (not 'Renaissance Literature from 1600 to 1700')? Sometimes reflecting on the period boundaries of your course will help you to understand an apparently arbitrary chronological marker. 1580 allows the inclusion of Marlowe and all of Shakespeare's plays in a study of Renaissance drama, for example. Sometimes a seemingly irrational adjective in a course title can be seen to have important implications: thus 'British' rather than 'English' alerts us to the presence of texts by Irish, Welsh and Scottish writers on a reading list. Equally, course parameters may reveal conscious or unconscious bias on the part of those who design them: 'Language and Gender in Contemporary American Fiction' clearly indicates that this is a course which addresses constructs of femininity and masculinity in literature; while 'The Rise of the Novel: 1688 to 1800' implies that the novel will be seen to

have developed formally over a historical period and also, perhaps, to
have consolidated its literary status relative to other genres.

Since course titles and programmes are presented to you in written
form and are by definition limited in scope, analysing the critical assumptions which underpin them is a relatively straightforward affair. Things
may seem rather more complicated when you begin to assess your tutors'
assumptions as conveyed in lectures, class discussions and comments on
your written work. Recognising the assumptions inherent in the opinions
of your fellow-students may be still more difficult, partly because a class
of ten, twenty or a hundred people will contain perhaps as many diverse
and even conflicting critical and theoretical viewpoints. It becomes obvious that some students belong identifiably to one or other critical or
theoretical camp, and clashes of opinion between rival perspectives can
give rise to some of the most engaging literary debates you will experience. Some women students will demand a reading of a text which is
sensitive to gender politics; others will draw attention to the social snob-
beries contained within a text which some readers perceive as entirely
universalist and unbiased. A teacher or lecturer might find her approach
to, say, Daniel Defoe's *Robinson Crusoe* (1719) or Joseph Conrad's *Heart
of Darkness* (1902) radically affected by studying them with classes which
include people of colour.

Because questions of gender, class and ethnicity are politically inflam-
matory outside the seminar room or lecture hall as well as within it, you
are likely to be on the alert for sexist, classist and racist prejudices when
they are manifested in the critical and theoretical remarks made by yourself, by other students and by teachers and lecturers. Other prejudices are
less easy to detect, often because they are virtually universal. For example, Terry Eagleton has written regarding the impact of the critic
F. R. Leavis that.

> There is no more need to be a card-carrying Leavisite today than there is
> to be a card-carrying Copernican: that current has entered the bloodstream
> of English studies in England as Copernicus reshaped our astronomical
> beliefs, has become a form of spontaneous critical wisdom as deep-seated
> as our conviction that the earth moves round the sun. (*Literary Theory: An
> introduction*, p. 31)

As this suggests, it will require special vigilance to identify your own
automatic deference to and rearticulation of Leavisite notions of, say, the
moral and intellectual pre-eminence of literature in society, or the feasi-

bility of a scientifically objective critical practice. These are ideas which form the basis of your decision to study literature and which you may not have thought you would ever need to justify. Alternatively you may feel that the charge of cultural elitism which his opponents have levelled at Leavis is so substantial a criticism that we no longer need to take seriously the English curriculum he proposed. Few college courses now adhere to Leavis's narrowly prescriptive canon of 'great' novelists. None the less, students still sometimes express a preference for 'Literature' over 'literature', and such preferences demand both reasoned explanation and an appropriately reasoned response.

As you learn to question and analyse the assumptions embedded in the choice of texts on your course and the discussions provoked by them you will also acquire an enhanced understanding of your own critical and theoretical interventions in such discussions, whether written or spoken. You may feel a passionate commitment to the works of a particular author, and gradually gain the assurance to justify it. You may feel, for instance, that the autobiography of Vera Brittain is unfairly neglected in literature courses relative to the work of contemporary male poets such as Siegfried Sassoon and Wilfred Owen. Or you may feel that John Webster and Thomas Middleton are as interesting as Shakespeare; or that literature courses generally make insufficient acknowledgment of the relationships between literary works and other art forms such as music and painting. You may also begin to flinch from some of your own less defensible critical and theoretical assumptions when you try to find an intellectual justification for them. What are your criteria for evaluating texts, and are they vulnerable to the very charge of subjectivity you might wish to avoid?

I do not want to imply that this self-examination is a simple and once-only matter; as I have said, you should expect and strive to revise and redefine your standpoint whenever you study literature. Studying literature over time promotes self-awareness, for you will start to realise that you have been more fascinated by certain ideas and issues than others, and ask yourself why this should be so. Certain aspects of literature will preoccupy you, while others will not: in writing on topics as diverse as pastoral or modernism you may find you are continuing an ongoing debate with yourself about the nature of realism, for example. You may feel an acknowledged personal investment in feminist criticism or postcolonialism. You may value literature primarily for its illuminations of human psychology, and wish to make this point expressly at the outset of any critical essay you write. You may, however, come to re-evaluate your earlier preferences for certain literary qualities rather than others, and wonder exactly what it was that you found so admirable in ambiguity, complexity, profundity or coherence – or, indeed, wish to reassert their importance, but from a sound theoretical base.

At the beginning of this chapter I emphasised that criticism and theory are inseparable, in the sense that criticism is always based on certain theoretical pre-suppositions and theory is only produced as a response to certain problems raised by criticism. And if theory and practice cannot be divorced, we would be mistaken if we thought it possible first to 'decide on' a theory and then to apply it to every text we read and studied. Such a procedure is, in fact, impossible, since theories do not appear from nowhere and they inevitably reflect our prior experience of literature. It is also an undesirable way of going on, and at odds with the central purpose of criticism and theory: to oblige us to think about what we do and guard against critical passivity (it is revealing that this last phrase is something of an oxymoron). Almost all the most creative and influential critics and theorists have altered their stances in the course of their careers, and express indignation when other writers unproblematically label them as belonging to this 'school' or that 'movement'.

To return to the earlier examples I gave of critical and theoretical texts which have had a significant impact on literary studies: we saw how such texts not only argue with one another (De Man with his Marxist opponents, for example, or Eagleton with the post-structuralists) but also how they initiate what we might term a dialogue with their readers. I shall conclude with an example of a critical issue which is very far from being resolved: how we go about studying women's writing. No less today than when it was first published, Woolf's *A Room of One's Own* exhilarates the reader with its call to arms:

> Therefore I would ask you to write all kinds of books, hesitating at no subject however trivial or however vast. By hook or by crook, I hope that you will possess yourselves of money enough to travel and to idle, to contemplate the future or the past of the world, to dream over books and loiter at street corners and let the line of thought dip deep into the stream. (p. 107)

The rhetorical power of this is undiminished by the decades since *A Room of One's Own* was first published. But from Woolf the newly politicised reader is likely to go on to explore a number of later critics, and then to discover that at some point feminist literary studies appear to have diverged in a number of directions. Elaine Showalter's *A Literature*

of Their Own[23] refers explicitly to Woolf in its title, and Showalter
alongside other critics has taken Woolf's essay as the starting-point for
what has been termed 'gynocritics'. Gynocritics asserts the individuality
of women's writing, its distinct preoccupations by contrast with those of
texts by men, its reflection of a female literary tradition entirely separate
to that of the mainstream, and even its exploitation of sentence structures
which are unique to women writers.

The brilliance of many works belonging to the gynocritics tradition,
such as Adrienne Rich's 'When We Dead Awaken: Writing As Re-
Vision',[24] Ellen Moers's *Literary Women*,[25] and Sandra Gilbert and Susan
Gubar's *The Madwoman in the Attic*[26] are likely to have an increased
impact on the reader in the context of closely related and widely dispersed
texts on non-literary feminist issues. Betty Friedan, Kate Millett, Ger-
maine Greer and popular novelists such as Marilyn French and Alice
Walker, have given currency to many of the ideas fundamental to gynocritics: that women's experience and, therefore, women's writing, are distinct
from men's, and that while women may have been excluded by patriarchal
systems of power from the dominant culture (literary or otherwise), they
have maintained a strong and succouring tradition of their own.

Yet gynocritics does not answer all the questions which may occur to
the feminist reader, such as the viability of defining what a female sentence might be; the extent to which female traditions can be recon-
structed for historical periods which leave us few records of women's
experience; and the nature of the relationship which exists between writing by women and writing by men. Gynocritics is also problematic in that
it supposes a continuity of experience between women of widely different
social, economic and ethnic backgrounds. From gynocritics, therefore,
the feminist reader may turn in a number of directions, for there is no
single dominant school with which to identify at the present time. She
may move towards what has been called 'feminist materialism', an approach which combines feminism with Marxism and which therefore
attempts to rehabilitate a progressive theory which has too often ignored
questions of gender. Or she may turn to the endlessly fascinating writings
of the French theorists Hélène Cixous, Julia Kristeva and Luce Irigaray
who rewrite Freudian and Lacanian psychoanalytic theories for the
woman writer and reader.

Whatever your critical preferences you should recognise that you are
not studying literature simply for its own sake but as part of wider
struggles about meaning and interpretation. Your class discussions and
written papers are a reflection of and contribution to such struggles and

can be related directly to them if you are sufficiently self-conscious about your practices as students of literature. A recent president of the Modern Language Association of America, one of the largest professional organisations for language and literature studies in the world, described his sudden perception that criticism and theory should aspire to what he terms 'a rigorous local pedagogy'; in other words, that teaching and learning about literature should take into account the particular contexts in which these activities take place. Houston A. Baker urges us to relate our readings of, for example, slave poetry to our own lives; for his own students this is 'as black women on the campus of the University of Pennsylvania'.[27] He explains that: 'Such a pedagogy draws on cultural studies propositions about "inside" and "outside" textualities; it assumes that local mapping cannot be separated from the development of anything approaching useful and practical reading skills for the twenty-first century' (p. 406). This sort of assertion may seem almost intimidating in its emphasis on the immediate relevance of your studies to your personal and political situations, but it also adds a new and exciting resonance to the educational term 'empowerment'.

Whichever critical and theoretical questions are currently vexing or beguiling us, we are all conscious of the need to answer certain pressing but seemingly insoluble problems concerning the nature of literature and society. If we all agree that literature is a good thing, none of us can say precisely why this is, or offer any satisfactory explanation of how literature can help us to remedy social injustice, end wars, halt nuclear proliferation, or promote environmental awareness, even though, when confronted, most of us would probably agree that one function of literature is, or should be, the betterment of society. Because these huge questions are crucial both to us as students of literature, and to society as a whole, they are bound to continue to generate strenuous and sometimes impassioned debate, and so ensure that criticism and theory retain their prominence in literature studies far into the future.

Notes

1. Tzvetan Todorov, *Genres in Discourse*, trans. Catherine Porter (Cambridge: Cambridge U.P., 1990).
2. Roland Barthes, 'Textual Analysis of Poe's 'Valdemar'' (1973), reprinted in David Lodge (ed.), *Modern Criticism and Theory* (London: Longman, 1988), pp. 172–95.

3. William Empson, *The Structure of Complex Words* (London: Chatto and Windus, 1951).

4. Raymond Williams, *Culture and Society 1780–1950* (London: Chatto and Windus, 1958).

5. Gillian Beer, *Darwin's Plots: Evolutionary narrative in Darwin, George Eliot and nineteenth-century fiction* (London: Routledge, 1983).

6. This example is discussed by John Guillory, 'Canon', in *Critical Terms for Literary Study*, eds Frank Lentricchia and Thomas McLaughlin (Chicago: Chicago U.P., 1990), pp. 233–49 (pp. 247–8); Guillory draws on the suggestions of Arthur Marotti in *John Donne: Coterie poet* (Madison: Wisconsin U.P., 1986).

7. Virginia Woolf, *A Room of One's Own* (1929; repr. Harmondsworth: Penguin, 1945).

8. *The Poems of Aemilia Lanyer: Salve Deus Rex Judaeorum*, ed. Susanne Woods (Oxford: Oxford U.P., 1993).

9. *The New Oxford Book of Seventeenth Century Verse*, ed. Alastair Fowler (Oxford: Oxford U.P., 1991).

10. *The Penguin Book of Renaissance Verse 1509–1659*, selected and with an introduction by David Norbrook, ed. by H. R. Woudhuysen (London: Penguin, 1992).

11. *Political Shakespeare: New essays in cultural materialism*, ed. Jonathan Dollimore and Alan Sinfield (Manchester: Manchester U.P., 1985).

12. W. K. Wimsatt and Monroe C. Beardsley, 'The Intentional Fallacy' (1946), repr. in Wimsatt, *The Verbal Icon: Studies in the meaning of poetry* (London: Methuen, 1970), pp. 3–18.

13. Roland Barthes, 'The Death of the Author' (1977), repr. in Lodge (ed.) *Modern Criticism*, p. 170.

14. Ian Watt, *The Rise of the Novel: Studies in Defoe, Richardson and Fielding* (1957; repr. Harmondsworth: Peregrine, 1983), p. 66.

15. Terry Eagleton, *Literary Theory: An introduction* (Oxford: Basil Blackwell, 1983), p. 107.

16. Paul De Man, 'The Resistance to Theory' (1982), repr. in Lodge (ed.) *Modern Criticism*, pp. 355–71.

17. A. D. Nuttall, *A New Mimesis: Shakespeare and the representation of reality* (London: Methuen, 1983), p. 29.

18. Jonathan Culler, *Structuralist Poetics: Structuralism, linguistics and the study of literature* (Ithaca, New York: Cornell U.P., 1975), p. viii.

19. David Lodge (ed.), *Modern Criticism and Theory* (London: Longman, 1988), p. xi.

20. Clare Brant and Diane Purkiss (eds), *Women, Texts and Histories 1575–1760* (London: Routledge, 1992), p. 9.

21. Henry Louis Gates (ed.), *Black Literature and Literary Theory* (New York: Methuen, 1984), p. 3.

22. Edward Said, *Orientalism* (London: Routledge, 1978).
23. Elaine Showalter, *A Literature of Their Own* (London: Virago, 1977).
24. Adrienne Rich, 'When We Dead Awaken: Writing as Re-Vision', *College English*, 34, no. 1 (1972), 18–25, reprinted in *Adrienne Rich's Poetry*, selected and ed. Barbara Charlesworth Gelpi and Albert Gelpi (New York: W. W. Norton, 1975).
25. Ellen Moers, *Literary Women* (1976; repr. London: The Women's Press, 1978).
26. Sandra Gilbert and Susan Gubar, *The Madwoman in the Attic: The Woman Writer and the Nineteenth Century Literary Imagination* (New Haven, Conn.: Yale U.P., 1976).
27. Houston A. Baker, 'Local Pedagogy; or, How I Redeemed My Spring Semester', *Publications of the Modern Language Association*, 108, no. 3 (1993), 400–9.

Further reading

Abrams, M. H., *A Glossary of Literary Terms*, 6th edn (Fort Worth, Tex.: Harcourt, Brace, Jovanovich College Publishers, 1993). (This glossary contains definitions of literary terms and a section with brief, clear accounts of modern critical theories. Introductory level.)

Eagleton, T., *Literary Theory: An introduction* (Oxford: Basil Blackwell, 1983). (Arguably still the most lucid and engaging account of modern criticism and theory, though some recent developments such as cultural materialism post-date this early survey.)

Easthope, A., *British Post-Structuralism Since 1968* (London: Routledge, 1988). (Explores the impact of post-structuralism on English and American culture, including film, the social sciences, music, philosophy and literature.)

Greenblatt, S. and Gunn, G. (eds), *Redrawing the Boundaries: The transformation of English and American literary studies* (New York: The Modern Language Association of America, 1992). (Leading critics summarise current preoccupations in period studies and various theoretical fields.)

Hawthorn, J., *A Concise Glossary of Contemporary Literary Theory* (London: Edward Arnold, 1992). (Despite its title, a comprehensive and sophisticated dictionary of current terms.)

Humm, M. (ed.), *Feminisms: A reader* (Hemel Hempstead: Harvester Wheatsheaf, 1992). (A valuable anthology reflecting the cultural and philosophical diversity of twentieth-century feminist theories.)

Lentricchia, F. and McLaughlin, T. (eds), *Critical Terms for Literary Study* (Chicago: Chicago U.P., 1990). (A stimulating and wide-ranging collection of short essays by prominent North American critics and theorists on key terms and concepts such as 'discourse', 'canon' and 'gender'.)

Lodge, D., *Working With Structuralism: Essays and reviews on nineteenth- and twentieth-century literature* (London: Routledge, 1981). (A helpful and accessible collection of structuralist readings.)

Lodge, D. (ed.), *Twentieth Century Criticism: A reader* (London: Longman, 1972). (An anthology of twentieth-century criticism up to 1966.)

Lodge, D. (ed.), *Modern Criticism and Theory: A reader* (London, Longman, 1988). (An anthology of major interventions in twentieth-century literary theory usefully arranged so that they may be read either in historical or thematic order.)

Marshall, D.G., *Contemporary Critical Theory: A selective bibliography* (New York: The Modern Language Association of America, 1993). (An overview of the major critical theories in terms of their most significant texts and authors. The latest citations are from works published in 1990.)

Sarup, M., *An Introductory Guide to Post-Structuralism and Postmodernism*, 2nd edn (Hemel Hempstead: Harvester Wheatsheaf, 1993). (A concise study which focuses exclusively on recent theorists such as Lacan, Foucault, Cixous, Irigaray, Kristeva, Lyotard and Baudrillard.)

Selden, R., *Practising Theory and Reading Literature: An introduction* (Hemel Hempstead: Harvester Wheatsheaf, 1989). (Selden briefly describes a range of critical approaches, and then illustrates them by applying them to various literary texts. Further exercises for the reader are included at the back of the book.)

Selden, R. and Widdowson, P., *A Reader's Guide to Contemporary Literary Theory*, 3rd edn (Hemel Hempstead: Harvester Wheatsheaf, 1993). (A more up-to-date but less readable introduction than Eagleton's.)

Conclusion

As students of literature where do you go from here? Clearly, much of what the future holds in store will depend on the precise nature of the programme you are following, on the exact stage you have reached within it and on the options available to you. With the widespread advent of semester-length modules many degree programmes involving literary studies offer a bewildering array of choices and combinations. In a good number of institutions now the student is able to shape the direction she wishes her studies to take. But whether you are in a college or university where the syllabus is very traditional, or in one where the courses on offer are radically innovative, or (perhaps most likely) operating in a framework which lies somewhere in between these two extremes, it will to a large extent be up to you to decide how you want to approach the study of literature over the next few years. One of the main aims in writing this book has been to force this realisation upon you. There are many possible critical positions, approaches and perspectives where the study of literature is concerned and they each have their associated sets of assumptions, ideas and values. There really is no critical practice without theory, as has been pointed out before now.[1] And it is important that you appreciate the significance of this fact if you are to be enabled and empowered as a student of literature.

Try to be as clear and explicit as possible – certainly to yourself, and preferably to others as well – about your interests, your values, your theoretical position, your critical approach. For many this may involve expressing frankly a large measure of uncertainty and scepticism not to say confusion. There is nothing wrong with any of this. Resist the intellectually lazy option, however tempting it may seem. Thinking your way through the competing claims of different theoretical and critical stances is not easy, admittedly. The Scylla and Charybdis of contemporary literary theory and criticism are the stubborn refusal to take account of recent critical and theoretical developments on the one hand, and the hasty and disingenuous adoption of the latest fashionable orthodoxy on the other hand. Ivan Turgenev, in a letter to Leo Tolstoy, wrote:

> Systems are only valued by those who do not possess the whole truth and want to grab it by the tail. A system is like truth's tail and truth is like a lizard – it will leave its tail in your hand, knowing very well that another will grow in its place.[2]

Perhaps there is something to be said for not striving for consistency too eagerly, too impatiently. Helpful as 'either/or' ways of thinking can be, the 'both/and' approach has its claims too. Ideas compete for our attention, but they can also be regarded as complementing and qualifying each other. While we are not recommending relativism, we would certainly wish to suggest that a healthy, open pluralism has much in its favour in that an awareness of the differences between critical positions, and of the issues that generate conflict and debate, if it encourages readers to think critically about their own practice is not something to be lightly dismissed. Most readers, after all, are intellectually in transit, outgrowing some positions, trying on for size a different set of opinions, feeling their way towards a tentative formulation which, they hope, will do greater justice to their complex sense of how reality is.

Finally, it is worth reiterating the belief that reading literature is – or should be – first and foremost a pleasurable activity, and that much of the pleasure depends on engaging critically with the literary text, and attending to detail as well as to the whole. It is, moreover, essentially interpretational in nature, and the most productive reading experiences are surely those where the reader interacts with the poem or novel or play creatively, dynamically and self-reflexively, alive both to the problematical, unstable nature of the text's medium – language – and to the complexities of both the context and the reading process itself. And if reading literature can be pleasurable, so too, we would argue, should be the activity of studying literature.

Notes

1. See Catherine Belsey, *Critical Practice* (London: Routledge, 1989), p. 4.
2. Quoted by Glyn Turton in *Turgenev and the Context of English Literature 1850–1900* (London and New York: Routledge, 1992), p. 115.

Index

Abrams, M. H., 14, 133
academy, 199
accent, 76, 80, 81
Adcock, F., 120
'A' level, xiv, 30, 71
Aitchison, J., 73
Albee, E., 179, 186
alliteration, 114
allusion, 14, 172, 202
anagnorisis, 187
anapaest, 133
anticipation, 165, 171
archaisms, 74, 137
Aristotle, 123, 127, 128
    Poetics, 125–6, 187, 197
Armitage, S., 129, 139
Arnold, M., 127–8
assertiveness, 22–3
attendance, 22
attitudes, 9–12
attitude studies, 83
Atwood, M., 172, 197
Auden, W. H., 91, 116, 121
audio-visual aids, 37, 193
Austen, J., 1, 11, 87, 171
    Emma, 99, 156, 158, 162, 163–4, 171
    Northanger Abbey, 151
    Persuasion, 101–2
Austin, J. L., 86
author, 102, 156, 159–60

death of, 205
autobiography, 150, 164–5, 205

Baker, H. A., 216
Bakhtin, M., 168, 199
Baldick, C., 137–8
Barthes, R., 197, 205
Bat Out of Hell, 28
Beardsley, M. C., 203–4
Beckett, S., 188
    Waiting for Godot, 103, 183, 189
Beer, G., 200
Beethoven, L. V., 37
behaviour, 18–23
Behn, A., 13
Bell, A., 85
Bible, 13, 14, 16
binary oppositions, 121–2, 123, 142, 147
biography, 61, 200–1
Birch, D., 178
Blake, W., 37, 89, 125
blank verse, 131, 142
Bond, E.
    Saved, 179, 182, 186
Booth, W. C., 160–1
Boulton, M., 13, 14
Bradford, R., 135
Brant, C., 208
Bridges, R., 89
Brittain, V., 213

Britten, B., 37
Brontë, C., 59
    Jane Eyre, 159, 162, 169, 200
    Villette, 11, 156, 164, 170
Brontë, E.
    Wuthering Heights, 105–7, 163
Browning, R., 137
Büchner, G.
    Woyzeck, 188
Byatt, A. S., 197
    Possession, 111
Byron, G. G., 137

canon, 2, 202, 208, 213
capitalism, 107, 206
caricature, 158
Carter, A., 197
    'The Snow Child', 5, 151–5
catharsis, 187
character, 36, 205
    'flat' and 'round', 158
    in prose fiction, 90, 153, 155, 163–4, 169
    in drama, 90, 181–4
    naming of, 157, 158
characterisation
    in prose, 156–9
Chaucer, G., 74, 87
    The House of Fame, 73
Chomsky, N., 77–8
Churchill, C.
    Top Girls, 183, 190
Churchill, W., 73, 145
Cixous, H., 215
class, 81, 203, 212
classicism, 122
closet drama, 190
Clough, A. H., 127–8, 137
code-switching, 83
cohesion, 90, 141
Coleridge, S. T., 126, 134, 197, 199
    'The Ancient Mariner', 37
colloquialisms, 63, 74, 145
Collins, W., 89, 95
communicative competence, 84
connotation, 136, 137
Conrad, J., 28, 212
context, 59, 101, 107–9, 115, 155, 201, 204
continuous assessment, 31, 39
creative writing, 2
creole, 82–3, 84
critical terms, 14, 209–10
criticism, 10, 57–9, 196–219
Culler, J., 207

cultural materialism, 203, 204
cummings, e. e., 89–90

dactyl, 133
Dalton, T. A., 72
Dante, A., 128, 197
Darwin, C., 200
deep structure, 78
defamiliarisation, 17
Defoe, D., 212
De Man, P., 206–7, 214
denotation, 136
denouement, 188
De Quincey, T., 185
Derrida, J., 108, 207
descriptivism, 72–76
diachronic, 81, 171
dialect, 15, 75, 76, 91, 145
dialogue
    as part of learning process, 25–6
    between reader and critical text, 214
    in drama, 90, 181–4
Dickens, C., 1, 25, 35, 95–6
    Bleak House, 157, 163
    Great Expectations, 95–6, 170, 205
    Hard Times, 57
diction, 116, 130, 142
    poetic, 135
diglossia, 83
direct speech, 167
discrimination, 11, 17
Dollimore, J., 202–3, 208
Donne, J., 109
    Songs and Sonets, 200–1
Doré, G., 37
Drabble, M., 15
drama
    derivation of word, 177
    distinguished from prose, 150
    semiotics of, 184–7
    structure and time in, 187–190
dramatic irony, 171–183
Dryden, J., 126
Du Maurier, D., 164–5
duration, 166

Eagleton, T., 102–3, 206–7, 212, 214
education, 12, 22, 23
elegy, 113
Eliot, G., 14, 197
    Adam Bede, 161
    Middlemarch, 20–1, 101, 159, 161
    The Mill on the Floss, 156, 168

Eliot, T. S., 26, 32, 38, 116, 128–9, 136–7, 197
Empson, W., 199–200
end-stopped, 142
enjambement, 142
essay, 34, 36, 38, 48–68, 76
  marking criteria of 49, 50, 55–9
  questions 50–4, 65–6
ethnicity, 81, 212
etymology, 15, 109
evaluation, 110–11, 169
exposition, 187–8

faction, 150
feminism, 202, 204, 208, 214–15
fiction, 150
figures of speech, 88, 130, 138
Fish, S., 103
Flaubert, G.
  Madame Bovary, 10
foregrounding, 17
Forster, E. M.
  Aspects of the Novel, 158, 169–70
  Howards End, 37, 98, 159–60, 161, 165, 166, 171
fourth-wall convention, 16
Fowler, H. W., 72
Fowles, J., 111, 170
Franklin, B., 19
free indirect style, 167
free variation, 82
French, M., 215
frequency, 165–6
Friedan, B., 215
Frost, R., 129

Gaskell, E., 51–4, 56
  North and South, 52, 56, 172
Gates, H. L., 208
gender, 81, 203, 206, 212
Genette, G., 164
genre, 87, 104, 150
Gissing, G., 61–2
Gilbert, S., 202, 215
grammar, 15, 64, 72, 75, 76–8, 79–80, 82, 88, 89, 132, 134–5, 137, 142
Gramsci, A., 198–9
Gray, T., 135
Greer, G., 215
Grice, H. P., 85, 86
Gubar, S., 202, 215
gynocritics, 215

half-rhyme, 131
Hardy, T., 91
Harrison, T., 120
  v., 139–40, 144–7
Hawthorne, N., 15
Heaney, S., 120, 124, 139
Heller, J.
  Catch 22, 30
heroic couplet, 131
higher education, xiv, xv, 19, 29, 34
Hofmannsthal, H. von, 180
Hollywood, 74
Hopkins, G. M., 14, 40–4
Horace, 197
humanism, 206
Hume, D., 207
Humpty Dumpty, 79
Hutton, R. H., 115

iamb, 133
iambic pentameter, 131, 133, 142, 147
ideology, 102–3, 110, 114, 198, 199, 201, 203, 205–6
idiom, 74, 145
imagery, 87, 114, 146, 147, 171–2
implicatures, 79, 86
implied author, 160–1
implied reader, 161
indirect speech, 167
individualism, 205
Ingarden, R., 178
intentional fallacy, 204
interior monologue, 167–8
interaction studies, 83–4
interpretation, 12, 103, 106, 110, 169
Ionesco, E., 188
intertextuality, 115, 172
Irigaray, L., 215
irony, 18, 107, 146, 163

Jakobson, R., 198–9
James, H., 16
  The Portrait of a Lady, 156, 163–4
  'The Turn of the Screw', 161
jargon, 14, 198, 209
Johnson, S., 76, 119
  The History of Rasselas, 122, 126
Jonson, B., 180, 197
Joyce, J.
  Dubliners, 171
  Ulysses, 167–8

Keats, J., 18, 37, 76, 134

Keats, J., (*continued*)
'Ode on a Grecian Urn', 88
kennings, 139
Kermode, F., 120, 138–9
knowledge, 12, 13–18, 177
Kristeva, J., 215

Labov, W., 81
language, 15, 26, 71–94, 101, 109, 116, 205
and literature, 86–91
of poetry, 120, 126, 127, 128, 130, 132, 135–9
of prose fiction, 166–9
langue, 81, 205
Lanyer, A., 202
Larkin, P., 119–20
Lawrence, D. H., 86
learning
active, 34, 44–5
from essays, 66–7
from lectures, 27–9
from others, 11
from seminars, 29–33
from small group work, 39–44
from student presentations, 34–9
from writing, 48
independent, xiv
Leavis, F. R., 91, 212–13
lecture, 27–9, 33, 39
Leech, G., 133–4
lexical items, 78, 116
library, xiv, 21, 23, 37
lighting effects, 186
linguistics, 71, 73, 87, 91, 121, 135
listening, 17–18, 25–7, 31
literary competence, 16
literary conventions, 16
literature
discussing, 25–47
reading, 95–118
studying, 9–24
writing about, 48–68
Locke, J., 80
Lodge, D., 207–8
How Far Can You Go?, 158, 165–6
Nice Work, 172
Lukacs, G., 198

McGuire, R. L., 10
magic realist, 155
Mamet, D.
Oleanna, 189
Marlowe, C., 13, 198, 211

Marvell, A., 40, 88
Marxism, 108, 199, 215
meaning, 15, 110
metaphor, 87–8, 114, 129, 137–9, 141, 146, 157
metonymy, 88–9, 138
metre, 113–14, 130, 132–4, 136, 137, 142, 147
metrical foot, 133, 134
Middleton, T., 213
Miller, A.
The Crucible, 30–1
Death of a Salesman, 184
Miller, J., 192–3
Miller, J. Hillis, 95, 96, 163
Millett, K., 215
Milton, J., 89
Paradise Lost, 108, 130, 131
mimesis, 123, 125, 127, 207
mnemonic, 131
modernism, 157
Moers, E., 202, 215
morphology, 76–8
Morrison, T., 91

Nabokov, V., 10, 15
Lolita, 159
narratee, 162
narration, 159–66
narrative, 150–1, 154, 155, 205
double, 163
multiple, 163
retrospective, 164
narrator
embedded, 163
first person, 159
omniscient, 160, 179
third person, 159–60, 163–4
unreliable, 161
national language studies, 82–3
neo-classical, 126, 147
neo-Victorian, 111
New Criticism, 203–4
note-taking, 17–18
novel, 87, 151, 156
endings, 170–1
modernist, 157
realist, 54
rise of, 119, 211–12
Victorian, 96, 122
Nuttall, A. D., 207

openness, 10

order, 164
Orwell, G., 75, 197
Osborne, J.
  Look Back in Anger, 108–9, 179, 185–6,
    189
Ovid, 14
Owen, W., 37, 213
oxymoron, 89, 138, 214

paradox, 88, 114
paraphrase, 51
parole, 81
performance, 177–8, 190–3
peripeteia, 187
persona, 112
personification, 88
phoneme, 81
phonology, 76, 79–80, 82
pidgin, 82
Pinter, H.
  Betrayal, 190
  The Dumb Waiter, 85–6
  The Homecoming, 179, 182, 186
  Moonlight, 186–7
plagiarism, 60, 210–11
Plath, S., 198
Plato, 123–6, 128
plays, 87, 90, 176–195
play-text, 176–7
plenary, 29
plot, 16, 90, 164–6, 170, 171, 187
poem, 121, 129–39
poetic language, 135–9
poetic licence, 137
poetry, 87, 89–90, 119–149
  and history, 119, 123–4, 125, 126, 128
  and philosophy, 119, 125, 126, 128, 129
  and politics, 123, 124, 129
  and religion, 124, 127, 128, 129
  classical conception of, 126
  differentiation from prose, 134–5, 136–7
  Romantic conception of, 122, 126
point of view, 163
Pope, A., 73
postcolonialism, 208–9
postmodernism, 96, 130
post-structuralism, 92, 206–8
Poulet, G., 169
pragmatics, 72, 79, 84–6
Pratt, M., 86
preparation, 20, 30, 48
pre-Raphaelite, 28, 37
prescriptivism, 72–6

prose fiction, 90, 150–75
prose language
  difference from poetry, 134–5, 136–7,
    150
pun, 146
Purkiss, D., 208

quatrain, 113, 132
questions, 27–9, 31, 32, 33, 38, 45, 106,
    109–10
quotations, 57, 64

reading
  aloud, 15, 44–5, 191–2
  basic, 16, 97, 98, 99–101, 105, 109
  critical, 17, 51, 97, 98, 101–2, 105, 107,
    109, 110, 111, 116–17
  in time for classes, 20–1, 30
  literary texts, 95–118
  plays, 176–95
  poetry, 119–49
  prose fiction, 150–75
reader, 25, 96
  active, 105
  common, 120
  ideal, 110, 161
  questioning, 109–10
  readerly, 105
  response, 87, 155, 169–72
  self-conscious, 95–7
  writerly, 105
realism, 53–4, 153, 180, 205
received pronunciation, 75
Renaissance, 119, 124, 125, 126, 132, 197,
    205
rhetoric, 2, 136, 137, 180
rhyme, 15, 114, 130, 131, 132, 134, 137,
    147
rhythm, 114, 116, 130, 134
Rich, A., 215
Richardson, S.
  Clarissa, 201
  Pamela, 102–3, 162
  Sir Charles Grandison, 201
Romanticism, 122, 124, 126, 127
Rushdie, S., 197
Russell, W., 37
Russian Formalism, 198

Said, E., 208
Sassoon, S., 213
Saussure, F. de, 81, 205
scene changes, 188–9

Index

Scholes, R., 170
Searle, J., 93
self-confidence, 11–12, 200
semantics, 76, 79–80
seminar, 23, 29–33
semiotics, 184–7
sentence, 72, 79, 132, 135
serial publication, 95, 157
setting, 104, 106, 153
Shakespeare, W., 13, 14, 15, 74, 76, 88–9, 109, 128, 180 199 202–3, 211
  Hamlet, 12, 86, 87, 90, 156, 181, 183–4, 187–8
  Henry IV, Part One, 180–1, 189
  Henry V, 176–7
  King Lear, 87–8, 203
  Macbeth, 89, 139, 185, 186, 189, 191–2
  Measure for Measure, 71
  Richard II, 204
  Romeo and Juliet, 85
  The Winter's Tale, 190
Shaw, G. B., 72, 180
Shelley, M., 11
  Frankenstein , 163, 198
Shelley, P. B., 125, 126–7
Sheridan, R. B., 108
Shklovsky, V., 198
short story, 150, 151–2
Showalter, E., 202, 214–15
showing, 168–9
Sidney, P., 119, 126, 197
simile, 88, 138
Simon, P.
  Hearts and Bones, 37
Sinfield, A., 202–3, 208
skills, 13–18, 34, 151, 172, 196
small group work, 27, 39–44
sociolinguistics, 81–4, 91
soliloquy, 183–4
Sophocles
  Oedipus Rex, 187
sound effects, 185
speech act theory, 86
Sperber, D., 85
stage directions, 179–81
Standard English, 76, 81
stanza, 130, 131–2, 134
Stein, G., 32–3
Sterne, L., 87
stichomythia, 190
Stoppard, T.
  Rosencrantz and Guildenstern are Dead, 28

stream of consciousness, 167
structuralism, 92, 204–8
structural linguistics, 89
student presentation, 34–9
studying
  etymology, 1
  literature, 9–24
Styan, J. L., 192
suspense, 95–6, 170
Swift, J., 74, 205
syllable, 132–3
symbolism, 87, 171–2
synchronic, 81, 171
syntax, 15, 76–8, 130, 132, 134, 137, 142–3

talking, 25–7, 105
Tannen, D., 84
telling, 168–9
Tennyson, A., 35–6, 37, 127
  'Break, Break, Break', 111–16, 139
  In Memoriam, 115
  'Tears, Idle Tears', 116
  The Princess, 36
text
  definition of, 198
  primary, 21–2, 59, 98, 203
  reading literary, 95–118
  secondary, 21–2, 203, 210
  in drama, 178, 180
  use of in essays, 57
Thackeray, W. M., 169
theatre
  of the mind, 178–81
  the theatrical medium, 176–8
theory, 110, 121, 196–219, 221–2
theme, 90, 102, 130
time management, 19–20, 50, 98
Todorov, T., 197
Tolstoy, L., 222
tone, 154
tradition of complaint, 72–5
tragedy, 187
trochee, 133
Trollope, A.
  Barchester Towers, 157
Turgenev, I., 222
tutorial, 27, 29, 45
Twain, M., 13

utterance, 72, 79, 86

vernacular, 63, 202
verse, 114, 130, 137

verse paragraphs, 132
Victorian, 115, 122, 127, 170
vocabulary, 137, 143, 154, 200
  and language change, 78
  in essays, 64

Walker, A.
  The Color Purple, 158, 215
Waller, E., 73
Watt, I., 205–6
Webster, J., 213
Wharton, E.
  The House of Mirth, 62
White, E. B., 80
Widdowson, H., 86
Williams, R., 200

Wilson, D., 85
Wimsatt, W. K., 203–4
Winterson, J.
  Sexing the Cherry, 40, 44, 104, 171–2
Woolf, V., 197
  A Room of One's Own, 201–2, 214–15
  'The Legacy', 36–7, 46–7
  To The Lighthouse, 157–8, 166–7
Wordsworth, W., 10, 63, 76, 120, 126, 137
  'Preface to *Lyrical Ballads*', 135, 136
  'The Old Cumberland Beggar', 139–43
writer, 102–3

Yeats, W. B., 50, 125

zeugma, 138

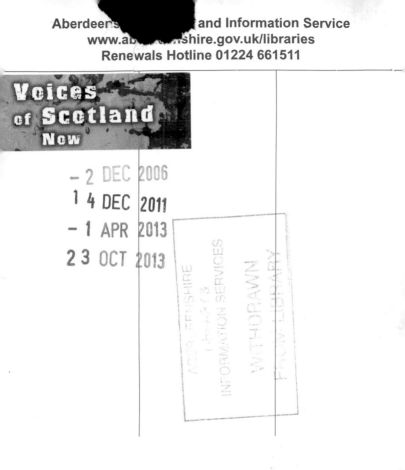
ROBERTSON, Robin

Swithering